A COMPANION TO

Plato's *REPUBLIC*

W9-ARQ-211

A COMPANION TO

Plato's *REPUBLIC*

Nicholas P. White

HACKETT PUBLISHING COMPANY

Copyright © 1979 by Nicholas P. White

All rights reserved
Printed in the United States of America
Fourth printing 1988

Library of Congress Catalog Card Number 78-70043
ISBN 0-915144-56-5
ISBN 0-915144-92-1 (pbk)

For further information, please address Hackett Publishing Company, Inc.,
Box 44937, Indianapolis, Indiana 46204

for L. P. W. and M. G. W.

Contents

Preface

When I first began to assemble the material that ultimately became this book, I did so for my own use in teaching various courses involving the *Republic*. At that time, I had the impression that the effort to trace carefully the argument of the whole work would be of use mainly to students and was too elementary an exercise to be worth pursuing for the sake of anyone else, or for scholarly purposes. I was mistaken. Both continued scrutiny of the *Republic*, and continued reading and rereading of the secondary literature on it, convinced me that an exposition of its main line of thought was essential not only for those approaching it for the first time, but also for those who must have read it many times over. This happy coincidence of pedagogical and scholarly usefulness inspired me to write a commentary suitable for students and general readers, which, at the same time, would serve as the vehicle for my own interpretation of Plato's work.

The book that results is not intended to be a full treatment of all aspects of the *Republic*. Rather, it is an attempt to follow step by step what I take to be the main argument, to show how that argument is articulated, to show the important interconnections among its elements, and, above all, to show thereby that there is a coherent and carefully developed train of thought which motivates virtually everything in the work. The contrary impression is common and understandable, because Plato was sometimes more concerned to make his work flow smoothly and attractively than to make plain its argumentative articulations. But the smoothness and attractiveness of his exposition are all the more remarkable when one realizes how thoroughly compatible he has made them with the meticulous tracing of a complex piece of philosophical reasoning. My main purpose is to show the structure of that reasoning and to demonstrate the way in which it informs the whole of the work.

The form of my presentation has a natural connection with this expository purpose. It would have been possible to present my claims about the coherence of the *Republic*, and my interpretation of the particular arguments within it, simply in the form of a continuous exposition, rather than writing the section-by-section summary and commentary which constitutes the major portion of this book. My reason for proceeding as I have, however, is this: I believe that the over-all argument of the *Republic* can best be seen, and mistakes about its components best avoided, when the argument is seen as a whole. More-over, I believe that this is the way in which one may gain from the work what is philosophically most interesting. Many recent scholarly dis-cussions of the *Republic* suffer from too much concentration on what are thought to be its crucial sections. The fact is that the details of Plato's arguments are often (not always) much less interesting than the overall scheme within which they are placed. Far more important is the basic structure of his position, which can frequently be defended through means somewhat different from the ones that he himself adopts (see, e.g., the end of Introduction, sec. 4). Furthermore, the whole point of the more detailed pieces of argumentation is easily missed if their places in the whole are not scrupulously attended to. I have therefore thought it best to interpret the *Republic* by taking the reader, or persuading him to take himself, step by step through the whole work. Not only will this procedure aid those developing a first acquaintance with the work; it will also, I believe, make it clearer to anyone.

In adopting my particular expository purpose I have had to exclude many others. First of all, because I believe that the main point of the *Republic* obviously has to do with ethics and political philosophy rather than metaphysics and epistemology, I have concentrated on the former. Plato certainly believes that his views on ethics have a metaphysical basis, and I have said something about what I think it is; but I have not discussed that basis completely nor argued extensively for my account of it. Second, I have referred very little to works other than the *Republic*. I believe that Plato intended it to be complete enough to be fairly well understandable by itself. (The main exception is that the metaphysical basis of the ethical argument is described only in bare outline.) By restricting myself to the *Republic* alone, I have tried to show how well Plato succeeded in making it a self-contained and coherent argument. For similar reasons I have refrained from treating historical, literary, and dramatic elements of the dialogue, for interesting and important as they are, they sometimes tend to distract one from the argument (although at other times they reinforce it). Moreover, these elements of the work have been well treated by other writers. Another restriction that I have adopted is to deal very little, in a direct way, with secondary literature on the *Republic*. I am of course on many points indebted to such work, and there are many writings which, although I disagree with them, should be consulted by anyone critically scrutinizing what I say.

Although I have not been able to give by any means all of the pertinent citations on such matters, I have tried to give a reasonable—though inevitably arbitrary—selection of what seem to me the most interesting or important passages by other authors on issues that I treat, or those that will best lead the reader to further consideration, *pro* or *contra*, of my interpretation. I believe that my interpretation is supported by a straightforward reading of the *Republic*, taken as a whole, and that it fits its parts. But rather than take up space arguing against rival inter-pretations, I have chosen to expound my own and to allow readers to examine the rivals and arrive at their own conclusions.

I had better explain, lest someone form the wrong idea, why the over-all coherence and meticulousness of Plato's argument strikes me as so interesting. Part of the reason is the spectacle of it, pure and simple. The argumentative structure of the *Republic*, quite apart from its soundness or lack of it, is simply a beautiful thing to behold, the more so because it has often been so difficult to uncover. (One learns not to be surprised when a formerly aimless-seeming Platonic passage turns out to be making a point essential to his argument; I am certain that there are many such passages that I have not noticed.) The other reason, however, has to do with a certain sympathy that I have with Plato's philosophical aims. This sympathy concerns extremely abstract features of his doctrine and argument. It emphatically does not mean that I agree with all of his ethical or political claims. Indeed, some of what I say in this book is an effort to expound views of his that seem to me wrongheaded and, in some cases, nearly unintelligible. But although I point out such diffi-culties, I do not dwell on them. Uncounted objections can be brought against Plato's arguments and formulations at almost every stage. It would be fruitless to try to discuss them all or to show how Plato might respond to them; and those that have been brought in recent writings on the *Republic* are not always the most interesting or notable. Rather, I have particular philosophical interests that make me wish to give special attention to this work. They are focused on a highly abstract feature of Plato's ethical doctrine with which I have some sympathy. It has to do with his treatment of the notion of goodness. I can indicate what that feature is only in the crudest manner here and in the rest of the book. I think, in the first place, that he was right to try to discover a single notion of goodness underlying the apparent multiplicity of our uses of the word "good," although I do not think that he was successful, or that the metaphysical theory on which he based his attempt can be upheld. I also think that he was right to try to give to the notion of goodness the kind of (to be very vague) preeminence that he did give it within his ethical system, though again I think that his attempt was foiled by important flaws in his metaphysics. Thirdly, I think that he was in *some* degree right to try to attach to the notion of goodness a certain kind of (to be very vague again) objectivity, in the sense of making the goodness of a thing less dependent, in a certain sense, on the capacity of persons to value it than is frequently done, particularly in ethical theories of the present day. I have not attempted to defend these views in this book (they receive brief explanation in section 4 of the Introduction), but I mention them here to give the reader some idea of the underlying motivations for the present work.

I have focused some fair amount of attention on the problem of the conflict between justice and self-interest, because this is Plato's own focus and because, as he saw, it is a good way of approaching his views. There are many points at which it might be tempting to compare what he says with modern ideas. I have chosen to make such a comparison only in one large-scale manner, by first dealing with Plato's views mainly on his own terms, and only then attempting to look at them against the background of more recent thoughts on the matter. I have set up the problem in an elementary way in section 1 of the Introduction. I have then in sec. 2 given a brief outline of the whole argument of the *Republic*. This outline covers very cursorily the same ground as the alphabetically-labeled notes forming the main body of the book, but it follows an order of exposition different from Plato's, and postpones to those same alphabetically-labeled notes the task of supporting my interpretation of Plato's argument. In section 4, I use this material to explain the structure of his ethical theory, and the way in which his response to the problem of justice and self-interest departs from most modern ways of looking at that problem. (Section 3 is an excursus on his theory of knowledge and metaphysics lying behind his ethical theory.) In section 5, I briefly explain the ways in which the structure of his ethical theory makes it difficult to classify and describe in contemporary terms. Finally, in section 6, I explain even more briefly what seem to me to be the broadest and most important grounds on which his theory should be assessed.

Partly because I have attempted to make this book useful to several different kinds of people, some of the material in it is presented more than once. For example, as I have just said, some of what is contained in the Introduction is also in the notes. Another kind of repetition occurs in the notes themselves, when I have found it necessary to harp on certain themes repeatedly, partly to show how important and pervasive they are in the *Republic*, and partly because those reading this book along with the *Republic* will find that, because it is quite a long work, they need to be reminded of what has gone before and made to anticipate what is to come.

Much of the material in this book has been in circulation, in different places and in different forms, since 1970, when much of the material in section 2 of the Introduction was presented to the colloquium of the Department of Classics of the University of Michigan. Further material was developed in classes in the Department of Philosophy. I am much indebted to the many, including students in various courses, who have offered their comments and criticisms. I am especially indebted to William K. Frankena for his help in numerous conversations about Greek ethics in general and the *Republic* in particular, and to the dedicatees for their extensive and valuable comments on an earlier draft. I am grateful, too, to the John Simon Guggenheim Memorial Foundation, for a fellowship which supported the final stage of the writing.

The Use of This Book

Different readers with different backgrounds and different needs and interests should read this book differently. The reader who has never read the *Republic* will perhaps wish to read the capitalized summary along with the *Republic* to help get some sense of the continuity of the argument. (Reading the summary *instead of* the *Republic* is a very bad idea; much is left out of the summary, which would not enable a student to pass an examination on the *Republic*.) The summary is not itself a translation of particular sentences in the text, although it follows the text and its phraseology fairly closely. It can be used, I believe, with any standard translation of the *Republic*, though special effort has been made to coordinate it with G.M.A. Grube's translation. (See Bibliography.) Readers of other translations will sometimes have to make adjustments to coordinate their translations with the summary, but these adjustments should not be difficult.

The notes, labeled with capital letters, vary in their degree of difficulty and in the level at which they are directed. The most technical are in small print. Some of the rest will be of interest mainly to philosophers and Plato scholars, but they shade off gradually into those aimed at persons with no specialized expertise. Here the reader will have to suit his interest and leisure. My belief, however, is that most of the notes will be of use to those who know the *Republic* well, including both Plato scholars and those other philosophers who happen to be interested in the work.

Those who wish a brief view of the *Republic* as I see it, particularly with regard to the interpretation of its ethical theory, might start by reading secs. 2 and 4–6 of the Introduction, along with sec. 1, which introduces (in a manner suited also to the elementary student) the main ethical problem on which I, following Plato, focus my discussion. It should be noted, however, that secs. 2 and 4, and particularly sec. 2, simply expound my interpretation, without the support for it contained in the summary and the alphabetically-labeled notes which constitute the main body of the book. Sec. 3 of the Introduction stands apart, being a partly conjectural account of how one might construe the connection, which Plato obviously believes to exist but does not spell out in detail, between his metaphysics and his ethics. Sec. 5 will be fully intelligible only to those with some knowledge of recent ethical thought, particularly in America and England. Sec. 6 presupposes no special expertise.

I urge readers of all kinds not to dwell too much on Book I of the *Republic*. It is an introduction and is not intended by Plato to be a complete, or even a fully cogent, treatment of the issues which it broaches (see 354a–c). In my experience, it is not even a good book to use in introductory courses in philosophy—a purpose to which it is sometimes put—because it annoys students more than it stimulates their thoughts, and it convinces them that Plato and Socrates were dishonest. Readers of the *Republic* should not allow themselves to become bogged down in it. For this reason, I have treated it quite briefly and have emphasized only the points on which it anticipates or foreshadows later discussion.

For my references to Plato's text, I have used the standard system of Stephanus numbers and letters (e.g., "473a", "608d–609c"). A few shoddily produced editions of translations lack these reference-marks altogether, and should be avoided. Some lack just the letters. They are serviceable, barely: almost all of the numbered sections (originally, pages) have five equal subdivisions, "a" through "e", and the reader can make rough estimates of where these begin and end. Occasionally, out of a need for precision, I add the line number of Burnet's Greek text (e.g., "583a4–6"). Those not using that text can find the intended passages, usually, by figuring on 9–13 lines for each letter-labeled subdivision.

The bibliographical references are made by means of authors' names, often with letters whose meaning can be deciphered by consulting the Bibliography at the back.

Introduction

Modern moral philosophers rightly believe that one of the central problems of ethics concerns the contrast between a person's interest, or what is good for him, and his moral obligations, or the things that he morally ought to do. This contrast figures, to some degree at least, in the lives of almost all of us. We are frequently confronted with situations in which it is clear to us that we have an obligation or duty to do a certain thing, such as keeping a promise or repaying a debt, while at the same time we know that doing that thing would be disadvantageous to us, or detrimental to our interests. For example, we might be able to keep what we owe, purchase something valuable with it for ourselves, and be practically certain both of escaping detection and punishment and of avoiding feelings of guilt which might outweigh the benefits gained. What this kind of situation seems to show is not merely that there is a *difference* between one's duty and one's interest, but also that the two can sometimes come into *conflict*. In situations of such conflict many of us are at least sometimes perplexed and feel pulled in two directions at once, toward duty and toward our own advantage. Moreover, we can see others similarly torn, though we can tell that sometimes they try to conceal the fact, even from themselves, just as we ourselves sometimes try to do. All of us sometimes wish that the world were otherwise, and that we could be free of such conflicts, with an easy harmony between obligation and advantage.

The world is not otherwise, however, and everyone—philosophers included—must deal with it as it is. But when such conflicts arise, what shall we do?

1. *Plato's aims: the problem of duty and interest.*

Like ordinary people, philosophers differ in their answers to this question, and not surprisingly the disagreements among the latter run parallel to those among the former. We all know that some people are of dutiful temperament and strongly inclined to do what they ought to do, even when their interests are sacrificed. We trust them to keep their promises, even when they will lose by it. Equally familiar are those who

9

tend in the opposite direction to one degree or another. Sometimes they simply evade their obligations or flout them, and sometimes they gain by doing so, as they hoped. At other times they perform their obligations, but we can tell that they do so only because they see that that is where their interests lie. That is, they can see that the situation is one in which duty and interest coincide rather than conflict, and they choose to follow duty because they will gain thereby. We do not begrudge people such happy coincidences, and ourselves prefer, as I have said, to have what we morally ought to do be the same as what we benefit from. But we do not fully trust those who do their duty solely (or even partly) in order to further their own interests, because we know that we cannot rely on them to fulfill their obligations to us unless they will be helped by it.

The temperaments of philosophers mirror those of ordinary people. Some philosophers have insisted that when duty and interest conflict, duty is the course to follow in spite of the sacrifice involved, and they have constructed elaborate arguments to show why reason or good sense must tend in this direction. The greatest philosopher to be commonly associated with this view is Kant, who attempted to show not merely that reason dictates choosing obligation over advantage, but that in strictness it is a mistake to allow the hope of advantage to be any part *at all* of one's motive for doing what one ought to do. On this view, roughly expressed, the reason for keeping a promise, for example, must never be even partially that one may gain or be made happy by doing so, but *purely* and *completely* that doing so is one's moral obligation. (Not even the satisfaction of having done one's duty is an allowable inducement.) Other philosophers of this general persuasion have been less extreme than Kant, but they all represent a tendency of a moralistic rather than advantage-pursuing kind.

The advantage-pursuing philosophers, on the other hand, come in two main types. One type is extreme and tends to think of morality as in general an irrational affair, which can and should be easily given up when one's interest conflicts with it, as they think it frequently does. Such philosophers lay stress on the attempt to show how or why the pursuit of one's own advantage or benefit is reasonable, and how or why its sacrifice is unreasonable. If duty conflicts with one's own advantage, then, according to them, so much the worse for duty. The other type is less extreme, and some of its members are less extreme by far. Such philosophers do accept the rationality of pursuing one's own good exclusively, but their tendency is to emphasize how frequently this can be done by following one's moral obligations. These are philosophers, that is, who stress how often there is coincidence rather than conflict between interest and duty. This can be done in various ways. For example, one may point to man's social impulses and the fact that he is often made happy by helping others. Or one may assert that there is punishment in the afterlife which will outweigh the benefits in this life of flouting obligations. Or one may adopt the view that when it is properly understood, one's benefit or welfare actually includes the performance of all, or some, of one's duties, so that the performance of these duties is a part of one's good, in roughly the way in which producing notes is a part of being a musician. This last view may take the form of maintaining that all of one's duties are included in one's welfare, and that all violations of duty are excluded by it, in which case the view denies that any conflict between duty and interest ever arises. But what this view has in common with the other views of this type is this: one's welfare is offered as the *reason* or *ground* for doing one's duty, so that if it is asked, "Why is my duty the thing to do?" the answer is that if you do your duty then you will benefit.

All of these views have one important thing in common. Although they disagree on the extent of the conflict between duty and interest, and about what to do when conflict occurs, they all take the distinction between the *notions* of duty and interest to be irreducible, as follows. They hold that we can set up a contrast between what one ought to do and what it would be beneficial to do, and that once this contrast is set up the next and *only* questions to ask are whether these two things can conflict and which should be chosen if they do. Moreover, once these questions are posed, all of the views thus far outlined agree that the only kind of answer that can be given is to *pick one or the other* as somehow overriding, and to show that considerations of reasonableness or rationality or some other philosophical arbiter come down on one side or the other. Perhaps the most characteristic feature of modern ethical thought is to see ethics as dominated by these questions, and ethical philosophers as forced to respond to them in one of these ways. The picture is of a choice between two alternatives, a choice that must be made in one way or the other unless something can show that the two can never conflict.

When viewed from this perspective, Plato has generally been regarded as taking the side of the advantage-pursuers against the view of Kant, particularly in the *Republic*. Probably the most emphatic and influential expression of this interpretation of Plato came from H. A. Prichard, almost fifty years ago, in his "Duty and Interest."[1] Prichard, who was

1. For full reference for this and all citations throughout this work, please refer to the Bibliography at the rear of the book.

on these matters of a strongly Kantian persuasion, in effect charged Plato with not really comprehending the notion of a moral obligation, on the ground that, Prichard said, Plato both attempted to show that keeping to one's duty would make one happy, and seemed to presuppose that unless he could show that this was true, then doing one's duty would be unreasonable. On this account, Plato is one of those mentioned above who thinks that if there is a conflict between duty and interest then reason must choose interest, but who also thinks that the coincidence between duty and interest is virtually complete, so that it is rational to do one's duty after all. On this account, too, it follows that Plato is one of those who regards himself as faced with a choice between duty and interest, and as required, therefore, to find considerations weighing to one side or the other.

The point is not much affected by the fact that, as Prichard saw, Plato does not talk in terms of duty (or of right—a somewhat different term that Prichard also employed) but in terms of justice (*dikaiosynē*). One difference between these two terms is that there are duties that are not, so to speak, duties of justice, but that arise out of different considerations. A further difference between duty and justice as Plato speaks of it is that whereas "duty" is a word that applies primarily to actions, "just," as Plato thinks of it, applies mainly to people (and their souls), and only secondarily applies to the things they do (443b–444a, n. C; Plato also has an important use of the word in application to cities). But in spite of these differences, the issues involved in Plato's contrast between justice and interest are much the same as those involved in the contrast between duty and interest, and so for present purposes we may treat the two as nearly interchangeable.

That said, it should be noted that the customary account of Plato's intentions involves a certain complexity. To find a coincidence, especially a complete or nearly complete coincidence, between duty and interest is not easy. Too many observable facts seem to point the other way. Those who wish to find such a coincidence are therefore often obliged to maintain that the ordinary notions of duty and interest are in some way mistaken. Thus, they say, it often *looks* to us as though we are harmed by performing our obligations and helped by avoiding them, but when this appearance is not caused by simple mistakes about facts, it is caused by confusion about what obligation really is, or, indeed, about what good or advantage for us really is. If we were not thus confused, and if we understood what our duty was and what was *really* in our interest, then, they maintain, we would realize that the conflict that we see between the two is an illusion. Plato is generally thought to have adopted such a view as this, not saying that duty and interest as we *usually* conceive them are coincident, but that as *correctly* conceived they are so. But even if we take account of this complexity, the picture is still one of a Plato confronted with much the same choice between duty and interest, and as forced to choose one or the other, with the result that when all is said and done he chooses the latter, and then hopes to get the former too, by denying significant conflict between them.

I do not think that this picture is correct, and one of the things that I shall try to do in the following pages is to show why. The correct picture is instead a more complicated one, one that is different from what modern perspectives on the contrast between duty and interest lead one to expect.

2. *The argument of the* Republic.

We cannot see the correct picture, however, until we have before us a sketch of the argument of the *Republic* in the terms in which Plato formulated it. I shall now give such a sketch, in outline and without here arguing for the interpretation embodied therein. (Support for the interpretation will be found in the main body of the book, in the alpha-betically-labeled notes on particular passages.) When the sketch is completed, we shall be able to return, in sec. 4, to our effort to under-stand Plato's overall view on the problem of duty and interest.

The aim of the *Republic* is very simple: to discover what justice (*dikaiosynē*) is, and to show that it is more beneficial, in a certain sense of that word, than its contrary, injustice (*adikia*). Book I is a prologue to this effort. The problem is then posed anew in Book II; and Books II–IV expound Plato's answer to the question, "What is justice?" which he considers an essential preliminary to discovering whether or not it is beneficial. Books V–VII deepen his account of justice and related matters, including certain points of human motivation, and connect them with a brief explanation of his notion of the Good. In Books VIII–IX he finally mounts his demonstration that justice is more bene-ficial than injustice. And Book X serves partly as an epilogue and partly as a completion of certain strands of the earlier argument. But of course this simple summary conceals much complexity.

*   *   *

The best method in approaching this complexity is to begin in the middle of the *Republic*, at the point at the end of Book IV where Plato has shown what he thinks justice is and is about to commence the further elaboration of Books V–VII.

By this time Plato has actually explained justice in two distinct applications, one to a city or *polis* and the other to an individual human being, or rather, as Plato sees it, to his soul (*psychē*). Both cities and souls, Plato thinks, are composed of parts and both can be viewed as tripartite. The city contains a class of rulers (who turn out in Book V also to be philosophers), a class of soldiers or auxiliaries, and a class containing all other citizens, particularly farmers and artisans. In parallel fashion the soul has three parts: the reason; the spirited part, which is the seat of anger and indignation; and the appetitive part, which is a motley collection of various cravings and desires. Given this view of city and soul, Plato holds that in both cases, justice is the condition in which each part of a thing performs the task to which it is in a sense naturally suited. In the city, justice is the condition in which the rulers rule, the auxiliaries perform the military parts of the task of protecting and preserving the city, and the members of the third class pursue their several occupations. In the case of the soul, justice is the condition in which the reason rules, the spirited part is indignant and angry at whatever contravenes reason's efforts, and the appetites exert themselves with a kind of moderation which has been developed by the supervision of reason. This brief description misses much, but it will do for the present.

It is crucial, however, to know not merely what Plato's account of justice is but also what his grounds for it are. Because of his double application of the term, Plato's grounds are complicated. He begins with an account of justice in the city, saying that it will help us to see what justice in the individual is (368c–369b). Of course, the latter is his main quarry, because he is trying to show that an individual is best off possessing justice. But the discussion of justice in the city contains certain essential elements of what he wishes to maintain. Accordingly, we should begin with it.

*   *   *

In outline, Plato's procedure for identifying justice in the city is to describe a certain sort of city, to discover that it contains justice, and to see what that justice is. In this procedure, a crucial role is played by his claim that the city in question is good, and indeed perfectly good (427e–428a). From this claim Plato concludes that it has all of the virtues or excellences (*aretai*—see *ibid*., n. E). He then goes on to identify a particular one of these, the attribute of having each of its parts performing its own proper task. And he argues that this is justice in the city (432b–434c).

Because a central role in his account of justice is played by his contention that his city is good, we must look thoroughly at this contention and his reasons for it. The contention is not accompanied by explicit argument at the point where it is enunciated; rather, the argument is contained in his whole description of the city to that point. So we must begin at the beginning.

The city was initially introduced as a necessary institution to provide for human needs, in view of the fact that individual human beings are not self-sufficient (369b–d). Some philosophers would proceed from this point to argue that therefore the best city is the one that most copiously provides for those needs, perhaps explaining this idea by saying that such a city would be that which produces the greatest net amount of satisfaction or good for its inhabitants. (Satisfaction or good might or might not be construed as pleasure, depending on whether or not the philosopher was a hedonist.) The goodness of the city would thus become a function of the quantity of satisfaction that the inhabitants receive. But it is obvious that Plato does not take this course. Nowhere does he suggest such a simple quantitative test for the goodness of his city, and although a part of the goodness of a city certainly involves its ability to minister to human needs, his main line of thought about its goodness goes in a quite different direction.

At the time at which Plato claims that his city is good, the fact about it that he has most stressed, and that he has claimed makes it the only institution worthy of being called genuinely a city and a desirable institution, is that, as it ministers to the needs of its citizens, it possesses a sort of cohesiveness and unity (422e–423d), along with a stability allowing it to keep that cohesiveness and unity (424b–e, 422a, and n. B on 412e–414b). In order to keep it a city, he says, we must make sure that its unity is preserved. He construes unity in a fairly straightforward way, as a lack of what we would ordinarily call strife or dissension (for civic strife was a constant problem in Greek city-states), and seems unconcerned with the possibility that the notion of unity might be construed in other ways. Accordingly, when he discusses defective forms of city in Book VIII, he maintains that the cause of constitutional alteration and decline is always dissension (545c–d, 547a), and he presents as a defect of an oligarchic city that it is "not one city but two" (551d). The idea that the goodness of a thing can be grounded in its unity and stability has important connections with elements of his metaphysical theory (see sec. 3), and with his analogous view that a certain kind of psychological unity is essential for human goodness and welfare (see below in this section).

While attempting to provide this ground for saying that his city is good, Plato is at the same time trying to commend his city in another way, by saying that his arrangements supply it with benefit or good (405a–410a, n. C, and 461e–462e). Many present-day philosophers will be strongly inclined to say that the uses of the word "good" in these two claims are quite different, and that they must not be confused. In saying that a city is good, they may claim, we (at least, typically) employ a notion of goodness differing from the notion employed when we say that certain events or arrangements will produce good or benefit. Moreover, many philosophers who do not recognize different notions of goodness in these two cases will hold that other uses of the word "good" do exhibit importantly different notions. For example, it is usual to say that there is such a difference between "good" in "He is a good carpenter" and the same word in "The new building program will produce a great deal of good (i.e., benefit) for the local carpenters"; or, between the uses of the word in "He is a good man" and "Athletics are good (beneficial) for human beings." In these pairs, the distinction is thought to be, roughly, one between something that performs up to standards appropriate to its particular type of thing, and something that confers benefit. That there is a such a distinction can be argued by citing the fact, e.g., that a man may be a good embezzler even though, as it happens, he produces more harm than benefit. Still another difference between uses of "good" is often seen between such sentences as "He is a good *man*" and "He is a good *carpenter*", which ascribes excellence at a certain narrower role that human beings may adopt. Very roughly again, the argument is that being a good man is not a matter of playing a certain role well or fulfilling a certain function well, but has instead a particular status that can be pointed to by saying that being a good man involves being *morally* good, whereas this is not the case for such things as being a good carpenter. Now I do not wish to endorse here any particular distinctions among uses of "good" or to give final arguments for drawing them. My aim is rather to remark, by alluding to these modern distinctions, that Plato adopts none of them. He does not recognize any significant difference in the meaning of "good," neither elsewhere in the *Republic* nor in the discussion of the city that concerns us here. And in fact the grounds that he offers for saying that his arrangements are good for the city turn out to be just the same as his grounds for calling it a good city. For in 461e–462e he says that the greatest good for a city is what binds it together and makes it one, while the greatest evil, or bad, for it is what pulls it apart and makes it many. Accordingly, in his attempts to see that the city be, as a whole, as happy as possible (420b, 519e), he concentrates on those measures that will preserve the unity of the city.

*   *   *

That is a sketch of Plato's grounds for thinking that his city is good. We must now try to see how he shows the presence of justice in it. To do this, we must look carefully at the way in which the city is constructed, because the basic principle of its construction turns out to be precisely the sort of justice that he finds in it.

Once he has introduced the city in 369b–d, he immediately advances the thesis, which is to dominate the rest of the *Republic*, that the needs of its inhabitants can best be met if each person in it performs that single task, and that single task alone, for which he is naturally suited (369e–370c; cf. 423d). The notion of a "natural task" is one that strikes many philosophers as obscure and philosophically suspect. But such scepticism about the notion was not a factor within the intellectual climate in which Plato worked, and he does not say anything explicit in the *Republic* to try to meet it. That there is a single natural task for each reasonably capable person seems to him amply evident from ordinary experience, and he does not expend energy trying to argue for it. (Like his views on the connection between goodness and unity, however, this view also is linked to elements of his metaphysics; cf. sec. 3.) This thesis, which can be called the Principle of the Natural Division of Labor, is then applied to the entire organization of the city.

It is essential to an understanding of the *Republic* to realize that almost all of the arrangements for the city are dictated by Plato's desire to adhere to this principle, in a way that will be evident in the commentary below. But it is equally essential to see that one particular application of the principle has a very special place within the whole scheme. It is the application of the principle to the guardians (*phylakes*) of the city, and to the rulers of it, who are a special class of guardians singled out and trained to be the most guardianly of guardians (412c10). The guardians are originally introduced as those who will protect the city from enemies (373d–374e), and from that point onward the description of the city is focused almost exclusively on them and their role.

Because of the centrality of the guardians' role in the city, the effort to explain how the city can be good turns out to be identical with the effort to explain what the task of guardianship is. The function of the guardian is to keep the city in being and to repulse all forces that might tend to overthrow it. As remarked, the rulers of the city are those guardians with the special task of overseeing this activity. As such, they are charged with the task of preserving the cohesiveness of the city against both external enemies and internal dissension. The way in which they do this is to make sure that the Principle of the Natural Division of Labor is adhered to strictly. For according to Plato, this principle is the chief factor in enabling the city to avoid dissension, which comes, he believes, when one element of the city attempts to perform the natural task of another, and roles are not assigned to their natural players (414b–415d, 545c–547c). For this reason, a special part of the rulers' task is to see to the selection and education of people for the various functions that need to be performed (401d–403c, n. B); the rulers, in other words, are the directors of education. (Another very special element of their task, as we shall see below, is to make sure that their own task of guardianship is properly carried out, which requires an understanding of that task—i.e. of the Principle of the Natural Division of Labor—and how it contributes to the good of the city.) To explain the guardians' and rulers' task, then, is simply to explain how the city can be kept in a good, i.e., cohesive and stable, condition by adherence of its citizens to the Principle of the Natural Division of Labor, overseen by those who will assign tasks, including their own, in the correct manner. Or, to put it the other way around: the explanation of how the city can be kept in a good condition is simply the explanation of how dissension and instability can be avoided by the properly overseen adherence to the Principle of the Natural Division of Labor.

One special aspect of the rulers' effort to preserve the unity of the city is that they must preserve their own internal unity as a group. According to Plato, the cause of internal change and instability is dissension among the rulers, and whenever they are free from dissension the unity and preservation of the city are guaranteed (465b, 547c–d). He therefore makes arrangements that will ensure the maximum possible cohesiveness within the class of rulers of his city. The relationship among them is to be like that of the parts of a living body, all of which suffer when any one of them is damaged (461e–462e—we are here anticipating some of Plato's elaborations in Book V), and Plato devises elaborate measures to bring about this state of affairs.

*　　*　　*

The foregoing remarks make evident the connection between justice as Plato explains it and both what is *good for* the city and the *goodness of* the city. What makes the city good is precisely the fact that it is made to adhere to the Principle of the Natural Division of Labor, according to which each element in the city performs its own natural task. But this, in its application to the three classes in the city, is precisely what Plato says justice is (432b–434c).

Of course, once Plato has identified this particular structural feature of his city, he needs an argument to show that it is properly labeled by the word "justice," because the ordinary Greek sense of the word *dikaiosynē*, even as applied to cities, might seem to be somewhat different. But although Plato's arguments on this point raise certain difficulties (see 432b–434c, nn. B–C—as the notes in the main body of the book are labeled), he apparently believes that the connection between the ordinary use of the word and his own is sufficiently close for his purposes.

*   *   *

Having arrived at an account of justice in the city, Plato proceeds immediately to his main destination in this part of the *Republic*, an account of justice in the individual, which he thinks must be an account of justice in the individual's soul. This sort of justice, as I have said, he identifies with the performance of its natural task by each part of the soul, and in particular the performance by reason of the task of ruling within the soul. As in the case of justice in the city, there are difficulties in his argument for using the term "justice" to apply to this condition of soul, but Plato does attempt to show that his notion of psychic justice is at least close to the ordinary one (441c–443b). He also attempts to show that a person with a just soul would be a person who performs his task in Plato's city (if, that is, he should happen to live in such a city), and vice versa (441c–442d, n. C).

As Plato makes clear at the end of Book IV (444a–e), he thinks that justice in the soul plays much the same role in making the soul (and the man whose soul it is) good that justice in the city plays in making the city good. And when he comes to his comparison of the just man and the unjust man in Book IX, it will become clear that he thinks that justice in the soul produces benefit and happiness for the soul in precisely the way in which justice in the city produces benefit and happiness for the city (see above). For as he thinks it bad and deleterious for a city to lack unity, so too he believes that a soul torn by strife among its parts cannot be either happy or good (see 443c–e and Book VIII, *passim*, esp. 554a–555a, with 576b–578b). Nor, he thinks, can a person of this sort perform a single task to which he is naturally suited, because he will be constantly pulled in different directions (559d–562a) or be dominated by some appetite which will in one way or another skew his activities (551b–552e, n. A, 573c–576b). According to Plato, the man in the best condition is one who organizes his life according to a single, coherent plan (519c), in accordance with which the whole soul may be made harmonious (443c–e).

*　　*　　*

Having given an account of what justice is both in the city and in the soul, and described what he takes to be a good city and a good man, Plato feigns readiness at the beginning of Book V to consider cities and men less just and less good. He eventually does precisely this in Books VIII–IX, but in Books V–VII he occupies himself instead with a further elaboration of his description of his city and its rulers. With tongue in cheek he presents this part of the work as a digression, and with tongue further in cheek he presents it as merely a response to pressure from Socrates' interlocutors to explain his statement in Book IV that the guardians will hold "wives and children in common." In fact, however, Books V–VII supply a foundation that has been missing from Plato's description of his city and its rulers in the preceding books.

The basic fact is that Books V–VII lead up to and present a discussion of the notion of the Good that is essential, according to Plato, to a clear understanding of justice and its role. The obvious connection between the Good and the earlier material on the city is the use of the notion of goodness that Plato has, we have seen, already made in his effort to identify justice. The city was said to be good, like the corresponding sort of man who ruled in it, and justice was one of the things that made them both good. But another connection, not yet plain in Book IV, has to do with the motivation of the rulers to rule the city as Plato says they must. In Books VI–VII it emerges that this motivation is their effort to see that the Good is exemplified in the city, in a way that explains their efforts to adhere, and to see that the city adheres, to the Principle of the Natural Division of Labor, and likewise their efforts to keep the city cohesive and stable.

Along with problems concerning the Good, Plato also treats another problem in Books V–VII, the question whether it is possible for a city such as he has described to be established on earth. This question may at first sight seem unconnected to problems concerning the Good, and also to Plato's description of the city in Books II–IV. But this is not so. The connection with the description of the city is as follows. The point of showing that his city could be established is not merely to show that he is not a utopian dreamer. For his contention all along, through his use of the Principle of the Natural Division of Labor, has been that his city is constructed simply by the exploitation of the natural capacities of human beings, that is, by allowing people to pursue the tasks for which they are naturally suited. If it turned out that there is no possibility of going from the actual state of affairs to an approximation of his city, then serious doubt would be cast on his contention that his city is indeed based on natural human capacities. The effort to show, then, that the establishment of something like his city is possible is an effort to show that the Principle of the Natural Division of Labor is true and has been correctly applied (472e–473b, n. A). It is true that from a certain perspective (see *ibid.*) it does not matter to him that his city actually be established. But the argument that it is in a certain sense possible is a necessary continuation of his description of it.

Another aspect of his effort to show that his city could be established is also connected with earlier material concerning the desirability of the city's being cohesively organized. One of his arguments is that the role of guardianship cuts across the boundary between the sexes, and that women may just as well be guardians and rulers as men. (This argument is his response to the first of three "waves" that he says threaten to overwhelm his argument; see 475a–c, n. A.) The other is that an arrangement is possible—and to the benefit of the city—under which spouses and children are held in common. The purpose of this arrangement is, as Plato emphasizes (461e–465b), to ensure the unity of the guardian and ruler classes and thus the unity of the city (465b). The arrangement involves an elimination of private family life and loyalty, and a system of breeding and education for future guardians and rulers, which will avoid attachments that might compete with the unity of the city. (Here Plato is responding to the second "wave"; the link between the two responses is that the system of eugenics involved in the second depends on the association of women with men in the class of guardians which is defended in the first.) To show that the establishment of the city is possible is to show that the kind of unity advocated in Books II–IV can in fact be attained.

It is the third part of Plato's discussion in Books V–VII (his response to the third "wave") that provides the most important connection between his views on the Good and the construction of his city. For he holds that, appearances notwithstanding, the only way in which his city could be established would be for philosophers to become rulers or rulers to become philosophers, philosopher-rulers being those who are naturally disposed and carefully trained to attain a knowledge of what the Good is (473b–474b, 504d–506a).

The most important thing about Plato's rulers is that through their knowledge of the Good they understand how to rule the city, i.e., how to preserve it in a good and just and happy condition, and are moved to do so (540a–b; cf. 505a–b, 520d–521b, with 519d–521b, n. E). But Plato has already explained, from Book II onward, that the way in which to preserve the city in a good condition is to keep it unified and stable in accordance with the Principle of the Natural Division of Labor. What a knowledge of the Good must give to the rulers, accordingly, is an understanding of how adherence to that principle, and the justice that emerges from it, is truly a good for the city and a virtue of it (505a–b). For, of course, if such adherence were not a good or a virtue (not that he thinks that this is a serious possibility), then Plato would not wish to recommend it.

Seen in this light, Plato's description of the task of the philosopher-rulers takes on a special importance and a special intricacy. The rulers must both understand the Principle of the Natural Division of Labor and oversee its application, and at the same time must act in accordance with it, by performing the task of true guardians and preservers of the city (412a–c). We shall now see what this entails.

The crucial fact that makes philosophers suitable rulers is that they have knowledge of the Good and of the realm of intelligible objects of which it is a part. But an equally important fact about them is that once they gain knowledge of such things, they find that the activity of exercising their intellects on these things is far more desirable than ruling the city (519b–d). Now this fact might seem to present an obstacle to the notion of a philosopher-ruler, on the ground that the motivations for ruling and philosophizing seem to pull in opposite directions, so that the tasks of the ruler and philosopher could not be combined in one person. But Plato thinks that this is not so. In fact, he thinks that this very conflict between the desire to philosophize and the necessity of ruling (421c, 520a, e, 539e, 540b) is precisely what makes philosophers natural rulers. For according to him, the only way in which the city can be well governed is to have rulers who *do not wish* to rule but have something else that they would prefer to do (520c–521a). If a city is ruled by those who wish to rule, he says, there will be dissension and strife over who shall rule, and this strife will cause strife in the city as a whole and the destruction of its constitution (*ibid.* and 545c–d). So it turns out that the very task of the rulers *requires* that they not wish to rule and that they prefer to do something else which would be better for them. Plato emphasizes that this is an important part of what enables them, by contrast to everyone else, to keep the city in a good condition.

Because Plato wishes to show that his city could be established, i. e., that it really is based on natural human capacities, he must, of course, show that the task of guardianship is a coherent one for which some human beings do have the capacity. This is why he spends so much time in Books VI–VII discussing the naturally philosophical tempera-ment, the way in which it is suited to rule, and the course of education that it must follow if it is to be fully developed and charged with the governing of the city. (In their capacity as overseers of education, the rulers are in charge of this whole process; see above and 401d–403c, n. B.)

Because it involves spending some time ruling, and thus not merely philosophizing, the task of a philosopher-ruler necessarily involves some sacrifice of the individual good of the person performing it. This is a point repeatedly emphasized by Plato, both in his general warning that he is not aiming for the maximum possible happiness of any one class in the city (420b–c, 421b–c, 519e), and in his specific statement about the rulers that they must view ruling as something necessary, as something they do because it is just, and as something less good than what they might otherwise prefer to do (520a, e, 539e, 540b, d–e). The point is often missed because readers think it incompatible with what they take to be his main aim in the *Republic*. That aim is, as is recognized, to show that justice is beneficial to its possessor. But it is important to attend to what Plato does and does not say he means by this. Sometimes he puts his claim loosely by saying that the just life is better than the unjust life, or that being just is better than being unjust (358c, e). But his official contention, which he states clearly at the beginning and the end of his argument, is that the *completely* just man is better off than the *completely* unjust man (see 358a–362c, nn. B, D). He does *not* claim that one gains a bit of happiness for every bit of justice that one ac-quires, and the case of the rulers constitutes an express counterexample to the idea that he does uphold such a claim. We shall see in sec. 4 how he explains this matter.

The rulers govern their actions in the city, and themselves, in accord-ance with their knowledge of the Good (540a–b), and this knowledge leads them to see that adherence to the Principle of the Natural Division of Labor, including the self-sacrifice involved in their own adherence to this principle as just described, is good. We must, of course, ask how they are motivated by their understanding of the Good, and particularly how this understanding or knowledge can motivate them to act against their own self-interest. Some part of an answer to this question will emerge in secs. 3 and 4, when we consider Plato's metaphysical theory and the structure of his ethical theory. For the moment, however, we may simply observe that in Plato's view, the reasoning part of the soul is regarded as having motivations of its own, separate from those of spirit and appetite. (This view stands in contrast to a conception such as Hume's, for example, according to which "reason" is the name of something that has no motivating force of its own.) Moreover, Plato appears to believe that the mere understanding of what the Good is, and of what would be involved in its exemplification in the world, is sufficient, without any additional consideration of *one's own* good or self-interest, to motivate a person to attempt to exemplify the Good in the world (see 519d–521b, n. E).

In these ways, therefore, the discussion of Books V–VII is an essential explanation of the description of the city in Books II–IV. It further explains how the preservation and cohesiveness of the city may be guaranteed. It shows further how the Principle of the Natural Division of Labor, especially as applied to the rulers, works for the preservation and cohesiveness of the city. It shows how the activity of the philosopher-rulers exhibits a genuine application of that principle, because it contains a description of the temperament and education that such a ruler must and can have. And it argues the possibility of there being people who are motivated to act as Plato's rulers must act, that is, in such a way as to preserve the city rather than their own maximum good. Furthermore, it argues that this sacrifice is itself an integral part of the function of a true guardian or ruler, the understanding of which fact is vouchsafed to the rulers by their knowledge of the Good. If Plato had not given this account of the role of knowledge of the Good in the governance of the city, he would not have described fully the fundamental basis of the city's operation, the Principle of the Natural Division of Labor and its application to the rulers, and his argument would have been rendered seriously incomplete. This incompleteness would have infected his whole account of justice in the city (and thereby his account of justice in the soul), which is, as we saw, simply an application of that principle to the roles of the three classes into which the city is divided.

*   *   *

By the end of Book VII, Plato has presented a very full picture of the completely just man, the philosopher-ruler, who will eventually be compared with the completely unjust and bad man, the dictator or tyrant described in Book IX, so that we can see which of the two is better off and happier.

But Plato does not describe the dictatorial man immediately. Instead, he proceeds to him through a series of steps in Book VIII, in which he describes types of city that are worse than his own, and corresponding types of man who are worse than the rulers of his city. The types are: timocracy and the timocratic man; oligarchy and the oligarchic man; democracy and the democratic man; and finally dictatorship, the portrayal of which ends Book VIII. In the overall economy of Plato's argument, the purpose of these sketches is to show how cities and men are progressively made worse, less just, and less well off, by progressive deviations from the strictures governing Plato's own city (which is called kingship or aristocracy, depending on the inessential detail, from Plato's viewpoint, of whether they have one ruler or more than one). These sketches lead us to an understanding of the state of the dictatorial man, as Plato sees him, and show us the structure and effects of his character and his resulting life, so that we may compare it with that of the kingly ruler of the good city.

In Book IX Plato finally gives us a description of the dictatorial man. The comparison of his life with that of the philosopher-ruler, or the "kingly" man, is meant to constitute Plato's first argument for saying that the perfectly just man is better off than the perfectly unjust man (580a–c).

We must be careful to understand the contrast between the philosopher's kingly soul and the dictatorial soul, and to understand what makes the former completely just whereas the latter is completely unjust. The first thing to observe is that according to Plato, it is a natural function of the reason to rule in the soul, to direct and train the other parts, and to determine what actions will be performed. In the philosopher's soul the reason rules and in the dictatorial soul it does not; so in the latter we have a violation of justice: one part of the soul fails to perform the task to which it is naturally suited. So far, however, the account is superficial and does not make clear why it is the task of reason to rule, and why the rule of lust or *erōs*, which prevails in the soul of the dictatorial man, is tantamount to a condition of complete and perfect injustice.

The explanation is that under the rule of reason, according to what Plato claims, all of the desires and impulses of the soul are given adequate scope and satisfaction (not counting certain desires which Plato deems unnecessary), and so will remain reasonably quiet and not interfere with the satisfaction of others either by becoming too insistent through lack of satisfaction or by being excessively indulged and so growing stronger. Under the rule of lust, on the other hand, all of the other desires of the soul are thwarted, and lust is overindulged to the extent of taking on unnatural and unnecessary forms. For lust, in Plato's view, is the most obsessive of desires and leaves the least room for the adequate satisfaction of other desires. Reason, by contrast, incorporates the desire that is most conducive to the balanced and harmonious satisfaction of all desires (including *erōs* itself, 458b–460b), namely, the desire to manage the whole soul well, so that it will be free of conflict, happy, and good as a whole. Under reason, each desire is sufficiently attended to so that none ever attempts to thwart the others; under lust, all desires have to struggle for a chance at satisfaction. Hence, the justice of the philosopher's soul consists, as it should, in each part's performing its own function and not, as it were, meddling in that of another; and the injustice of the dictatorial man's soul consists in the fact that none of its parts adequately performs its own function.

This state of affairs in the completely unjust soul, Plato says, must result in misery. His argument for this contention—the first of his three arguments in Book IX for the preferability of the just life (see 576b–578b, n. A)—is made to depend on the analogy between the city and the soul which goes back to Book IV. The dictatorial man may present a superficial show of happiness, Plato says, but if his condition is like that of the dictatorially governed city, we must conclude that he is enslaved and miserable (*ibid.*, n. B).

In addition to this argument based on descriptions of kingly and dictatorial men, Plato offers two further arguments for thinking justice more beneficial than injustice, one in 580c–583a and the other in 583b–587b. The first of these arguments supposes that people fall into three types corresponding to the three parts of the soul, and that a person of a given type will advocate a life consisting of pleasure derived from the corresponding part of the soul, the part by which he is dominated. The argument that Plato then gives is an argument for accepting as true the judgment of the man dominated by reason, who advocates a life of the pleasures derived from reason. The other argument, in 583b–587b, is more closely tied to Plato's metaphysical theory and rests ultimately on the claim that the pleasures of reason are in a sense more "real" or "true" than those having to do with the body. The conclusion of both of these arguments is that the man dominated by reason, who is perfectly just and kingly, has the most pleasant life. (It is noteworthy that these arguments, unlike the first, explicitly employ the notion of *pleasure*; though the transition to this notion is made without warning or explanation, and one does not know for certain what Plato's reason was for making it—see 580c–581e, n. A.)

*   *   *

It is perhaps not too difficult to see in a general way why Plato believed that his kingly man is so much better off than the dictatorial man. But his account does leave one important point unclear. When he says that reason governs the soul so as to provide it with the greatest benefit, he does not make it explicit whether he is talking of a maximization of total welfare or happiness of the different parts of the soul, or, instead, of some other condition involving not merely total welfare in some straightforwardly quantitative way, but also the balance or distribution of welfare among the different parts. This issue is the analogue of the one raised above with regard to the welfare of the city, where we saw that the good of the city as a whole, in Plato's view, seemed not to be construed simply as the total quantity of the citizens' satisfactions. The question here raised is whether the good of an individual—of his entire soul, that is—is simply the total net satisfaction or welfare (or the like) of the parts of his soul, or something different. Just suppose, for example, that A has more total satisfaction than B. Does it immediately follow, on Plato's view, that A is better off, all things considered, than B? Or are there other considerations to be weighed? For example, suppose further that A's satisfaction is distributed very unevenly among the parts of his soul, so that reason has very little and appetite has a great deal, whereas B's satisfaction is distributed in a more desirable way, though it remains *in toto* less than A's. The question is: if such a circumstance occurred, would Plato say that B might be better off than A? Or would he say that the total amounts of satisfaction of A and B, regardless of anything else, were the decisive factors in determining which was better off? (In the case of the city, the question was whether the total sum of the happiness of the individual citizens is the decisive factor in how well off a city is, independently of distribution or anything else.) Plato's remarks do not provide an unambiguous answer to this question. Some of his remarks, such as 587b–588a, suggest that all that is in question is the total quantity of pleasure gained by an individual. But other parts of his argument suggest, on the contrary, that the way to the best life is not the maximization of the happiness of the soul's components, but through an appropriate balance of satisfactions of the different parts (see esp. 576b–578b, n. C). My own view is that Plato did not fully settle his mind on this issue in the *Republic*. (The *Philebus*, I believe, is primarily an effort to do so.) Accordingly, when we ask wherein lies the superiority of reason as ruler of the soul, from the standpoint of the welfare of the person, the answer may be either that reason can contrive the greatest possible total happiness of the parts of the soul, or else that it contrives the most harmonious arrangement and balance thereof.

*   *   *

Although Plato believes that one is in the best condition if reason rules one's soul, he also believes that not everyone is endowed with a reason strong enough, in some sense, to prevail over the other parts. Education, to be sure, can be used to correct some conditions of the soul, but apparently he thinks that many are irremediable. Whence it comes about that the rulers of a good city are inevitably in a very small minority (491b–494a). In such a city, a person who is not ruled by his own reason is put in a better condition by being ruled from outside, by the reason of someone else (590c–591a). The effect of this arrangement, of course, is to control the desires of the lower parts of the soul, and at least to approximate the condition of the rulers' souls in some degree. The exact degree to which members of the lower classes will be pleased with this arrangement, like the exact degree to which they will under-stand its rationale, is left somewhat unclear by Plato, though he does say that in his city there will be agreement about who should rule (430c–432a). On the whole, one must say that Plato has given us more substantial reflections about the psychology and motivation of his rulers than of the members of the other classes of citizens. One of the major objections, of course, to his claims about the possibility of establishing his city, and to its goodness, revolves around his neglect in this regard. He is too sanguine about the idea that the task of guardianship really answers to a natural human capacity and could in fact be performed; and he pays so little attention to the motivations of most people that he does not realize that because of their likely views about living in such a city as his, much more serious argument is needed to show that that city really can be called happy as a whole, and good, if indeed it can be.

*   *   *

Book X is both an epilogue that balances the prologue that is Book I, and a completion of some of the ideas that are left aside in Books II–IX. At the beginning of Book II, Plato says that he will show that justice is good both "for its own sake" and "for its consequences" (357b–358a). The distinction between these two kinds of goods is somewhat difficult to interpret and is not precisely what the modern reader might take it to be (358a–362c, n. C). Briefly put, it comes to the distinction between saying that justice is welcomed for what results solely from *it*, apart from any surrounding circumstances, and that it is welcomed because of what results from it in conjunction with surrounding circumstances. The principal surrounding circumstance that Plato has in mind is that of reputation, i.e., a person's reputation for being just or unjust. And he wants to show that justice is more beneficial than injustice, quite apart from what reputation the person may have (362d–368c). In other words, it is more beneficial independently of what other people may think or know about the just person. This is what he has tried to do in the part of the *Republic* that I have dealt with so far, namely, in Books II–IX.

In Book X he turns to the other project, of showing that justice is better than injustice, even when it operates in conjunction with other surrounding circumstances, such as the reputation for being just (612a–e). Or rather, he turns to this project in the middle of Book X, after dealing with certain other issues arising in Books II–IX, notably with whether or not poetry should be allowed in his projected city in the unrestricted manner in which it is allowed in actual cities. In Book III Plato has argued, on grounds having to do with the guardians' education and the need for them to fulfill their task, that poetry should not be allowed, and that they should be taught poetry only of a restricted sort. The discussion of Book X broadens the issue and tries to show Plato's metaphysical basis for the restriction (595c–605c).

Another issue raised in Book X is the question whether the soul of an individual is immortal (608c–611a). Plato believes and argues that it is, but a problem is raised by the conjunction of this view with his earlier contention that the soul is tripartite. For he sees reason to accept the principle that what is immortal cannot be divided into parts at all (611a–612a). But rather than pursuing this issue in detail, Plato shelves it by observing that he has treated the question sufficiently for his present purposes, which have to do with the status of the soul when embodied (612a).

These points discussed, Plato finally arrives at his argument that justice is beneficial by its operation with its circumstances as well as by its operation in isolation from them (612a–e). He contents himself with two brief treatments, one of the reputation of the just man among men and the other of his reputation among the gods. The conclusion is quickly arrived at in both cases that the just man is made better off by his justice than the unjust man by his injustice (612e–614a). If it seems that Plato reaches these conclusions rather hastily and without sufficient proof, one must remember that, as the challenges posed in Book II clearly show (358a–368c), he conceived himself to be facing opponents who thought that to show injustice more beneficial than justice, their best strategy was to admit that the existence of punishment for injustice does generally make the course of justice a prudent one, but to assert that if one were not *discovered* and *reputed* to be unjust, injustice would surely be more advantageous. So the argument in Books II–IX is the important one as it shows that justice is more beneficial to a person than injustice, quite apart from what is known or believed about that person. And Plato can take his opponents to be much less tenacious about insisting that injustice is advantageous even if one is recognized to be unjust.

Plato concludes the work with a myth, the Myth of Er (617d–621b), whose effect and purpose is not to prove that justice is beneficial, but rather to illustrate the way in which he believes this to be so, and with an exhortation to take seriously the decision whether or not to live a just life.

3. *The Theory of Forms and the Form of the Good.*

The relation of Plato's theory of knowledge and metaphysics to the main argument of the *Republic* is a difficult and tantalizing problem. On the one hand, he says enough to make clear that the relation is close and important, but on the other hand he says too little to allow us to see exactly what it is. Understanding of the Forms is said to be necessary for the rulers to know the Good and to perform their task of ruling properly (504d–506a), and enough is said about the status of the Good in Books VI–VII for us to be sure that Plato had some elaborate thoughts about it. But neither the *Republic* itself nor Plato's other writing, nor what we can attempt to glean about Plato's unwritten views (as in Krämer), gives us anything like a fully clear picture of what those thoughts were. They do not even make clear whether those thoughts were fully worked out or, as I am inclined to believe, sketchy in important respects.

Nevertheless, it is worthwhile to try to reconstruct some of the metaphysical and epistemological ideas that go along with Plato's views on ethics and political philosophy. For there are certainly hints permitting us to see at least the general direction of Plato's line of thinking, if not

all of the details. The following account is inevitably somewhat speculative (at certain places, as I shall indicate, more so than at others), and
little will depend on it elsewhere in this book (e.g., especially in sec. 4),
but it seems to me a likely way of pulling Plato's views together into a
fairly coherent whole. Lest confusion arise, I should emphasize the
independence of my main line of interpretation of the bulk of the
Republic from this discussion of the Theory of Forms. For example, that
Plato closely linked the notion of goodness with unity and stability as he
construed them, and regarded a thing's being unified and stable as an
important ground for calling a thing good, seems to be incontestable
when one examines the ethical argument in the *Republic*. That he
thought this fact to have some kind of metaphysical basis seems to me
equally incontestable. What is in doubt, on the other hand, is just what
he thought that metaphysical basis was. The present section is primarily
a suggestion about how that question might reasonably be answered.

*   *   *

I begin with a general account, very briefly expounded, of what Plato
thought that his Forms were; for these entities lie at the center of his
doctrine. This account is of course not the only one that interpreters
have put forward (it has been developed extensively in recent times,
particularly by Owen and Vlastos, though its leading idea can be found
earlier—see 476d–480a, n. C, *fin.*), but it seems to me the likeliest
description of what Plato had in mind.

Plato's initial notion of a Form, as expounded in *Rep.* 476–480
and 523–525 and in other dialogues such as the *Phaedo*, is the notion
of a thing that bears predicates (in the sense of predicate-expressions)
unqualifiedly or without qualification, by contrast to sensible objects,
which bear predicates only qualifiedly or with qualification. The
relevant notion of a qualification is a somewhat unclear one and is best
conveyed by example. One type of example is given by predicates
having to do with size, such as "large." Sensible objects, plainly, are
large only *compared to* other sensible objects, just as they are also small,
compared to different sensible objects. Thus we cannot correctly say
that any sensible object is large, *simpliciter*, without some further
addendum or completion referring to some thing by comparison to
which it is large. Another type of example is provided by the term
"beneficial," or the term "good" when it is used in the sense of "beneficial." A thing in the sensible world cannot be good in this sense without being good or beneficial *to* or *for* someone, a reference to whom

must be added as a completion to any attachment of the term "good" in this sense to a sensible thing.

Thus Plato views the matter. But along with the need for qualification or completion goes another idea, which is that sensible objects can have predicates attached to them only with qualification, precisely because the *same* sensible objects that bear one predicate with a certain qualification will also, perhaps inevitably, bear the *contrary* of that predicate, with a different qualification. Simple examples are that a single thing will be large compared to *A* but small compared to *B*, or beneficial to *X* but harmful to *Y*.

As one can see from these examples, the qualifications vary in type. Some arise because certain predicates are overt or disguised comparatives, such as "large." Others arise because of other sorts of relativity of predicates, as in the case of "beneficial." Still others arise for still other reasons. For example, Plato treats numerical words such as "one" as predicates requiring completion, as when he says that Socrates may be one man but is nevertheless also many parts, as Plato is willing to put the matter at (*Parm.* 129c–d). The boundaries of the class of predicates that Plato counts as incomplete in this manner are uncertain, and it may be that he changed them during his career. It has been suggested, for instance, that he at first did not but later did recognize a need for *temporal* qualifications on all predicates in their applications to sensible objects, on the ground that whatever predicate might attach to an object at some particular time must at some other time, whether earlier or later, not attach to it (Owen, ·*PPI*, p. 307). The basis for this latter idea could be the view that if all sensible objects are subject to generation and destruction (see, e.g., *Rep.* 546a), then even such predicates as might attach to a sensible object during the object's entire period of existence would have to be thought of as failing to attach to it before and after that period. The question whether this was indeed Plato's line of thought is subject to debate, as is the question of the exact boundary of the class of incomplete predicates. But however we answer these questions, and however we explicate the notion of incompleteness or predicates, the notion has a degree of rough comprehensibility that is sufficient for our purposes.

*   *   *

Certain important points, however, remain uncertain. For instance, sometimes the bearers of qualified predicates in the sensible world appear to be *particular* sensible things, whereas at other times they might be construed to be *types* of sensible things.

Thus, when Plato says that the same thing can appear to be both just and unjust (479a), it might be supposed that he means that of a given type of action (say, keeping a promise) some instances are just and others are unjust (see Irwin and Nehamas). Alternatively, he might think that the particular instance of keeping a promise is or appears just according to certain laws or standards (*e.g.*, Athenian standards, or yours) while at the same time appearing or being unjust by other standards. Or—a third possibility—he might not have attended to this issue. This last is recommended by the fact that he nowhere draws the relevant distinction, particularly when the matter arises (as in 479a–b and, even more strikingly, 523c *sqq.*); I take it that the likelihood lies here, though the point is not crucial to what concerns us now.

A more important point has to do with the difference between something's *being* both thus-and-so, with one qualification, and not thus-and-so, with another qualification, and its *appearing* both thus-and-so and not thus-and-so (with different qualifications). Though the matter is difficult, Plato seems to think that sensible objects both *appear* to and *do* hold their predicates only with qualification and along with their contraries. (See 479a–b with 476d–480a, n. C; the problem is that he might be taken to have illegitimately inferred that they do from the mere fact that they appear to, as remarked by Gulley, p. 29.) Thus, he not only thinks that the same thing will *appear* both large and small depending on its surroundings and the size of the objects in them (in the way in which the moon *appears* large when seen next to a star but appears small when seen next to a mountain over which it is rising), but also that it is correct to say it *is* both large and small, with the due qualification added (in the way in which the moon *is* large, compared to a penny, and *is* small, compared to the sun). And analogously for other predicates.

In contrast to sensible objects, which appear to and do bear their predicates only with qualification and along with their contraries, there exist objects that Plato calls, among other things, Forms (*eidē*). Plato's reasons for thinking that such objects must exist are not our concern here. What matters here is rather, in the first instance, that Forms are thought of as bearing their corresponding predicates *unqualifiedly* or *absolutely*, and without the accompaniment of their contraries. (To take account of certain passages in, especially, the *Sophist*, this interpretation requires either certain restrictions on this statement or else the supposition that that dialogue represents a later stage of Plato's views.) The effect of the lack of qualification varies, depending on the nature of the qualification involved, and in some cases will seem odd (as it did to Aristotle). Thus, whereas it may not be strange to think of the Form of the Beautiful as absolutely beautiful in this way (though many would disagree), it certainly seems peculiar to think that something is large without reference to some standard of comparison or other, as the Form of Large would have to be. (Of course, it might not seem peculiar to think that something could be larger than everything; but after all, if it is equal in size to itself and thus only larger than everything *else*, it would seem not to be truly large without qualification.) Likewise, it seems odd to suggest that something could be double without being double *of* something, and similarly for "half." And some philosophers, though not all, would also claim that nothing is absolutely one or unitary, but must always, as Aristotle insisted, be one in some specifiable way (e.g., one *of* some particular sort of thing). It may be that some of these oddities caused Plato to alter his theory later in his life, and certainly, as noted, they provoked criticism from Aristotle. But at the period of the *Republic*, Plato evidently believed that if they were indeed oddities, they were a reasonable price to pay for a powerful and general metaphysical theory. Although he regarded his theory as arguable on the basis of facts open to everybne's observation (517c–518d and, e.g., *Phaedo* 72–75), he never suggests that the finished theory itself must be straightforwardly commonsensical. On the contrary, he emphasizes the difficulty of philosophy and the necessity for long training to master it (531d–534d, 536b–540c, *Symposium* 209–212). One should not fall into thinking that all philosophers insist that their doctrines must cleave to what seems believable to the ordinary man or to the philosopher in his more ordinary moods. One antidote to this tendency might be to recall some of Russell's remarks in *The Problems of Philosophy*: "it is difficult to know that even the strangest hypotheses may not be true" (p. 24), and "whoever wishes to become a philosopher must learn not to be frightened by absurdities" (p. 31).

We have seen that the Forms, according to Plato, are not the same as the objects that we apprehend with our senses. But rather than saying, as some modern philosophers would say about objects that are not somehow "directly" sensible, that the existence of the Forms, and the truth of certain statements about them, must be *inferred* from what we do apprehend by sense, Plato instead believes that the Forms are themselves apprehended in some manner directly, by the mind rather than by the senses (see e.g., White, pp. 91–93). Sometimes this apprehension can come as the result of sensory cues (523a–524d, *Phaedo* 72–75), but it is still in important ways independent of sensibles. Attention to sensibles, he thinks, can indeed positively hinder one's apprehension of Forms (475e–476d), and the education recommended for philosophers consists of studies designed precisely to redirect one's attention away from the senses (523ff.).

*   *   *

I want now to begin to show how this interpretation of Plato's theory helps us to understand his views about ethics and value as they appear in the *Republic*. At the center of the discussion will be his conception of the Good, *i.e.*, the Form of the Good.

A direct corollary of the foregoing is that the Good *is good* without qualification or absolutely. By this is meant not just that the Good is unqualifiedly identical with itself, but that it is unqualifiedly good in the *predicative* sense of (as *we* might say) having the property of being good. We shall see in sec. 4 that the absence of qualification on the goodness of the Good has important repercussions on the attempt to understand Plato's ethical theory in modern terms. At present, however, the notable feature of this absence of qualifications is the fact that the Good is good *apart* from any reference to any particular person's tastes, likes, desires, or beliefs about what is good, and is not a notion of what is good or beneficial *to* or *for* someone or other. Rather, the idea of the Good is the idea of something that is good somehow independently of that reference to a benefited subject that is implicit in the notion of benefit as it is usually understood. This does not mean that the Good is bad for anyone. Nor does it deny that someone with a clear understanding of the world *must recognize* and *value* the Good. It means that, as Plato views the matter, the notion of the Good is the notion of something that can and should be recognized to be good apart from any consideration of something that is benefited. It is analogous to Plato's notion of the Form of Beauty, which, although it must be recognized to be beautiful by anyone with full knowledge or understanding, is nevertheless beautiful apart from any consideration of any particular thing or person in which or in whom some effect arises because of its beauty (*Symp.* 209–212). This notion of absolute goodness is hardly uncontroversial. To many philosophers it seems either abhorrent or incomprehensible, because they think that nothing can be conceived good apart from some sentient creature's interest in it. A classic example of a philosopher holding this view is William James, and the view has become so common among philosophers nowadays that many even find it hard to imagine that anything like Plato's conception of the Good has ever been seriously entertained. I am far from pretending that what I have said constitutes an adequate explanation of that conception, or is enough to show that the conception of absolute goodness is in the final analysis a defensible one. For the sake of philosophical broadmindedness, however, it is salutary to remind oneself that something much like it has been adopted by notable philosophers beside Plato, two good examples in the present century being Moore and, at a stage of his career before he was dissuaded by Santayana, Russell (see Moore; Russell, *EE*, and Schilpp, p. 470).

A closely connected point is that for Plato there is only *one* Form of Good; there are not different Forms, one for Benefit and one for some other sort of Goodness that is not benefit (e.g., Moral Goodness). Rather, benefit (or advantage or profit) is made to fall under the notion of goodness, represented by the Form of the Good (see 357b–c, 358e, 360c, 364a, among many other passages illustrating Plato's indiscriminate use of the word for "good," *agathon*, along with words meaning "profit" and the like), which is at the same time used to cover with equal propriety the notion of a virtue or excellence (*aretē*; see 427e–428a). Unlike many philosophers of more recent times, Plato does not believe in a plurality of notions of goodness, one of benefit, one of moral goodness, one of excellence, one of perfection, and whatever other possibilities there may be. The wide importance of this fact will emerge in sec. 4. For present purposes its relevance is just that one will search in vain for any sign in the *Republic* of a recognition that there is a relative notion of benefit, benefit *for* someone, that cannot be subsumed somehow under the notion of good *tout court*. The fact that this is so can only confirm the view that for Plato the Good is good absolutely in the sense explained.

Thus understood, the Good turns out to have what can be called a kind of "objectivity," in the following sense. The notion of benefit for a person seems inextricably tied, in one manner or another, to the particular desires and needs of that person, and to the pleasures and satisfactions that correspond to those desires. It is viewed as so tied by Plato in Book IX of the *Republic*, where the effort to show that justice is more beneficial to its possessor than injustice takes the form of showing that the former brings greater happiness, satisfaction, and pleasure than the latter (see sec. 2). To the extent that people's constitutions differ so as to produce differences in their desires and satisfactions, and to the extent also that circumstances never cease to produce conflicts between the full satisfaction of one person and that of another, different states of affairs will be beneficial to different people, and the same state of affairs will sometimes be beneficial to one person and harmful to another. To the extent, further, that these facts are reflected in people's views about what is as a matter of fact good, to that extent there will be disagreements about what is good. If one regards the matter in this way, then the notion of an unqualified and absolute good can naturally seem to offer a way of settling such disagreements, at least in theory. Stated simply, the point is that if I tend to call good what satisfies me and you tend to call good what satisfies you, and if there is bound to be conflict between us with respect to what states of affairs satisfy us, then we shall seem to fall into disagreements over what things are good, which would apparently be resolved if we could arrive at a notion of good that did not depend on our thus potentially conflicting views (see further sec. 4). The idea that there is a notion of the Good independent of such conflicts therefore can seem to offer an objective way of settling these disagreements. One problem, of course, is to show not merely that there is such a notion, but to show how it will help us in determining what things, over which disagreements may arise, really are good or as close to it as possible. Another problem, closely connected with this one, is to show what link there could be between grasping this notion of goodness and actually being moved to do the things that are seen, in the light of it, to exemplify it in some degree. Plato addresses both of these problems in the *Republic*, especially in Book VII (see sec. 4), though it is of course a matter of philosophical controversy how successfully he does so.

*   *   *

But Plato's general theory of Forms itself helps to provide some of the content of the notion of the Good, which will help him to address the problem just mentioned, and to try to vindicate the idea of a Good that is independent of any particular person benefited.

The first step on our way to seeing this involves something else about the relationship between sensible objects and Forms. On the basis of the idea that sensibles bear qualifiedly those predicates that Forms bear unqualifiedly, Plato is willing to say that in a certain manner sensibles are *copies* or *imitations* of Forms, suggesting that they have a resemblance to the Forms but that they fall short of perfect likeness. In some cases he may have in mind that sensibles approximate Forms in the way in which an imperfectly drawn circle approximates being perfectly circular. In the main, however, the idea is simply that the bearing of a predicate with whatever qualification, whether one of relation or a temporal one or some other, constitutes a failure on the part of the object to match perfectly the unqualified bearing of the predicate by the Form (see *Phaedo* 75a–b and *Tim.* 48e with Vlastos, *DRP*). In this sense, Forms exhibit perfectly or fully the attributes that sensibles exhibit only imperfectly, and are paradigms that sensibles replicate to only a limited extent. Qualifiedly beautiful sensible things are *only* qualifiedly beautiful; they are imperfect copies of what is unqualifiedly and purely beautiful without any admixture of ugliness (*Symp.* 211a), i.e., imperfect copies of that which most properly deserves the appellation "beautiful" (*Phdo.* 100–102 and White, pp. 74–75).

In addition to being models or paradigms, the Forms also have two other important properties. One is the property of stability and immunity to change, by contrast to sensibles, which are constantly altering (485b, *Phdo.* 78d–e)—this is a central tenet of Plato's theory. It is not clear whether Plato wishes to say that a Form is free of *everything* that could conceivably be called a change (such as even relational changes such as coming-to-be-better-apprehended-by-Socrates) or merely free of changes of some restricted class. One thing is clear, however, and that is that the Form of *F* is not stable in the sense of never having come to be *F* and never ceasing to be *F*. Rather, it is *F* without reference to time, or timelessly. (Not, that is, always or at *all* times—no more than the Form of the Large is large compared to everything—but somehow *independently* of time; in *Timaeus* 37–38 Plato expresses this idea by calling time only the image of eternity, and saying that no "was" or "will be" but only "is" applies to Forms; cf. Owen, *PTP.*) A sensible object, on the other hand, will be *F* only with some kind of temporal qualification, as noted.

The other important property of a Form is that this is thought of as somehow unitary or "one in form" (*Phdo.* 78d, 80b, *Symp.* 211b, e: *monoeidēs*). It is doubtful that this is meant to imply that each form is in *all* respects atomic and indivisible (although it is sometimes believed that this is so and that Plato was here under Parmenidean influence). But it at least implies that the Form of *F* is not in any sense a plurality of *F*s, but rather in some strong sense a single *F*.

Both of these properties of Forms can be readily derived from the idea that the Forms are unqualified bearers of predicates. In the first place, that the Form of *F* is (predicatively) *F* without any temporal qualification immediately entails that it does not alter in respect of being *F*, that is, change to or from being *F*. In the second place, the requirement that something be *F* unqualifiedly prevents it from being at the same time not *F*; and this, Plato believes, means that it cannot be many *F*s or a plurality of *F*s, for the reason that if it were, then there would be a way in which it would be correct to say that is was not *an F* (cf. Owen, *PNB*, p. 226, n. 8). In a passage of the Republic to which we shall return again, 422e–423a, he says that a thing does not properly deserve the title "city" if it is in fact two cities rather than one, but must be called something else. Moreover, Plato also regards the property of being unitary as derivable from the stability of a Form. He frequently pictures the source of destruction of a thing (which is what would befall the Form of *F* if, *per impossible*, it altered in respect of being *F*) as its being in some way composite, so that its elements can be split asunder, and he likewise views immunity to destruction as resulting from a lack of parts that might thus be divided (*Phdo.* 80b, *Rep.* 381a–b).

           *   *   *

Having seen these features of Forms, we can now consider their role in Plato's ideas about value and goodness in the *Republic*. Here the major relevant facts are two. First, Plato treats his city in certain respects like a Form, although it cannot strictly be a Form, and gives it the properties that we have seen attaching to Forms, at least to the extent possible. Second, he uses the possession by the city of these properties as his chief grounds for calling it good and his arrangements for it beneficial.

The first point emerges in Plato's frequent emphasis on the idea that his city is as unified and as changeless as it can be. Its unity is first stressed in 422e–423a, d, just cited, and reappears often throughout the work (422e–423d, n. B). Its stability is equally prominent, particularly in his insistence that any innovation be discouraged (422a, 424b). And he also makes a connection between unity and stability, in his claim that dissension (*stasis*) is what leads to change of constitution (545d). Moreover, Plato speaks of his city as a model or *paradeigma*, using the word that he often applies to Forms as a way of indicating that his city is to be regarded as a kind of exemplar (592b, 472d–e). But in spite of these resemblances to a Form, he makes it plain that the city is not a Form. He says that it is liable to destruction, like all sensible, created things (546a), and he frequently makes explicit the fact that it is an institution designed to deal with the imperfections of the sensible world (369b–d, n. B), particularly because its unity as a city is to some extent an enforced one, which must be established against important centrifugal forces within it (590c–591a, n. C). (It is another question whether he thought that there is or could be such a thing as the Form of City.)

In addition, however, Plato views the unity and stability of his city as the basis of its goodness and desirability as a political institution, as we saw in sec. 2, in the course of the argument establishing his identification of justice. That is, his ground for calling the city good, and saying that it possesses virtues or excellences, is its cohesiveness and consequent resistance to destruction (427e–428a, nn. B, E). Not only does the goodness of the city have its basis in this unity and stability, but the same features provide the ground for his assertion that his organization of the city is responsible for good or benefit *to* the city: for he says that the greatest good for the city is what holds it together and makes it one, and the greatest evil what pulls it apart and makes it many (461e–462e, n. B).

Moreover, the same ideas applied to the city are also applied to the individual human being. The desirability of an individual's being one or unified has two aspects. One has to do with Plato's Principle of the Natural Division of Labor. The idea here is that a person with a single task is better at it, and in general better off, than a person who divides his time among many activities (423d, 397e, 394e). The other aspect is connected with Plato's theory of the parts of the soul: the man whose soul is harmoniously bound into a unity is, as we have seen, regarded as better and happier than one whose soul is full of dissension and conflict, and this claim is the nerve of Plato's first argument in Book IX for the superiority of the just life to the unjust life (580a–c; cf. 554d).

* * *

So for Plato, being unified and stable is closely connected with being in a certain sense good. Perhaps we should simply take this as a brute fact, to be partially explained by remarking that other philosophers also have thought of unity and changelessness as associated with goodness. But if we are willing to be a bit more speculative, we can use another apparent element of Plato's theory of Forms to provide the fact with an explanation.

We begin by noting once again that the good-making properties relied on by Plato are, as we saw, properties that attach to Forms, and we then ask whether their being properties that attach to Forms is in any way responsible for their being good-making in Plato's eyes. On a certain interpretation of Plato's theory, the answer is affirmative. If we accept this interpretation, therefore, we shall be able in some measure to explain why unity and stability should seem to Plato to make his city, and the corresponding kind of man, good. But it should be noted at the start that the interpretation of Plato's theory is—like all interpretations of this part of his theory—quite speculative, and that it encounters at least one significant difficulty.

In being an unqualified specimen of F, the Form of F is quite clearly regarded by Plato as being in a certain manner a perfect and nondefective specimen of F, whereas a sensible object is merely a poor or defective specimen of F (e.g., *Phdo.* 75a–b). Pursuing this hint, we may perhaps accept the suggestion that Forms are perfect and in that sense *good* specimens of the very attributes of which sensibles are less perfect or good specimens (see Hare, pp. 35–37, with 507a–509c, n. B). This notion of goodness is partially adumbrated at the end of Book I of the *Republic* (352d–353c), where Plato explains the virtue or excellence (*aretē*) of a thing in terms of its effective performance of its "function" (*ergon*). Here, having the excellence of an *F* amounts to performing the function of an *F* well (353b–c). The notion of goodness that I am discussing amounts to a kind of generalization of the idea in Book I, to all things corresponding to which there are Forms, even those which are not idiomatically said in English or Greek to have a function or *ergon*. If we think of goodness in this manner, then we shall say that the Form of *F* is a good specimen of *F*, *i.e.*, good of its kind *as* an *F*. But if to be the Form of *F* is in and of itself to be a good *F*, then it is clear why Plato should regard his city as a good city, even though his city, as I have said, is not itself a Form. For as it is as close as possible to being unqualifiedly a city, through being a unified and stable city (notice esp. 422e–423a), it is as close as possible to being a good city, under the interpretation just expounded. In the same way, any specimen of *F* will be regarded as the better for being more unitary and less changeable, and thus for being more like the Form of *F*.

It will have occurred to the reader already that there is paradox lurking in the account of Forms just suggested, because there are some Forms that we might call "bad Forms," such as the Form of the Bad (Evil) and the Form of the Unjust (476a; cf. Cherniss, *ACPA*, p. 266, n. 175), and there is a certain strangeness in thinking of such things as good. This difficulty with the present interpretation might seem to be palliated by the reflection that, after all, in calling the Form of Bad good we mean to say only that it is *unqualifiedly* bad, and so only in *that* sense a "good" sample of the bad. Whether this is a successful response to the problem is a question too involved for discussion here, as is the question whether we can reasonably believe that Plato adopted either it or some other response to the difficulty. For if we cannot believe this, then of course the credibility of this part of the interpretation of his theory must suffer. I am inclined to believe that certain things that he says do suggest some such response on his part, but I shall have to reserve argument on the matter for the present, and I therefore reiterate that this part of the interpretation must be taken as conjectural.

Waiving this difficulty, we might still see a problem in the fact that merely by showing that his city is good in the sense of being good *as* a city, he does not thereby show that it is necessarily a desirable political institution to have or live in. But Plato has tried to close off this line of attack against his argument (an attack that could be mounted quite apart from the foregoing interpretation) long before he claims in

Book IV that the city is good (427e–428a). For the initial description in Book II of the way in which the city arises is designed precisely to show that it *is* a desirable institution, both in being a response to human needs (cf. sec. 2), and in arising in a natural rather than an arbitrary or externally imposed manner (369e–370c, n. C). Plato feels himself then free to go on, granted that a city is what is wanted, to show what the best possible city is like.

Aside from the problems reviewed just now, the present line of interpretation has the advantage of supplying us with an explanation, arguably superior to others, of Plato's statement at 509b that the Good is responsible for the very being of knowable objects, namely Forms, as well as for their being known. For if the form of F is in and of itself a good F, then (see Hare) it is plausible to say, at least on certain assumptions, that the being of the Form includes goodness; and if to understand the Form of F is to grasp what it is to be a good F, then knowledge of the Form must involve the knowledge of the Good. Someone might object to this line of reasoning on the ground that when we speak of a good F, different notions of goodness are involved depending on what term takes the place of "F" (thus Hare). But as we have seen and shall see further in the next section, Plato is convinced that there is a single kind of goodness in all cases, the Form of the Good. Much more serious is the difficulty mentioned earlier, that "bad Forms" would have to have the Good somehow involved in their being. (Cherniss, *SEAP*, p. 253, rightly points out that there is no paradox involved in saying that knowledge of the Good is required for knowledge of such Forms; but I am sceptical of his suggestion in n. 34 that 517c3–5 cancels the implication of 509b as I have just reported it.)

There are of course numerous further links that Plato sketches in Books VI–VII between his views on the Good and various parts of his doctrines of knowledge and metaphysics, particularly those parts having to do with dialectic, and his criticisms of the procedures of geometers and arithmeticians of his day (esp. 511a–d, 533b–e). At certain points he seems to suggest that knowledge of the Good will provide us with a method of demonstrating what those practitioners take for granted in the form of axioms or postulates. But the basis of this suggestion, and of other elements of his doctrine on these matters, is left unexplained (as he well realizes—509c), and in any case lies to the side of our concern with his ethical views.

*   *   *

Whether or not we try to explain it along the foregoing lines, there is obviously a connection in the *Republic* between unity and cohesiveness and stability on the one hand and goodness and benefit in both a city and an individual on the other. This connection helps Plato present his attributions of goodness as having the kind of "objectivity" that we earlier saw him to want. The criterion of goodness in the city is not, as he describes the matter, the desires and likes of any particular people in the city, but rather the way in which the parts of the city avoid dissension and dissolution (427e–428a, n. B), and the same holds for the individuals said to be good (444a–e, n. B). By making us see this, Plato attempts to show us how an understanding, however incomplete, of what the Good is can help us to make more reliable judgments about what things are good than we would be able to make on the basis of our own unconsidered preferences. And this understanding, carried further by the education that the rulers of the city undergo, is what makes them able to guide their administration of the city in the way that Plato thinks they should, in contradistinction both to those who merely act by whim, like the democratic man (559d–562a, n. A), and to those who try to follow the whims of the majority, like the demagogue or the sophist (491b–494a). For part of the goodness of the philosopher-ruler, appropriately, is that he has a single, unified plan by which his actions are directed, namely, his understanding of the Good (519b–d). It is now time to see how this conception of his plan is to be pulled together and connected to his own benefit and to the notion of justice.

4. *The structure of the ethical theory of the* Republic.

In section 1, we saw a sketch of the view that Plato is usually thought to have adopted about the relationship between duty and interest. It was that when there is a conflict between the two, reason must choose the latter, but that, fortunately, there is very little conflict between them, so that we are rationally justified in following duty. According to this interpretation, Plato held that this coincidence of duty and interest would be clear to anyone who understood what duty and interest really consist in, and that the only reason for seeing conflict between the two is a failure adequately to grasp these two notions.

But this interpretation involves a misunderstanding of Plato's meaning in the *Republic*, as the foregoing two sections have already begun to show. We must now see what the true nature of Plato's views on this matter is. There are two reasons for doing so, one historical and one philosophical. The historical reason is simply to discover what the point of his ethical view actually was. The philosophical reason is that his view, correctly interpreted, turns out to have a special character which distinguishes it from theories that have become prevalent in recent times. I myself believe that in its structure—though not in its substance—Plato's theory shows us the correct way in which to construct a theory of ethics. But I shall not argue this claim here. What I shall do is simply to try to explain the alternative sort of theory that Plato presents, and how it shows us that the type of theory that contemporary philosophers tend to accept is by no means the only possibility. Even if the contemporary tendency be the correct one, to understand why it surpasses this Platonic rival would be to gain a deeper understanding of its foundation.

*   *   *

We have already seen, in sec. 2, the most significant case in which Plato believes that people should and do act against their own interests (or would if they could), for the sake of justice and the good of a society as a whole. This was the case of the rulers in Plato's city, who ruled in the city even though it would have been better for them not to. About other people, including other people in his city, he says much less, because in the *Republic* he is more interested in the capacities and motives of the rulers in his city than in those of anyone else. But the existence, not to mention the importance, of this case suffices to show that he does not think that the only possible or reasonable motive for acting justly is to increase one's own happiness.

On the other hand, it remains true that the main purpose of the *Republic* is to argue, against people such as Thrasymachus, that being just is beneficial to its possessor. And it remains likewise true that in certain places, for example at the end of Book IX and in the latter part of Book X, he concentrates his attention on those circumstances in which being just does increase one's happiness (see esp. 591a–592b, n. C). So even though he believes that there are motives for being just other than self-interest or the desire for one's own happiness, it nevertheless cannot be denied that he is very much interested in the benefits to be gained by being just.

The juxtaposition of the facts set forth in the foregoing two paragraphs should lead us to realize that the picture is more complicated than we might have expected or hoped. Plato's notion of the relationship between justice and one's own good needs much more careful scrutiny.

What part does he think that the effort to gain one's own good plays, and what part does he think it should play, in one's effort to be just and act justly?

*   *   *

Another complication is the fact that the gap between Plato's actual view and what is generally attributed to him is even greater than what I have just said would lead one to suspect. As I remarked in sec. 1, the general interpretation of Plato follows the usual philosophical view of the problem of duty and interest in its manner of construing what that problem is. It supposes that we have at our disposal two concepts, in some sense independent of each other, one of duty (or the like) and one of self-interest or one's own good (or the like). Conflicts between duty and interest are regarded as at least conceivable. When there are such conflicts, or when we are asked to say how we should resolve them if they occurred, our answer must consist in letting the concepts stand as they are and showing how one is to choose either what falls under one or what falls under the other, that is, to choose one's duty or one's own good. It is accurate to say, I think, that the most popular candidate, among philosophers at least, for the task of making this choice is *reason*. Some philosophers might formulate this view by saying that there is a faculty of reason that is the appropriate faculty to decide whether in cases of conflict we are to prefer duty or interest. Others would express it, without talk of "faculties" or the like, by saying that when one is presented with this choice, the task is to decide what is the reasonable or rational course to take. Standards of rationality are then assumed or somehow arrived at, and the choice is made. But—and this is still the crucial point—when the choice is made or described, it is portrayed as being between two independent concepts, that of duty and that of one's own interest, neither of which is in any sense reduced to the other. This description will become clearer when the Platonic view of the situation is contrasted with the modern one here sketched.

We may begin to see why Plato's view of the problem of duty and interest differs from this modern one as soon as we reflect briefly on the most striking fact about the scheme of ethical notions that appears in the *Republic*. It is the unique and preeminent position of the notion of goodness, or, as Plato thinks of it, the (Form of the) Good, taken as a single notion covering all types of goodness.

In the present context, what this preeminence of a single notion of goodness means is—to summarize briefly what we shall see at greater length—that choices ordinarily viewed as those that reason must make between duty and interest are regarded by Plato as decisions about what is, in a very broad sense, good or best, i.e., what exemplifies the good to the greatest extent. In short, Plato holds that we must know what is *best* in order to adjudicate between duty and one's own good as those things are conceived by modern philosophers.

*   *   *

To see how Plato thinks that he can explain this position satisfactorily, we must look more closely at his notion of the Good. The problem for him is to develop a notion of goodness that is sufficiently clear for us to see how, when we ask in specific cases whether we are to choose to perform our obligations or to pursue our own good, we can answer such questions by asking, and answering, the question which course of action or state of affairs is the good or best one.

The first essential fact is that, as was already apparent in secs. 2 and 3, Plato allows only one notion of goodness, and not the several that many modern views are inclined to insist on (see also 504d–506a, n. C, and 519d–521b, n. E). Contemporary reflections on uses of the word "good" have led to the opinion that several different notions of goodness, or meanings or uses of the word "good", ought to be recognized. The main ones are as follows: a notion of goodness or *benefit for* a person, a notion of *moral* goodness applicable to people (along with a somewhat different notion of moral goodness applicable to actions and some other things), a notion of *excellence* (often thought of as goodness-of-a-thing's-kind, applicable to things as falling under certain types—e.g., an excellent swimmer), and a notion of *perfection* (often not distinguished from excellence, and often also applied to things as falling under certain types). This list is not exhaustive, but it is sufficient for our purposes.

Plato's belief in a single Form of the Good does not allow for any irreducible differences between notions of goodness. Some interpreters are inclined to say for this reason that he has confused distinct senses of the word "good." But this is the wrong way to look at the matter. Although it is true that he has been insufficiently attentive to significant linguistic distinctions, it is better—and more conducive to philosophical illumination—to see him as actively *trying* to construct a theory in which such distinctions among notions of goodness will be, as it were, transcended. The point of having such a theory is not at all hard to see. It is one way of trying to avoid the possibility of a conflict in practical reasoning. As we know, conflicts can arise if we recognize claims on us of irreducibly different notions of goodness, and we shall be in doubt about what to do or how to be. Thus, the claim of goodness in the sense of moral goodness may struggle with goodness in the sense of benefit for ourselves, or for someone else for that matter; and a claim of some other sense of excellence, or of some kind of perfection (e.g., artistic), can struggle with both. As we saw too, it is possible to invoke some criterion of reasonableness or rationality to make the choices thereby rendered necessary. But Plato tries to cut off the issue earlier, treating the notion of goodness as providing the final criterion to be used in the exercise of practical reason, and endeavoring to show how we can resolve real or apparent conflicts between seemingly different types of goodness, as well as other conflicts, by understanding what the Good is and seeing how it can be exemplified in the physical world. Not that reason or rationality is absent from Plato's scheme. For it is the task of reason to apprehend the Good and to plan strategy for action (esp. 540a–b). But as Plato views the matter, the proper activity or reason is to be explained as its correct apprehension of the Good and use of this apprehension, and it is the concept of the Good, rather than the concept of rationality, that he thinks we must primarily and directly scrutinize when we wish to understand fully how to live and act.

* * *

Plato does believe that the notion of the Good in fact has the features necessary to guide us in our efforts to determine what to do and how to form our characters. He tries to put himself in a position to compare justice and benefit for oneself as two kinds of goods, which we may examine in order to discover which, in a sense to be explained, takes precedence over the other. On the one hand, justice is treated as a virtue or excellence (*aretē*), that is, as an attribute whose presence in a thing makes it good, or as, so to speak, a way of being good or a kind of good-ness (see 427e–428a, n. E). The notion of benefit or advantage, on the other hand, is thought of as having to do with what is *good for* some person or some other type of thing (such as a city, as in 461e–462e). The question now is, which of these goods is overriding in the kinds of circumstances to which Plato is attending?

Here his metaphysical theory is supposed to provide the answer. In the case of the philosopher-rulers, obviously, the answer is that they are to choose justice and the good of the city, and eschew the life that would be best for them. For the Form of the Good is, analogously to all Forms (cf. sec. 3), good unqualifiedly. By contrast, other things that are good are so only with some qualification of one sort or another. But it would be through the addition of some qualification that the notion of benefit or good relative *to* something would arise, the addition of a reference to some person benefited being treated as a qualification in the relevant sense. The Good is accordingly good without qualification, whereas various benefits are good only *to* or *for* someone or other, because the thing that is good for one person is capable of being bad for or harmful to another (sec. 3). Now the management of the city, as Plato emphasizes (419a–421c, 519d–521b), involves seeing to the benefit of the city as a whole, and is therefore as far as one can get, in the circumstances offered by nature (369b–d, n. B, and 472e–473b, n. A), from simply benefiting some people while harming others. That the good of the city is in this way more of an unqualified good than one's own good, which must in general be sought at the expense of others, is obviously linked with the idea of the unity of the city, which makes it possible, to a considerable extent, for the whole city to be benefited together (461e–462e, 419a–421c, 519d–521b). The upshot is that the good of the city is the more unqualified good than one's own good. But because the former good can be maintained only by the maintenance of the justice of the city, the claim of justice takes precedence over the philosopher-ruler's self-interest. The philosopher-ruler himself is supposed to understand this fact, because he fully comprehends the notion of the Good and is motivated to act accordingly.

It is clear that this particular manner of dealing with the conflict between justice and self-interest is rooted in certain metaphysical views, and that someone not accepting those views would have to approach the problem in a different manner. But that does not mean that such a person could not regard the problem essentially as it is posed by Plato, that is, as a problem of telling what sort of good is in a certain sense overriding. (For a view that is somewhat along these lines, see Reiner, *GS*, whose way of interpreting Plato, however, is different from mine.)

*   *   *

But before we conclude our examination of the structure of Plato's theory, we still must understand why the *Republic* has the main purpose that it has, namely, to show that the fully just man is better off than anyone else, especially the fully unjust man. Given the other things that he says, why should Plato be interested in making this claim?

Let us begin to answer this question by considering the motivation of the philosopher-ruler to rule in Plato's city. The philosopher-ruler, at the end of his education (531d–534d), is able to comprehend the Form of the Good and to see that, so to speak, his own benefit or good is not really an unqualified good in the sense that the Form of the Good is, and that it is in this way less a good, i.e., less close an approximation of the Good, than the good and justice of the city.

It is very important to realize that in Plato's view, this understanding will provide the rulers with an overriding motive to rule the city, without their going through any further step of discovering that this is good for themselves, and indeed, in spite of their discovering that it is not (519d–521b, n. E). Plato does not give a full explanation of how the apprehension of the Good motivates. It is clear that in his doctrine, reason is not a passive thing, as it is in Hume's view, and that it can set the person in motion without the aid of the rest of the soul. I am inclined to believe, in fact, that Plato thought that the mere apprehension of the Good could move a person to action without *any* other further step of *any* kind, and that, for him, to apprehend the Good fully along with a situation in which it might be exemplified *simply is* to have a desire overwhelming all others to see that instantiation take place. (This seems to me—though this is not the appropriate place to explore the matter—Plato's version of the Socratic view that no one "willingly sins.")

Not everyone, Plato thinks, is situated and disposed as is the philosopher-ruler. Many of us, he is aware, are disinclined to do things or to try to alter our characters if we do not believe that we shall gain some benefit thereby. Moreover, even those with a capacity to be philosopher-rulers pass through a long stage in life during which they do not have a clear apprehension of what the Good is and are moved strongly by consideration of their own interests, and Plato's plan of education explicitly makes provision for this fact. For the earlier stages of education of guardians and rulers is governed by the idea that they must perceive a community of interest between themselves and their city, so that they will undertake without hesitation to benefit the city (412d–e). Only when they reach a full understanding of the Good, and are therefore fit to take on the task of ruling in its entirety, are they prompted by the desire to see the Good exemplified, apart from their own interest (519d–521b, 531d–534d, 540a–541b).

There is therefore plenty of scope for a person to be usefully moved by self-interest in the direction of justice, and indeed Plato may well think that appreciation of one's own self-interest, and other limited sorts of goodness, are in some way a necessary preliminary to a full understanding of the Good itself (cf. the progression in the appreciation of types of beauty in *Symposium* 209e–210d). In any case, it is evident why he could think that there was a clear point in showing how justice produces benefit for its possessor.

Yet the question is not merely why Plato thought it worthwhile to argue that justice is beneficial, but whether this claim is fully consistent with the idea that philosopher-rulers sacrifice their own interests to some degree in ruling their city. The question is, accordingly, whether this idea commits Plato to holding that there are men who are not perfectly just and yet are better off than perfectly just men. This would not be shown simply by citing non-ruling philosophers who are happier than the rulers in Plato's city. One has to show further that these non-ruling philosophers are less just than the philosopher-rulers. Now for Plato, the presence of justice in an individual means that the parts of his soul are performing their own natural tasks without interference from the others. So the question is whether a non-ruling philosopher would be less just in this sense than a ruling one. Offhand, there seems no reason why he should be. He may simply live in a city in which he has not been called on to rule and so merely live withdrawn from political concerns, as Plato says in concluding Book IX (591a–592b). In that case we could not cite him, against Plato, as a man who is not perfectly just and yet better off than a ruling philosopher.

Some sort of problem clearly is raised for Plato, however, by the fact that it is *just*, he says, for his philosopher-rulers to rule (540d–e, 520e). What is plainly meant, in the first instance, is that a failure by the philosopher-rulers to rule would lessen or destroy the justice in the city. But it does seem reasonable to think that this event would either cause, or turn out to be caused by, a lessening of the justice in the souls of those rulers in whom the failure occurred. Thus there is a possibility, it seems, that a philosopher-ruler in Plato's city might, because of some failure in his education, retreat into philosophy and thereby become better off though less just. If this happened, then, we would have a case in which justice was not altogether beneficial for its possessor.

Although there are various ways in which one might try to allow Plato to avoid this difficulty, he does not seem to have availed himself of them, because in spite of appearances, the mentioned possibility is not at all a serious one for him, and there is no reason why he should not have tolerated it with equanimity. The only people who could be tempted by it to retreat from justice are philosopher-rulers, who had reached the point of being able to philosophize in the fullest and most rewarding manner. No one else would be in a position to gain greater benefits by being less just. Yet these philosopher-rulers are precisely the people, as we have seen, who have come to an understanding of the

Good, and are motivated by that understanding in a manner that overrides their tendency to be moved by their own interests. All others will be in a position, Plato believes, to benefit themselves by becoming more just. The case of the philosopher-ruler, therefore, is not a damaging one for Plato in his effort to convince people to be just by showing them the rewards of being so. Nor is it an important exception to the view that justice brings benefits, because he regards the life of the philosopher-rulers as very, very good indeed, in spite of the sacrifice that they must make (465c–466c).

Plato's theory of ethics, along with his view of our motive to abide by correct ethical injunctions, thus turns out to be more complicated by far than we might have realized. According to him, the ability to understand and be moved by the notion that he makes central to his system, the notion of the Good, is vouchsafed to only a few. For others, he must argue a coincidence between benefit and justice, and this is what he tries to do. It is unclear, however, whether he expects, or can legitimately expect, that this argument will be convincing to those who are neither capable of grasping nor inclined to accept, his notion of the Good, at least to some fair degree. In fact, as we have seen (sec. 2 and 576b–578b, n. A), he gives three distinct arguments for the superiority of the completely just life over the completely unjust life. The first depends heavily on his account of the virtues or excellences in a city and a soul. This account in turn depends on his claim that his city is good and on his description of the rulers' role in it, and might well seem to rest heavily on some comprehension of his notion of goodness. The same would appear to be true of the third argument, in 583b–587b, which relies on his metaphysical theory and its claim about which pleasures are more "real" or "true." The second argument, in 580c–583a, is less obviously subject to this difficulty. It is the argument for accepting the judgment of the man governed by reason that his life is more pleasant than any other life. Although it involves Plato's overall theory to a lesser degree than the others, the non-philosopher who accepts it must still understand the reasons given for saying that the judgment of the man governed by reason is to be accepted, and this understanding, if really complete, might well be claimed to require that he himself be a philosopher after all.

At this point it becomes difficult to speculate about what Plato's intentions were, and whether he would have agreed that there is some truth in the idea that the whole argument in Books II–IX really can be convincing only to philosophers (i.e., those of the philosopher-ruler type) and not to those who are without this capacity. Even if he would have agreed, however, it would not follow that the argument has no point, because we saw that even future philosopher-rulers begin by being taught a coincidence of their own interests with the claims of justice (412d–e), and so the argument of Books II–IX as a whole may be thought of as addressed to those who have the potential to be philosopher-rulers, and who have some ability, though incomplete (506b–507a), to understand the notion of the Good. This interpretation would also explain the role of Book X in the economy of the work. For that book would turn out to be addressed to those not addressed in Books II–IX, that is, to those without the capacity to understand the philosophical concepts involved in them. I have in mind, of course, not the discussion of poetry in 595a–608b, but the arguments in 608c–621b, which are designed to show that the consequences of justice are superior to those of injustice (612a–e, n. A). It is not hard to see that those arguments are weaker and less elaborately and carefully constructed than those in Books II–IX (612a–e, n. B), and that they depend little on a clear understanding of the notion of justice which Plato has explained, and of its relationship to the Good. It is therefore perhaps reasonable to follow those who have regarded Book X as an essentially popular argument rather than as one appealing to full philosophical understanding. (This is *not*, however, to deny that Plato believes much of the content of these arguments, but only to deny that he thinks that they have full rigor and cogency.)

Still, whether or not we accept this view of the status of the various arguments in Book X, there turns out to be an important difference between genuine philosophers and others, in Plato's view, with regard to the way in which they are motivated to act on the claims of justice.

*   *   *

The most distinctive feature of Plato's ethical theory is the preeminent position that he gives to the Good, and the way in which he allows the good of an individual to be, as it were, submerged in it. This will seem to many the most unreasonable element of his doctrine. It does not seem natural to most contemporary philosophers to think of one's own good (especially if this is distinguished from what one happens to want at the moment) as comparable to a partial view of some objective value, the Good, which can be seen from a somehow wider perspective and even cause what will seem to be damaging to one's interests.

On closer consideration, however, this idea does not appear any more difficult to accept than the idea that one's own self-interest can be legitimately overridden by moral *obligation* or *duty* as they are normally conceived. Impossible though it is to discuss this issue fully here, I think that it can nevertheless be seen, when the proposition is placed before one (especially in the light of the difficulty in showing *how* duty can override one's interest), that the notion of an overriding good that outweighs one's own good is not intrinsically less intelligible than that of a categorical duty that does the same thing. In fact, it seems to me that the advantages are on the former side, and that one's acceptance of the very claim that one's good is overridden by duty depends on one's notion of a good, in some sense independent of one's own good, involved in doing one's duty (cf. Reiner's use of the concept of *Werte*, in his *GS*; for a discussion of a different way of subordinating duty to goodness, see Frankena, *PEV*).

To be defensible, such a theory as Plato's must, of course, resist the objection that it is really tantamount to a theory representing the final claims on behalf of things or actions as claims of duty or obligation. Such an objection would say that if the attribution of goodness to something is said by this theory to be *"overriding,"* then that must be to say that it is *to be* preferred, which can only mean, in turn, that the thing *ought* to be preferred, or that there is a *duty*—indeed, an overriding duty—to prefer it. Such an objection might indeed gain support from a Platonic passage such as 352d, where it is said that the topic at issue is the question how one *must* or *should (chrē)* live. On behalf of the theory, the response to the objection need not be to deny that things that are good ought to be done. What the theory maintains, however, is that this is not the (in some sense) *basic* fact about them. The basic fact is rather that they are good, and their being obligatory, if they are, is a somehow derivative fact that follows from this. They are, so to speak, obligatory (if they are) *because* they are good, and not the other way around. If Plato's insistence on the preeminence of the Good, even over Justice, is to mean anything at all, it would seem to have to be upheld in this fashion.

An analogous defense of the preeminence of the Good must be mounted against the idea, already discussed, that the final judgment about matters of value is one not of goodness but of rationality. I have already observed that, for Plato, the task of reason is to apprehend the Good. The Good is apprehended by reason, but—so to speak again—it is not good *because* it is apprehended by reason; rather, reason is regarded as operating *correctly* when, and because, it succeeds in apprehending the Good. Moreover, by analogy to what was said in the previous paragraph, the basic fact that one cites in approving an action must, for

Plato, be that it is good, not simply that it is preferred by reason. Of course, it *will* be preferred by reason operating correctly, but this is to say—once more—that it will be preferred by reason when reason has succeeded in apprehending the Good and applying that apprehension to the task of choosing actions. It is not difficult to see that Plato's view must be uncongenial to those who would prefer to rely in the final analysis on a criterion somehow "internal" to the operations of reason, rather than on some standard of faithfulness to something outside of itself. That preference is easily understandable and can be defended by powerful arguments. But it is not Plato's preference.

Plato's tradition in ethics, then, gives a special place to a single, undivided, objective concept of goodness, and makes all other evaluative concepts subordinate to it. I would regard this tradition as detachable from the metaphysical theory with which Plato links it. If one does not accept that metaphysical doctrine, then one is free to try to formulate the notion of an overriding good different from his notion of an unqualified good. One must also show why such a good is overriding, and how we may tell which things manifest it more or less, so that the notion of an overriding good will help us decide what to do and what traits of character to foster in ourselves.

5. *The structure of Plato's theory contrasted to certain modern theories.*
Interpreters of the *Republic* frequently make efforts to classify Plato's ethical theory within the scheme of classification that is commonly used in the Anglo-American world for contemporary theories. More often than not, however, the efforts are both unsuccessful and even somewhat halfhearted. Many other interpreters simply eschew the effort altogether. We have now seen enough of Plato's theory, however, to understand what the difficulty is, and why the theory seems to resist classification in these contemporary terms.

Let us begin by seeing how the theory differs from two contemporary theories to which it is sometimes assimilated. When we have done this, we shall be able to give a deeper and more general characterization of the important differences between Plato's theory and others.

First, consider ethical egoism. I shall not attempt to distinguish all of the various forms of ethical egoism, and I shall gloss over the difficulties that arise when one tries to state what ethical egoism is. I shall consider ethical egoism to be a doctrine that recommends, in one set of terms or another, the pursuit of one's own good as the correct way of conduct. Given this much, it is easy to see that Plato's view differs from this one. For we have seen that the rulers in Plato's city are enjoined to do quite the opposite. But there is another contrast. When I speak of *ethical egoism*, I have in mind egoism as a theory of *obligation*, that is, a theory that says that one *ought* to follow one's own good. Plato's theory, however, is not, taken as a whole, simply a theory of obligation. Instead, as we have seen, it is a theory whose main aim is to articulate, not what is obligatory or what we ought to do, but what is, all things considered, good. Moreover, Plato adopts a particular notion of goodness that makes his theory differ from another theory that might be labeled egoistic. This theory, rather than trying to lay out our obligations, maintains that the only good for anyone to pursue is his own, on the dual ground that 1) there is no such thing as an "absolute" good, as distinguished from a relative notion of what is good *for* one individual or another, and 2) it is irrational, or perhaps impossible, for anyone to pursue anyone else's good, except insofar as it coincides with one's own good. Plato disagrees with this view primarily in denying 1), and maintaining, as we have seen, that there *is* a notion of non-relative goodness, the apprehension of which can motivate people. (Plato thus centers his attention on 1) and ignores 2), as many have noticed who have observed that altruism and fellow-feeling have little place, if any, in the *Republic*—cf. 545c–547c, n. D.)

Let us now consider utilitarianism. Utilitarianism, too, has many forms. Nowadays, it is generally advanced as a theory of obligation, according to which (to gloss over some distinctions among varieties of utilitarianism) one has an obligation always to do what will produce the greatest net sum of utility in the world as a whole. Once again, it is clear from the foregoing that Plato's theory is different from this one, because it is not primarily a theory of obligation. It is possible, however, to advance a form of utilitarianism that is a claim, not about obligation as such, but about the overriding good. (Indeed, it has been suggested by Lyons that Mill's view, or part of it, was of this sort.) That is, it is possible to maintain that the good, the overriding good, is the maximization of overall utility.

Plato's view has important affinities to this latter view, but great care must be exercised in tracing the relation between them, because a great deal depends here on what we take "utility" to mean. Some utilitarians would hold that utility is pleasure, and would thus, as hedonistic utilitarians, urge that the good is the maximization of pleasure in the world. (Many hedonistic utilitarians, of course, have advanced their view as an account of obligation, but we have now left accounts of obligation aside.) Other utilitarians might give other characterizations of utility, by calling it, e.g., happiness, or satisfaction, or something else of that general type. Now although Plato believes in the effort to increase the exemplification of the good in the world, he does not construe the good in these ways (see 519d–521c, n. E, 504d–506a, n. B, 419a–421c, n. D, 427e–428a, n. B). Instead, he holds a conception of the good that makes the advancement of the good include, in a certain sense, the advancement of justice in the city (cf. sec. 4). In this way, his view is similar to a form of utilitarianism which allows utility to include moral goods as well as non-moral goods such as pleasure. If this is done, then it can be claimed that the overall, overriding good is the maximization of a kind of combination of many sorts of utility in a broad sense (including, perhaps, happiness, knowledge, beauty in the world, and even, in addition, a particular distribution thereof; see Frankena, *E*, p. 42).

When these matters are taken into account, Plato's view can be seen to be something similar to the view just described. But there is still one important difference, arising out of the fact that Plato confines his view to a single city or *polis*, and says nothing about how the effort to have the good exemplified might be extended beyond these limits to embrace the world as a whole (cf. 469b–471c, n. A). Thus, Plato might be seen as advocating a partial version, aiming to consider only a single city, of the kind of utilitarianism just described, which adopts a certain special conception of utility which subsumes the various features that he wishes to see his city exemplify, and which is framed not as a theory of obligation but as an account of the good. (In the particular form that Plato gives it, of course, his conception of the good makes a close connection between goodness and unity—cf. secs. 2–3 and 422e–423d, n. B.)

When we compare Plato's doctrine to this version of utilitarianism, however, we must also be careful to take into account the traditional contrast between utilitarianism and intuitionism, which contrast was first explored thoroughly by Sidgwick (*ME*, pp. 83–87). Once again, exposition is made difficult by the great number of versions of both of these doctrines, but certain outlines are clear enough. After explaining the contrast between utilitarianism and intuitionism, Sidgwick argued that there was no incompatibility between the two (he, in fact, wished to support the former on the basis of the latter, pp. 496–7). Although there are enormously important differences between Plato and Sidgwick, and even between the ways in which they can be said to combine the two views, Plato is nevertheless best seen as having combined the special sort of utilitarianism just described with importantly intuitionistic elements. At least this is so if the method by which Plato thinks that we can apprehend the goodness of the features of his city can be correctly described as a method of intuition. Here we encounter yet further difficulties. For "intuition" has in recent times been most frequently used as a term to describe a way of determining the rightness of obligatory character of actions, rather than as a way of determining goodness. If, therefore, we are to ask whether Plato's overall theory is intuitionistic, we must be willing to transfer the use of this term from the case of obligation to that of goodness. Let us suppose that we do this. Even so, however, we are left with a further problem. Plato's own epistemological theory is rather different from the sort of theory within which the modern usage of the terms "intuition" and "intuitionism" have been formed, and this fact makes it hard to know whether the goodness of, in particular, the features of his city is to be determined by what we call intuition or not. Rather than try to expound his epistemology to the extent necessary to answer this question I shall confine myself to the following remarks. First, Plato did not attempt to assess the goodness of his city by a straightforwardly empirical investigation of the extent to which it produced satisfaction in its individual citizens (see 419a–421c, n. D, 427e–428a, n. B). This fact might tend to make us regard his theory as intuitionistic. On the other hand, his investigation of the city, and of the features that make it good, does seem to involve a certain important amount of empirical investigation of human beings and the needs that they have in the sensible world (369b–370c). This fact might tend in the other direction. The end result, I think, must be that his account shows certain intuitionistic tendencies and certain tendencies in the opposite direction. Plato does believe that we apprehend the Good and other Forms by means of the faculty of reason, but his investigation of the city does not seem to proceed by means of this faculty alone. We must therefore concede that he does not allow us straightforwardly to ascribe to him either an intuitionistic or an anti-intuitionistic view.

It will have become gradually more evident that, as I began this section by saying, Plato's ethical theory is not easy to classify in modern terms. First, he is not primarily advancing an ethical theory that is simply a theory of obligation, because for him the good is the pre-eminent ethical concept. Second, although his theory resembles a form of utilitarianism taken as a theory of the overall good, it still deviates considerably in other ways from modern forms of that doctrine. And, third, his epistemological views make it unclear whether his quasi-utilitarianism, if we may call it that, is to be regarded as substantially allied with intuitionism or not. There are two morals to be drawn from these considerations. One is how difficult it is to use modern classifications to describe a remote philosophical theory. The other, however, is that in the case of a particular theory we are able, with some effort, to gain an understanding of *why* such description should be so difficult.

6. *A brief assessment of Plato's ethical theory.*

A full-scale assessment of Plato's theory is impossible to give here. I confine myself to a few points that seem to me the most important.

In the first place, let me reiterate what I maintained in sec. 4, that aside from the *substance* of Plato's views about the good, and aside from the metaphysical theory in which they are embedded, he seems to me correct about the *place* that he assigns to the notion of goodness within his ethical theory. I am not able here to do more than state this view, but I would hope to argue for it elsewhere, and to persuade philosophers that it at least ought to be taken more seriously than trends in recent ethical thought have allowed it to be. It seems to me that this is one of the most neglected, most salutary, and most philosophically stimulating of Plato's contributions to philosophy.

I have tried throughout this introduction, and throughout the following commentary, to offer as little negative criticism of Plato's views as I could, so as to allow his views to come through with as little interference as possible. I have done this even in the many places where my own views correspond not at all with Plato's. On the substance of his views on the good and on justice, however, it seems to me that he has made such central mistakes that a treatment of the *Republic* should say something about them. I therefore conclude with some remarks about them.

To speak broadly, Plato's ethical theory exhibits two tendencies, one good and one bad. The good tendency is a push toward a kind of objectivity (sec. 4). The bad tendency is a failure to realize the extent to which the desires and satisfactions of the bulk of mankind must be taken into account in any satisfactory ethical and political doctrine.

Plato's push toward objectivity arises largely from a revulsion toward the seemingly endless conflicts that one encounters when one collects together the views of mankind about the states of affairs that they wish to obtain, and sees the enormous incompatibilities among them (see White, pp. xiii–xv, 3). In reaction to this situation, he endeavors to develop a conception of a society, a city, in which these incompatibilities can be resolved, so that people can live together in a unified and harmonious manner (422e–423d, n. B, 461e–462e, n. B, 465b, n. A, 545c–547c, n. A). The goodness of such a society seems to him apparent, and he simultaneously develops a conception of the good—the Form of the Good—that has an important connection to the sort of unity whose social benefits, caused by the lack of strife in a unified city, seem to him so important (422e–423d, n. B, Introd., secs. 2–3). The fundamental idea is that if we can find a notion of the good, and of the good society or city, which shows us how conflict may be avoided, we shall have a notion of goodness, and of a good society, that is certified by something more than the contingent likes and dislikes of people with no authoritative claim to knowledge or expertise.

But the effort to carry out this idea has its price. Plato's attempt to construct a society that is free of conflict leaves us with a society in which basic needs are provided for by classes of people, who are directed by the rulers, and who are given no credit for a full understanding of the principles on which the society is based (that is, those principles deemed necessary for freedom from strife). Plato is vague about the attitude of these citizens toward the city in which they live (see 590c–591a, nn. C–D), and about the motives that they would have to cooperate in its maintenance. This is a weakness on which many democratic and egalitarian critics of Plato have seized. And rightly. For it is hard to deny that these citizens would object to the institutions in force in Plato's city. And it is hard to deny that their desires and needs are taken into account only so much as to keep them from disrupting the stability and unity of the city, but not so much as to provide them with as much satisfaction as they are capable. Plato would demur, because he thinks that his arrangements do provide sufficient happiness to suit the capabililties for happiness of all of the citizens (this seems to be the import of 421c). But his demurral would fail to convince many. Their objection would persist that the happiness of a large number of people is being taken insufficient account of, in the service of an ideal of unity and unanimity which is not in fact sufficiently valuable to balance the neglect of that happiness. Plato, they would say, has been too single-minded in his attempt to avoid disruptive conflict and too prone to think that unanimity, unity, and lack of dissent are sure signs that an objective characteristic of goodness has been achieved and agreed on (see esp. 422e–423d, n. B). Moreover, they will deny that Plato's arrangements really do ensure unity at all. Contrary to Plato's belief, they will maintain, people are simply not so constituted as to acquiesce in being ruled as he recommends, or to allow the city to remain stable and free of strife, no matter how unified the class of rulers itself might remain (545c–547c, n. A, and 590c–591a, nn. C–D).

This is the most important front along which a defense of Plato's position must be mounted, but it does not seem to me that it can be mounted successfully. In his assessment of the goodness of his city, he simply places too much weight on such formal features as unity, and too little weight on the desires and satisfactions of those who must live in it (cf. 427e–428a, n. B). In his effort to develop a standard of goodness which he thinks can be regarded as objective, he discounts too severely the opinions of those who will dissent from it.

It goes without saying that, as many have realized, this criticism can be extended to Plato's account of justice, and through it to his argument that if one is just then one will be happy. Plato's argument for his account of justice makes essential use of the claim that his city is good (427e–428a, n. C, 432b–434c, nn. B–C). It also requires us to accept that account as a fairly close reflection, in some sense, of the concept of justice with which we ordinarily deal (*ibid.*, and 442d–443b, nn. B–C, 590a–c, n. B). If we are in disagreement with him on these points, as it seems to me that we should be, then we shall have to say that he has shown neither what justice really is nor that one benefits by being just. Moreover, a more accurate account of justice—and of obligation in general—will have to do what his notion of the goodness of his city fails to do, which is to take greater account of the needs and interests of more people. He is concerned, as we saw, with the greater exemplification of good in the world (secs. 4 and 5). He does not, however, realize the extent to which the greater exemplification of both good and justice requires the broader and more equal exemplification of happiness.

Summary of the REPUBLIC

Book I

*"what is justice?" opening question
several arguments follow*

As noted in the Preface and the Introduction, Book I is a kind of prologue to the *Republic*. In a preliminary way it sets up the main issues to be discussed, and, I believe, shows the state of the discussion as Plato saw himself taking it over from Socrates. It is not a complete discussion of those issues in its own right and should not be read as such. For in the rest of the work Plato shows clearly that he wishes to approach those issues in a quite different and much broader manner. In the notes on Book I, therefore, I have concentrated on calling attention to matters that will appear later.

Some interpreters have believed that Book I was originally written as a separate dialogue, and that Plato added later the remaining nine books. See 346e–347e, n. B.

327a–328c: THE SCENE IS SET. SOCRATES, RETURNING WITH GLAUCON TO ATHENS FROM A RELIGIOUS FESTIVAL IN THE NEARBY PORT, THE PIRAEUS, IS ACCOSTED BY POLEMARCHUS, ADEIMANTUS, AND OTHERS. THEY RETURN TO THE HOUSE OF POLEMARCHUS.

A.   The discussion that constitutes the *Republic* is not made to seem to be of Socrates' own making. He is pictured as reluctant to speak and uncertain of the truth of what he is saying. However much this trait may be derived from the character of the historical Socrates, Plato uses it in this work to underline the difficulty of the problems that he is treating and the incompleteness of at least some aspects of his own discussion (see, e.g., 506b–507a, 436b–437a).

B.   One of the most striking and effective things about the *Republic* is the characterizations of the people in it. (Of course an understanding of the characterizations should not be viewed as a substitute for an understanding of the ideas and arguments that they present, any more than the latter is a substitute for the former; as I have said in the Preface, this book deals with ideas and arguments rather than the characterizations or other dramatic and literary elements.) Socrates is the most important figure and virtually always serves as a mouthpiece for Plato. Plato himself is absent from the dialogue. He was in his teens at the time at which the conversation is portrayed as having occurred, which scholars usually place approximately a dozen years before Socrates' death in 399 B.C. Socrates' first interlocutor, when the dialogue begins in earnest at 328c, is Cephalus, who is the father of Polemarchus, the next interlocutor (331d–336a). (Cephalus was also the father of the orator Lysias.) Thrasymachus, who continues the conversation with Socrates from 336a, appears to have been one of the people known under the blanket term "sophist" (see 494a–496a, n. A). Socrates' main interlocutors, however, are Glaucon and Adeimantus, both older brothers of Plato himself. In an interesting manner, they alternate in the task of conversing with Socrates for the main part of the *Republic*, Books II–X. [Diès, pp. xxii–xxvi.]

328c–331b: SOCRATES STRIKES UP A CONVERSATION WITH POLEMARCHUS' OLD FATHER, CEPHALUS. CEPHALUS ACKNOWLEDGES WELCOMING OLD AGE AND THE MODERATION OF LIFE WHICH IT BRINGS. HE SAYS THAT IT MAKES ONE CONSIDER DEATH AND WORRY THAT AFTER DEATH ONE MAY PAY PENALTIES FOR WRONGS COMMITTED IN LIFE; BUT HE HOLDS THAT MONEY IS A GREAT HELP IN THE AVOIDANCE OF WRONGDOING.

A.   Cephalus presents a fairly conventional view of wrong action and the fear of being punished for it after death. Plato agrees in holding that one should be concerned about one's fate in the afterlife, a matter he discusses in Book X (608c–621d). But the main part of his argument, in Books II–IX, develops a quite different rationale for pursuing justice.

B.   Several themes touched here are developed later. In particular,

Cephalus voices a predilection for moderation, which Plato shares (e.g., 430c–432a, 441c–442d). But Plato's notion of moderation is far more elaborate than the conventional one of Cephalus (430c–432a, 441c–442d). Another is the question of the usefulness of money for a good man (331a–b). Contrary to Cephalus, Plato will deny that claim of usefulness (421c–422a, 550c–552e; cf. 547d–548d, n. B).

C. Although the conventional ethical conceptions of Cephalus are different from the ones that Plato will develop, we shall see that Plato finds it necessary not to depart *too* radically from them (see 442d–443b, n. B)—i.e., not so radically as to be irrelevant to actual debates about ethical issues couched in ordinary terms.

331c–d: SOCRATES PRESSES ON CEPHALUS THE QUESTION "WHAT IS JUSTICE?" HE ASKS WHETHER IT CONSISTS SIMPLY IN FOLLOWING SUCH ORDINARY PRESCRIPTIONS AS SPEAKING THE TRUTH AND REPAYING ONE'S DEBTS. CEPHALUS WITHDRAWS AND LEAVES THE DISCUSSION TO SOCRATES AND POLEMARCHUS.

A. Plato makes Socrates focus the conversation on the notion of justice, which will be the main topic for the rest of the work. This focus, Plato thinks, is proper because of the central role of that notion in problems about conduct (see esp. 433b–d), and because of the widespread mistake, made by people such as Thrasymachus (336b*sqq.*), about whether or not justice is beneficial to its possessor.

331d–334b: POLEMARCHUS IS MADE TO ARGUE FOR AN AC-COUNT OF JUSTICE WHICH IS ATTRIBUTED TO THE POET SIMONIDES. THE ACCOUNT IS THAT JUSTICE IS TO GIVE EACH WHAT IS HIS DUE, WHICH IS INTERPRETED TO MEAN THAT JUSTICE IS TO BENEFIT ONE'S FRIENDS AND TO HARM ONE'S ENEMIES. POLEMARCHUS IS ARGUED, ON THIS BASIS, FIRST INTO THE POSITION OF SAYING THAT JUSTICE IS USELESS AND THEN INTO THE POSITION OF SAYING THAT IT IS IN PART THE ABILITY TO STEAL.

A. The main purpose of this argument (which is too briskly framed to be cogent) is to point to problems latent in treating justice in certain ordinary ways. The problems arise chiefly because of the effort to treat justice as a kind of skill or craft (*technē*) viewed in everyday terms (first it is pushed into uselessness by other skills which appropriate all of the territory it might cover, and then it is shown to be capable, if it is an ordinary skill, of being put to bad uses). Books II–IX will argue for a conception of justice that is far more elaborate, particularly in its connection with goodness (504d–506a).

334b–335a: SOCRATES THEN PRESSES ON POLEMARCHUS THE QUESTION HOW THIS ACCOUNT OF JUSTICE IS TO DEAL WITH THE FACT THAT ONE CAN SOMETIMES BE MISTAKEN ABOUT WHO IS HELPFUL TO ONE (AND IN THAT SENSE FRIENDLY) AND WHO IS NOT, AND WITH THE POSSIBILITY THAT THE ACCOUNT MIGHT COMMIT US TO HARMING GOOD PEOPLE IN ORDER TO BE JUST.

A.   Once again we have a brisk argument designed to raise a problem rather than to settle an issue. The problem involved is the relationship between justice and goodness, and particularly the question, to be made explicit in the following section, whether justice can involve doing harm. The present passage demonstrates in a cursory way that there are difficulties in reconciling the efforts to help both those who are one's friends in conventional terms and those who are good. Further problems about the relation between justice and friendship are raised in 351d.

335b–336a: SOCRATES ARGUES THAT IF IT IS A VIRTUE OR EXCELLENCE, AS HE MAINTAINS THAT IT IS, JUSTICE CANNOT INVOLVE HARMING PEOPLE. HE CLAIMS THUS TO REFUTE THE ACCOUNT OF JUSTICE ARGUED FOR BY POLEMARCHUS.

A.   Plato bases the present argument on the contention that justice is a virtue or excellence (335c). This contention is denied below by Thrasymachus (348c) and is apparently argued for by Plato in Book IV (see 432b–434c, n. B). It is also supposed to be the function (*ergon*) of a good man not to harm people but to benefit them. (On the notion of "function" see n. A on 352d–354a.) This thesis is never argued for in so many words by Plato, but some approximation of it is clearly accepted by him (see esp. 519d–521b, esp. n. E). The very strong claim in 335c, that anyone who is harmed must necessarily become more unjust, seems not to be taken up later. But as remarked in the previous note, the point of this passage is to raise issues rather than to settle them conclusively.

B.   On the notion of "virtue" or "excellence" (*aretē*) see n. E on 427e–428a, and n. A on 352d–354a.

336a–337c: THRASYMACHUS LEAPS INTO THE DISCUSSION, OBJECTING BOTH TO SOCRATES' PRACTICE OF REFUTING THE VIEWS OF OTHERS WITHOUT EVER STATING AND DEFENDING HIS OWN, AND TO THE KIND OF ACCOUNTS OF JUSTICE THAT HAVE BEEN GIVEN SO FAR.

A. Thrasymachus' impatience with the foregoing discussion foreshadows the effort, portrayed as being both his and Socrates', to reveal what the real problem about justice is. That problem will have to do with the question for whom, if anyone, justice is something good.

B. We do not know how much of what is attributed to Thrasymachus here was actually maintained by a particular historical person, just as we do not know how much of what is put into Socrates' mouth in this book was actually advanced by him. It is Plato's main interest here to present two opposing lines of thought in an illustrative manner.

337d–339b: THRASYMACHUS TURNS OUT TO HAVE AN ACCOUNT OF JUSTICE OF HIS OWN TO OFFER: THAT JUSTICE IS THE INTEREST OR ADVANTAGE OF THE STRONGER, OR SOMETIMES, OF THE ESTABLISHED GOVERNMENT, OR, LATER (343c), OF SOMEONE OTHER THAN THE PERSON WHO IS JUST. HE MAINTAINS THAT GOVERNMENTS ALWAYS SET UP LAWS AND PRACTICES TO BENEFIT THOSE WHO GOVERN, AND APPLY THE TERM "JUST" TO THOSE LAWS AND CUSTOMS TO PERSUADE OTHERS TO ABIDE BY THEM.

A. Thrasymachus' position is framed in a somewhat confused manner, reflecting, no doubt, Plato's opinion that those who hold such positions do not generally articulate them very well. We are given three versions of the position, which are closely allied but nevertheless distinct. The fact that there are so many positions being advocated by Thrasymachus produces a certain amount of confusion for the reader, which is not completely dispelled by Socrates' arguments. Once again one must remember that the purpose of Book I is to raise issues.

B. What Plato takes to be central to views like that of Thrasymachus is later expressed more clearly in Book II, when Glaucon and Adeimantus present what Plato takes to be the primary problem that Thrasymachus was trying to articulate (358a–362c, 362d–368c).

C.   Within Thrasymachus' position—but apart from his effort to give a full-dress definition of justice—there are two crucial elements. One is that the prescriptions labeled by the term "justice" are in some important sense arbitrary, that they are set up by rulers to accommodate what happens to be their interests, and that they exhibit no significant common feature but this. The other is that it is generally against one's interests to do what is labeled "just." The qualification "generally" is necessary for two reasons. One is that presumably the rulers of a city, according to Thrasymachus, are sometimes benefited by their own observance of the laws which they have laid down in their own interests (though perhaps he would deny even this). More important is the fact that those in a city who are weak are apparently better off doing what is just simply because they will be punished if they do not. The petty wrongdoer, Thrasymachus claims (344a–c), may well be harmed by injustice.

   The connection between these two elements of Thrasymachus' position is the assumption that generally rulers are able to set up laws, or standards of justice, that will in fact work to their advantage. For if this were not so, then those who are ruled might well benefit themselves and harm the rulers by obeying the dictates of justice. Questions raised by the possibility that rulers may err are taken up in the following passage. [Shorey, WPS, p. 210; Cross and Woozley, pp. 25–41.]

339b–341c: SOCRATES RAISES THE PROBLEM CONFRONTING THRASYMACHUS IN THOSE CASES IN WHICH THE RULER ERRS ABOUT WHAT IS IN HIS OWN INTEREST AND THEREFORE PROPOUNDS RULES OF JUSTICE NOT TO HIS ADVANTAGE. THRASYMACHUS' REPLY IS THAT IN THE STRICT SENSE OF "RULER," A RULER DOES NOT ERR, AND HE MEANS HIS ACCOUNT OF JUSTICE TO HAVE TO DO WITH RULERS IN THE STRICT SENSE.

A.   Thrasymachus' insistence on a certain strict sense of the term "ruler" considerably changes the force of his position. Socrates endeavors in what follows to take advantage of the change.

341c–342e: SOCRATES CHALLENGES THRASYMACHUS' VIEW OF WHAT IT IS TO BE A RULER IN THE STRICT SENSE AND MAINTAINS THAT EVERY CRAFT OR SKILL AIMS NOT FOR THE GOOD OF ITSELF BUT FOR THE GOOD OF ITS OBJECT. HE CONCLUDES THAT EVERY FORM OF RULE AIMS AT THE GOOD OR ADVANTAGE OF THOSE OVER WHOM IT RULES.

A. Plato here foreshadows what he will say in Books III–VII about the proper role of rulers (introduced in 412a–c). What he will later maintain is that the ruler has the task of providing for the good of the whole city (see esp. 519d–521b, 419a–421c).

B. Here Plato attempts to derive his claim about the skill of ruling from a broader claim about skills in general. He does not do this later. His present argument has the notable difficulty that it does not distinguish between a skill's aiming at "its own" advantage and its aiming at the advantage of its practitioner (a skill's doing the latter would not clearly be indicative of any defect in it, such as is mentioned in 342a–b). This difficulty is absent from the treatment of rulership later in the work.

343a–344c: THRASYMACHUS SUGGESTS THAT HIS POINT HAS BEEN MISUNDERSTOOD. HE ASKS SOCRATES SIMPLY TO OBSERVE THE FACT THAT THOSE WHO PRACTICE JUSTICE COME OFF WORSE IN ANY DEALING THAN THOSE WHO PRACTICE INJUSTICE. HE SAYS THAT THIS FACT IS EVIDENT FROM CONSIDERATION OF INJUSTICE IN ITS COMPLETE OR PERFECT FORM. FOR ALTHOUGH HE ALLOWS THAT PETTY WRONGDOERS MAY SUFFER BY BEING PUNISHED, HE MAINTAINS THAT A MAN WHO IS UNJUST ON A LARGE ENOUGH SCALE WILL AVOID BAD CONSEQUENCES.

A. Thrasymachus' decision to rest his case on the consideration of complete rather than partial injustice foreshadows Plato's own way in Books II–X of discussing the comparative benefits to be gained from justice and injustice (see 358a–362c, n. B), in which he presents the question as one to be answered by comparing the results of *complete* justice with those of *complete* injustice. As we can see from this passage, he does so partly to give the partisan of injustice what such a person views as his strongest possible case.

B. It appears that in the present passage Thrasymachus drops his attempt to give a definition of justice and instead confines himself to indicating what he takes to be the central fact about it, namely, that it is disadvantageous to its possessor. We shall see that in the following section Socrates allows the ground to be thus shifted (see also 354a–c, n. B).

344d–345b: THRASYMACHUS INTENDS TO LEAVE, BUT SOCRATES URGES HIM TO STAY, SAYING THAT WHAT CON-

FRONTS THEM IS THE IMPORTANT QUESTION HOW ONE MAY
LIVE BEST AND MOST ADVANTAGEOUSLY. IN OPPOSITION TO
THRASYMACHUS, HE DENIES THAT EVEN COMPLETE INJUSTICE
IS ADVANTAGEOUS TO ITS POSSESSOR.

A.   Socrates now proposes to argue the question whether justice helps
one to live better and more advantageously than injustice. For the rest
of Book I neither he nor Thrasymachus attempts to support or refute
any particular account of what injustice is. In 354a–c, however,
Socrates reproaches both of them for this procedure, contending that
arriving at such an account is a necessary preliminary to determining
whether being just is advantageous.

B.   Socrates' remarks in this passage make us wonder whether he is
considering the question how much *advantage* one gains by being just,
or the question to what extent being just enables one to *live well* in some
other, perhaps moral, sense. The same apparent ambiguity seems to
crop up again in 353e–354a. We are naturally led to wonder whether
Plato will later resolve this ambiguity and point out the difference
between the two questions. In fact, however, although he keeps them
apart to some extent (see esp. 461e–462e, n. B), his overall view of the
notion of goodness encourages him to regard them as in many ways not
genuinely separate. On this complicated matter, see esp. Introd., sec. 4,
and 504d–506a, n. C.

345b–346e: SOCRATES INSISTS THAT EACH CRAFT OR SKILL IS
TO BE DISTINGUISHED FROM THAT OF MONEY-MAKING OR
WAGE-EARNING. TAKEN BY ITSELF AND APART FROM WAGE-
EARNING, NO SKILL PRODUCES BENEFIT FOR ITS PRACTI-
TIONER. HE MAINTAINS THAT THIS GENERAL CLAIM APPLIES
TO RULING, IN OPPOSITION TO THRASYMACHUS' VIEW THAT
THE TRUE RULER GAINS ADVANTAGE FROM RULING.

A.   Socrates recurs to the claim that he made in 341c–342e, though he
is now more careful to make clear his main point, that no skill, taken by
itself, should be thought of as aiming for the benefit *of its practitioner*
(see *ibid.*, n. B). His method of supporting this claim here is to try to
convince us that when monetary benefit appears to be caused by the
practice of a skill, that benefit is actually caused by the practice of the
skill of wage-earning which "accompanies" or "follows" the other skill.

B. Plato here (345e) foreshadows his very important discussion later in the *Republic* of what motivates a ruler, in the strict sense, to rule (see esp. 412a–c, n. A, 412d–e, n. A, and 519d–521b, n. E).

346e–347e: SOCRATES MAINTAINS THAT ONCE WE SEPARATE THE SKILL OF WAGE-EARNING FROM OTHERS, WE SEE THAT NO ONE GENUINELY WISHES TO RULE, AND THAT IF THERE WERE A CITY OF GOOD MEN, THEY WOULD COMPETE *NOT* TO RULE. IF THEY DID RULE, HE SAYS, IT WOULD BE NEITHER FOR MONEY NOR FOR HONOR, BUT THEY WOULD UNDER-TAKE RULE AS SOMETHING NECESSARY, BY SOME KIND OF COMPULSION OR PUNISHMENT, THE GREATEST PUNISHMENT BEING TO BE RULED BY SOMEONE WORSE THAN ONESELF.

A. This passage gives a preview of one of the most important claims that Plato will make about the rulers of the city he will describe in Books II–VII, namely, that they will rule unwillingly, through a kind of compulsion and in spite of the fact that there is something else more desirable for them to do (see esp. 519d–521b, nn. D–E, and Introd., secs. 2, 4). (The exclusion of money and honor as proper incentives to rule looks forward to the descriptions of the timocratic and oligarchic cities in Book VIII, 545c–548d and 550c–552e.)

B. Socrates' statement in 347e–348a that he will look into this matter later is most naturally read as a direct allusion to 519d–521b, 540d–541b, and like passages. There are some interpreters, however, who believe that Book I of the *Republic* was written as a separate dialogue, before the rest of the work. This seems to me unlikely, but whether it is true or not, the fact remains that Book I contains many indications of issues, notions, and contentions that will appear in the remaining nine books. [Dìes, pp. xix–xxii, cxxii–cxxxviii; Shorey, *Rep.*, I, p. x.]

347e–349a: SOCRATES ELICITS FROM THRASYMACHUS THE ACKNOWLEDGMENT OF THE BELIEF THAT INJUSTICE IS NOT A VICE OR DEFECT BUT A VIRTUE OR EXCELLENCE, AND A KIND OF WISDOM, AND THAT JUSTICE IS A KIND OF FOOLISH-NESS. HE PROFESSES TO SEE AT LAST HOW DIFFERENT THRAS-YMACHUS' VIEW IS FROM OTHER PEOPLE'S OPINION.

A. Thrasymachus here calls into question the assumption that Socrates had employed in his argument in 335b–336a (see nn. there), that justice is a virtue or excellence. Socrates therefore turns to this matter in the following passage.

B.   By the end of Book IV, Plato feels that he can assert that justice is a virtue or excellence (444a–e with 427e–428a). In view of Thrasymachus' denial of that proposition here, it would appear that Plato is not entitled to take it for granted but must find some argument to support it (see 432b–434c, nn. B–C). [Adkins, pp. 255–6, 259–60; 278, *et passim*.]

C.   At 348b Plato again alludes to the fact that he will ask us to choose between justice and injustice by asking us to decide whether complete justice or complete injustice is more desirable (see 343a–344c, n. A).

349a–350c: SOCRATES ADVANCES AN ARGUMENT DESIGNED TO SHOW THAT INJUSTICE IS A SPECIES OF IGNORANCE AND BADNESS, AND THAT JUSTICE IS A MARK OF WISDOM, EXPERTISE, AND GOODNESS. THE ARGUMENT IS BASED ON THE CLAIM THAT THE JUST MAN, LIKE THOSE WITH EXPERTISE, DOES NOT ATTEMPT TO OVERREACH OR GET THE BETTER OF THOSE WHO ARE LIKE HIM, WHEREAS THE UNJUST MAN IS LIKE THOSE WITHOUT EXPERTISE, IN ATTEMPTING TO OVERREACH OR GET THE BETTER OF BOTH THOSE WHO ARE LIKE HIM AND THOSE WHO ARE NOT.

A.   The idea that injustice involves an attempt at overreaching and getting the better of others anticipates a point that will be made next in Book II, 358a–362c. Against the defense of injustice offered there by Glaucon, Plato will argue that it is a mistake for a person constantly to be seeking to outdo others and to try to gain more and more without limit (see n. E *ad loc.*).

B.   An important kind of expertise that Plato will show to be involved in justice is, accordingly, an understanding of various kind of limits to be placed on human action in a well-ruled political community (see esp. 422e–423d, n. B).

350c–352c: AGAINST THRASYMACHUS' CONTENTION THAT THE MOST POWERFUL CITY WILL BE THE MOST COMPLETELY UNJUST, SOCRATES ARGUES THAT ANY COMMON COURSE OF ACTION REQUIRES THOSE WHO ARE ENGAGED IN IT TO

OBSERVE JUSTICE TO SOME DEGREE IN THEIR DEALINGS AMONG THEMSELVES. FOR OTHERWISE THERE WILL BE DIS-SENSION AMONG THEM, AND THEY WILL ACCOMPLISH NOTHING. HE MAINTAINS, TOO, THAT THE SAME THING APPLIES TO A SINGLE PERSON, BECAUSE SOMEONE WHO IS IN A STATE OF DISSENSION WITHIN HIMSELF AND NOT OF ONE MIND WILL BE AN ENEMY OF HIMSELF AND LIKEWISE ABLE TO ACCOMPLISH NOTHING.

A.   Much in this passage reflects views that Plato will develop. Most notable is the idea that justice involves a kind of unanimity among distinct parts of a thing, which enables them to accomplish a common purpose and also requires that they not constantly attempt to get the better of each other. This idea will begin to emerge in 369b–370c and will eventually be incorporated in 432b–434c into an account of what justice is in a city.

B.   Another anticipation of later ideas is Plato's claim that there is an analogy between the workings of justice in a group with a common enterprise and its workings in a single person (352a). For an analogy of this sort will be crucial when he develops the notion of justice in an individual human being (441c–442d with 434d–436b and 368c–369b).

C.   Against Thrasymachus (351b), Plato will hold that the best city is the most completely just (427e–428a), and that the worst city is the most completely unjust (576b–578b).

D.   In connection with the points made in n. A, notice that Plato's claim here about the undesirability of dissension (*stasis*, 351d, 352a) fore-shadows numerous further restatements of the same point by means of the same term (e.g., 547b, 465b). That a well-ruled community requires friendship (*philia*) and being of one mind (*homonoia*, 351d, 352a) is also repeated later (432a, 442c, 547b–c). And the idea of having a common enterprise (see *koinēi*, "in common," at 351c, d) is close to one of the central themes of Plato's description of the way in which a city ought to be ruled (449a–550c, n. A).

352d–354a: THE FUNCTION OF A THING, SOCRATES SAYS, IS THAT WHICH THE THING ALONE DOES OR WHICH IT DOES BETTER THAN ANYTHING ELSE DOES; AND THE EXCELLENCE OF A THING IS ITS PERFORMING THAT FUNCTION WELL. ON

THIS BASIS, HE ARGUES THAT BECAUSE A FUNCTION OF A
SOUL IS TO LIVE, AND BECAUSE A FUNCTION OF A SOUL IS
ALSO TO MANAGE THINGS, A SOUL THAT IS UNJUST AND THE
MAN WHO HAS IT MUST LIVE BADLY, AND THEREFORE BE UN-
HAPPY, WHEREAS A JUST MAN MUST LIVE WELL AND BE HAPPY.

A.   Objection can be raised against many of the steps of this argument,
but, once again, the purpose of the argument is to raise certain issues
which Plato will discuss further. The notion of a thing's function (*ergon*)
has already appeared (335b–336a), and it will appear later, particularly
in the idea that each element of a society—in particular, each person in
a city—should have his own single task to perform (369e–370c, n. F,
374e–376c, n. A, 422e–423d, n. A, and 601b–602c, n. B). [Grote, pp.
169–70, 178, *et passim*; Shorey, *Rep.*, I, pp. 100–1.]

B.   In 353e Plato alludes to prior agreement that justice is a virtue or
excellence of the soul. (The ensuing argument *seems* to rely, illegitimately, on something stronger than this, namely that justice is *the* single
virtue or excellence of the soul.) Presumably, Plato has in mind the
argument in 349a–350c. (The question, however, is whether Plato now
thinks himself entitled to take this claim as proved or rather regards
himself as needing to support it with a stronger argument; see 335b–
336a, n. A, and 369e–370c, n. F.)

354a–c: THOUGH HE HAS NOW GIVEN AN ARGUMENT THAT
INJUSTICE IS NEVER MORE ADVANTAGEOUS OR PROFITABLE
THAN JUSTICE, SOCRATES REPUDIATES IT. HE REPROACHES
HIMSELF FOR MOUNTING SUCH AN ARGUMENT WITHOUT
FIRST DISCOVERING WHAT JUSTICE IS. UNTIL THEY ANSWER
THIS QUESTION, HE SAYS, THEY WILL NEVER BE ABLE TO
KNOW WHETHER OR NOT JUSTICE IS ADVANTAGEOUS.

A.   The general methodological point made here, that one must know
what a thing is before one can know certain other things about it, is
also made by Plato elsewhere (e.g., at the end of the *Meno*). [White,
pp. 10–19.]

B.   As we saw (343a–344c, n. B), it was in 343a–345b that Socrates
made the mistake, as he regards it, of turning from the attempt to discover what justice is to the premature attempt to say whether it is
advantageous.

C.   This passage clearly shows the preliminary nature of the argument in Book I. The serious part of Plato's discussion of justice is to follow, in Books II–X, where he will try to supply the lack noted here, first giving an account of what justice is (432b–434c, 441c–442d), and on that basis arguing that it is beneficial to its possessor (591a–592b, 612a–e, n. A; cf. Introd., sec. 2). [See, e.g., Adam, I, p. 61.]

Summary of the REPUBLIC

Book II

[handwritten marginalia:]
— arguments on justice continue
— justice of polis & individual   > origin of polis
— human nature / division of polis
— education of guardians

357a–b: GLAUCON IS DISSATISFIED WITH SOCRATES' ARGU-
MENT THUS FAR. SOCRATES EXPRESSES THE DESIRE TO BE
MORE CONVINCING.

Those who are made uncomfortable by the cursory quality of the
arguments in Book I are quite right. Plato makes clear that it was
only a prelude to the main argument, and did not itself give us
adequate grounds for conviction (though it did give hints of fuller
arguments to come). The serious argument begins here.

357b–358a: SOCRATES DISTINGUISHES THREE CLASSES OF
THINGS THAT ARE GOOD: (1) THOSE THAT WE WELCOME FOR
THEIR OWN SAKES, NOT FOR THEIR CONSEQUENCES; (2) THOSE
THAT WE WELCOME FOR THEIR OWN SAKES AND ALSO FOR
THEIR CONSEQUENCES; AND (3) THOSE THAT ARE "WEARI-
SOME" BUT THAT WE WELCOME BECAUSE OF THEIR CONSE-
QUENCES. HE MAINTAINS THAT JUSTICE BELONGS IN THE
SECOND CLASS, WHICH HE SAYS IS THE BEST.

A. As a signal that the argument is about to become more elaborate
and more serious, Socrates draws a distinction among three kinds of
goods. It is against the background of this distinction that Plato makes
Glaucon (358a–362c) and Adeimantus (362d–368c) expound, in a
calmer manner, the view that Thrasymachus has been advocating. That

view is, in effect, that to the extent that justice is a good at all, it belongs in the last of the three classes that Socrates has distinguished, but that for those who can gain the beneficial consequences of justice in some other manner, justice itself can be entirely dispensed with.

Plato's position, on the other hand, is that justice belongs in the second, the "best," class of goods. Showing that justice is to be valued over injustice for its own sake occupies him until the end of Book IX (the present passage is alluded to in 588–592, esp. at 588b, 589b–c). In Book X, at 612b–d, he undertakes to show that justice is to be valued over injustice for its consequences, as well.

B. The distinction among kinds of goods that Plato draws is itself of interest, especially because what he says seems to contradict the expectation that he here creates in many modern readers. When he says that justice is to be welcomed not only "for its conse- quences" *(apobainonta)* but also "for its own sake" *(hautou heneka)*, we naturally suppose that in arguing that it is good for its own sake, he will not appeal to any of what we would call its consequences or results. But in the part of the *Republic* in which he does try to show this, which occupies Books II–IX (see 612a–e, n. A), he does appeal to what we would regard as consequences of justice, as when he claims that if one is just one will have happiness *(eudaimonia,* 580a–b) and pleasure *(hēdonē,* 583a, 587d–e), and he uses these claims as crucial elements in his effort to praise justice apart from its consequences. Is there any way in which we may remove this seeming contra- diction? Because Plato does not further explain his contrast here, we must rely on what he says later, in the challenges laid down by Glaucon and Adeimantus, who press Socrates to defend his claim that justice belongs to his second class of goods. Let us therefore postpone consideration of the contrast until we see what that challenge amounts to (see n. C on 358a–362c). [See Prichard, Sachs.]

C. Before we proceed any further, we should ask a question that has undoubtedly occurred to many readers of the *Republic* long before now. As we can see in Book I and in the challenges of Glaucon and Adeimantus that follow the present passage, Plato is challenged to show that being just (including acting justly) brings greater benefit to the person who is just than being unjust. Plato takes up this challenge and tries to show this. Why does he do this? Why does he not reject that challenge as misconceived, as Prichard and others have maintained that he should have done. In their view, the point of being just has nothing to do with whether or not one will thereby benefit. They claim that it is possible to act out of other motivation than the effort to seek one's own benefit, and that one must do so if one is to be genuinely just. (Prichard and others nowadays talk of doing one's duty or obligations rather than of being just, but for present purposes the difference does not matter; see Introd., sec. 1.) They claim that to ask for a self-interested reason to be just is to misunderstand the notion of justice altogether, on the ground that part of being just is, precisely, *not* acting out of desire for one's own benefit. They therefore accuse Plato of making a mistake, and indeed a mistake that shows that he himself did not fully grasp the concept of justice, because if he had then he would have rejected the challenge as irrelevant.

We shall see that this charge against Plato contains some misapprehensions about his views (358a–362c, n. D). Plato does in fact allow for actions that are not motivated by self-interest, and indeed seems to have thought that acting against one's interest was an essential part of perfect or complete justice, as it is manifested in the rulers of the city that he describes in Books II–VII (see esp. 519d–521b, n. E, and Introd., secs. 2, 4). That this is so will emerge in due course. For now, however, we may note only that from the mere fact that he tries to show that being just is to one's benefit, it does not follow that he thought either that all actions are motivated by self-interest, or that the *only* reason that one could have for being just is that being just brings benefit to oneself. [Prichard; Adkins, esp. chs. XII–XIV.]

358a–362c: GLAUCON FORMULATES THE CHALLENGE CONFRONTING SOCRATES: TO SHOW THAT THE JUST LIFE IS BETTER THAN THE UNJUST LIFE, AND THAT PEOPLE ARE WRONG IN THINKING THAT JUSTICE IS NOT A GOOD BUT IS ONLY TO BE FOLLOWED WHEN ONE IS CONSTRAINED TO DO SO. THE VIEW OF MOST PEOPLE IS THAT IF ANY JUST MAN WERE PUT IN THE POSITION OF GYGES AND COULD ACT UNJUSTLY WITHOUT BEING DETECTED, HE WOULD DO SO AND WOULD ENGAGE IN THE PURSUIT OF GAIN; FOR THIS IS REGARDED AS THE GOOD, WHICH MEN FOREGO ONLY BECAUSE OF THE EXISTENCE OF LAWS AND CUSTOMS, ON WHICH THEY HAVE AGREED BY CONVENTION. TO SETTLE THE ISSUE, THEN, BETWEEN THESE PEOPLE AND SOCRATES, WE MUST COMPARE A MAN WHO IS PERFECTLY JUST WITH A MAN WHO IS PERFECTLY UNJUST, TO SEE WHICH HAS THE BEST LIFE.

A.   Glaucon's speech expounds the view that Socrates must combat. It is presented as a restatement of the position of Thrasymachus (see 358cl) in Book I.

The speech contains two main ideas. One is that injustice *(adikia)* and gain *(pleonexia,* 358e3, 359c5—see n. E) are good for the person possessing them, whereas justice is bad (358e3–4) for the person possessing it, and that anyone who had a choice unencumbered by extraneous considerations would opt for a life of injustice and gain. The second is an explanation of how people come nevertheless to act justly, and of how laws arise that make it advantageous in certain circumstances to be just (see esp. 358e–359b). The explanation is that because the harm of being unjustly treated outweighs the benefits of treating others unjustly, those who are weak and often suffer injustice but have little chance to gain the benefits of perpetrating it, will have an interest in preventing injustice in general. They do this by joining together to make laws and conventions, calling their provisions "lawful and just," and arranging for those who violate them to be punished. The upshot is that it is often advantageous to be just, but only because of the consequences resulting from the conventions thus established, and not for any other reason— on the contrary, those who are able to avoid these consequences will find that committing injustice is preferable. Thus, on this view, justice turns out for those who are weak to be only a good of the third class, which Plato has distinguished in 357b–358a, as "wearisome" though welcomed because of their consequences, and not a good at all for those who are strong enough to avoid the conventionally created disadvantages of being unjust (cf. 337d–339b, n. C).

B. Glaucon then suggests a method of settling the dispute between Socrates and the advocates of these ideas. It is to compare the lives of the perfectly just man and the perfectly unjust man (or, as they are sometimes simply called, the just man and the unjust man—compare, e.g., 360e with 361d1). This comparison governs the remainder of the *Republic*, which is an effort to compare these two extreme types, and to demonstrate that the just, or perfectly just, man is better off than the unjust, or perfectly unjust, man (cf. 580a–c with n. A thereon). See further n. D below.

   In framing the issue in terms of the extreme types of complete justice and injustice, Glaucon is following the line of thought originated in Book I by Thrasymachus. According to it, the greatest obstacle to the unjust man, and to his enjoyment of the fruits of his labors, would be any failure to go far enough in his injustice. Being only halfway unjust, that is, is dangerous, because you may be punished. To avoid this result, you must be willing, e.g., not merely to rob, but also to lie about your robbery, and to indulge in whatever further injustice is necessary to avoid punishment. Thus the bad consequences of partial injustice are pictured as being avoidable by carrying the injustice further; and complete injustice is pictured as having no bad consequences at all.

Accordingly, the exponent of this view wishes to extol the benefits of complete injustice, and not anything short of it. He wishes to recommend a thoroughgoing policy of injustice, and he sees the consequences of partial injustice as consequences of extraneous circumstances, not as consequences of injustice itself.

Plato here accepts this view for the sake of argument, and allows the completely unjust man to be compared with the completely just man. For the view expounded by Glaucon has pictured the apparent benefits of justice as really the benefits of the conventional system of rewards and punishments, without which justice would in no way be worthwhile. In both cases, then, the idea is to examine the just man and the unjust man, and to allow us to ignore the extraneous effects of avoidable circumstances, i.e., of circumstances that could be avoided by a person while still remaining just or unjust. Plato is therefore allowing the terms of the comparison to be set by his opponent, and as favorably to his opponent as his opponent thinks they can be made. For the opponent is given the advantage of having the unjust man avoid the punishments laid down by convention, and also the advantage of having the just man lose the rewards that convention allots to justice. It will turn out, however, that in Plato's view, his opponent is hurting his case by asking for complete injustice to be pitted against complete justice; for it will emerge by the end of Book IX that, according to Plato's argument, the completely unjust man is the worst off of all.

C. We are now in a position to turn back to the problem that we earlier noted in Plato's classification of goods (n. B on 357b–358a), which was that although he says that he will praise justice apart from its consequences, he nevertheless seems to do this by arguing that if one is just then one will have happiness and pleasure, which appears to be a way of praising justice *for* its consequences rather than *apart* from them.

Various suggestions have been made about how to remove this difficulty. One is to say, with Mabbott, that although we may think that the happiness and pleasure that Plato speaks of are consequences, he himself does not think that they are consequences of it but rather that they are identical with it. It seems on balance implausible, however, that Plato should have presupposed, entirely without argument or explanation, so extraordinary-sounding a thesis as that justice and happiness (let alone pleasure) are identical. Another suggestion is that rather than thinking that happiness is a consequence of justice, or identical with it, Plato instead thinks that justice is in some sense a part of happiness (Irwin). It is, however, almost as difficult to suppose that Plato would have relied on this contention without explanation, and to understand why, if this is what he is doing, he does not avoid giving the impression that he thinks that happiness *is* a consequence of justice. Moreover, it seems implausible to think that, even if he did sometimes regard justice as a part of happiness, he could have thought that justice was a part of *pleasure*, rather than having pleasure as a consequence—unless, again, we could find some considerable explanation of this idea, which we do not. But not only does Plato argue that if you are just then you will have more pleasure than if you are unjust (583a, 587d–e); he also makes this argument a part of his argument in Books II–IX that justice is to be welcomed for its own sake, and that the just man is better off than the unjust man (357b–358a, n. A, 588b, 589b–c, with 580c–581e, n. A). In one way or another, therefore, Plato is praising justice for what we would call its consequences, in that part of his argument which is devoted to praising it for its own sake.

A more promising way in which to remove the difficulty is to say that by his phrases "for its own sake" and "because of its consequences" (357b), as the Greek expressions are translated, Plato does not intend the same contrast that we translate and understand him to intend. But if that is so, then what other contrast would he have in mind? Glaucon's speech gives a quite clear indication of his intent. The important distinction there is one between what ensues on being (un)just and is not due to any extraneous and avoidable circumstances, and what ensues on being (un)just but is due not to one's (in)justice but to such extraneous and avoidable circumstances (see n. B.). Expressed in another manner, the distinction is between what (in)justice produces independently of the circumstances and what it produces in conjunction or cooperation with the circumstances. (An example of the latter sort of case is the benefit that comes when one is just *through* the reputation for justice that one gains as a result, in part, of being just.) Accordingly, we are dealing with a distinction between two different sorts of consequences of (in)justice, those that it brings about *by itself*, and those that arise from it adventitiously, through the cooperation of circumstances which could be avoided even while the (in)justice remained. (This account in all essentials is the one given by Grote, p. 117 (but perhaps not at p. 102), and Sachs, pp. 39–42.)

There is a reason why Plato's contrast does not leap to our minds or strike us as natural. It is that we, or many of us, are nowadays accustomed to think of causes as never producing their effects "by themselves," but only in conjunction with certain "standing conditions," or the like. To those who adopt this view, Plato's distinction will appear to make little sense. (Plato does have a notion much like that of standing conditions or auxiliary causes—see *Phaedo* 99a–b and *Timaeus* 46c, but he never suggests that they are indispensable in all causal situations.) [Grote, pp. 101–2, 117; Sachs, pp. 39–42; Mabbott, pp. 60, 64–5; Irwin, PMT, pp. 254ff.]

D.   As we have seen in n. B, Plato poses the issue confronting him by comparing the perfectly just man and the perfectly unjust man and asking which is better off. An important question is raised by this formulation of the issue: even if the former is better off than the latter, does Plato hold in addition that, *quite generally*, the more just one is the better off one is? Evidently, the second proposition does not simply follow from the first. Frequently, however, interpreters assume that because Plato is trying to "praise justice," he must be contending that a person's happiness must always increase in proportion with his justice, so that every additional amount of justice must produce a corresponding increase in happiness. But Plato does not say this.

What he believes is something close to it but crucially different. He does believe that, as a rough generality, the more just one's character, the better off one is. He shows this belief in his descriptions in Books VIII–IX of the different types of human character, where he plainly intends to make it plausible that their happiness decreases as their degree of justice does (580a–c, n. A). On the other hand, he never suggests that for each and every additional degree of justice, one gains some additional happiness. Rather, he confines himself at most to a rough generalization about the degree of justice in one's character. There is, moreover, a certain vitally important exception to a complete proportionality of justice and welfare. This is the case of the philosopher-rulers who govern the city described in Books II–VII (see Introd., sec. 4, with n. E on 519d–521b), who turn out to suffer a loss of welfare by engaging in the just task of governing rather than doing something else that would make them better off.

E. The view that Glaucon expounds differs from Plato's not merely in what it has to say about justice. It also contains quite different ideas from Plato's about the *good*. According to Glaucon, it is "(undue) gain" (*pleonexia*, 359c5, 362b7, 365d6) that "every creature by nature pursues as a good" (359c5). The claim being reported here is that left without interference, any man—or indeed any creature—will aim at mere *increase* of what he has, particularly an increase over what his fellows have and quite probably at their expense. The point on which this view differs from Plato's is in denying that there is, so to speak, any *natural limit* on what a man will aim to acquire. On this view, whatever a man has, he is always after *more*. Plato will argue, on the contrary, that there are natural limits on human beings' rational aims, and that for this reason cooperation among them is possible (see n. C on 422e–423d, and n. B on 555b–557a).

362d–368c: ADEIMANTUS REFORMULATES THE CHALLENGE TO SOCRATES, MAINTAINING THAT GLAUCON HAS NOT STATED IT SATISFACTORILY. HE RESTATES THE ATTACK ON JUSTICE THAT GLAUCON HAS REPORTED, EMPHASIZING THE BENEFITS OF BEING REPUTED TO BE JUST (AS OPPOSED TO REALLY BEING JUST), BOTH AMONG MEN AND AMONG GODS.

A. It would be wrong to think that Adeimantus' version of the challenge to Socrates differs importantly from Glaucon's. What Adeimantus does is to emphasize one factor or circumstance that can influence the benefits gained or lost in a life of justice or injustice. That factor is reputation *(doxa)*. On the view that he and Glaucon are reporting, the benefits that arise from justice, and the harms that arise from injustice, really arise only because of the customs that men have, of praising and rewarding justice, and doing the opposite to injustice. But for anyone who could gain the reputation of justice while still acting unjustly, life would be far, far better. And the claim is that not only can reputations among men be contrived, but reputations among the gods can be also, so as to ensure a pleasant afterlife even for the unjust (363d).

B. That Plato should emphasize this particular extraneous factor is not surprising. He himself has a strong tendency to be suspicious of the mere opinions or beliefs of the majority of people (the word *doxa*, which is translated by "reputation," is also Plato's standard for "opinion" or "belief" as contrasted with "knowledge"—see 476d–480a). He would not wish to say that a person's reputation for justice or injustice is a reliable indication, by itself, that the person really is just or unjust. For this reason he is particularly inclined to agree with his opponent here that the effects of reputation should be discounted when we compare the lives of justice and injustice.

C. From the fact that Plato is so willing to discount a person's reputation, we can see another way in which he disagrees with the conception of justice represented in the speeches of Glaucon and Adeimantus. The view they expounded was that justice is created, so to speak, by certain conventions governing conduct, and that it is only in virtue of violating these conventions that one can be called unjust. Plato's view, on the contrary, is that justice and injustice are *neither* merely a matter of human convention *nor* simply a matter of action or outward behavior. The latter point will become evident when we look at his notion of justice in the soul, and see the precedence that it seems to take over justice in actions (see n. B on 443b–444a). The former point will become equally evident when we see that, in his view, justice is a condition of a thing the presence of which can be determined quite independently of what the human conventions in a given locality, or indeed anywhere, happen to be (see *ibid.*, n. C). For Plato, being just is emphatically not merely a matter of abiding by the conventions which happen to be in force; for even if the real dictates of justice do substantially coincide with strictures that are laid down by society (see *ibid.*), it is nevertheless possible that they should diverge from those strictures. Being just does not merely *consist in* a tendency to observe them. (Cf. 443b–444a, n. D, and 491b–494a, n. B.) [Cf. Crombie, *PMA*, pp. 135–6, 142–3; Ritter, *EPP*, pp. 82–3; Shorey, *Rep.*, I, pp. 46, 114–7; Krämer, *APA*, p. 119. On the general matter of Plato's epistemological anti-conventionalism, or realism, see White, *passim.*]

368c–369b: BEFORE CONSIDERING WHETHER JUSTICE IS MORE BENEFICIAL THAN INJUSTICE, THE FIRST TASK IS TO DISCOVER WHAT JUSTICE IS. SOCRATES PROPOSES TO DO THIS BY FIRST ATTEMPTING TO DISCOVER WHAT JUSTICE IS IN A CITY (*POLIS*), ON THE GROUND THAT IT WILL BE EASIER ON THAT BASIS TO DETERMINE WHAT IT IS IN AN INDIVIDUAL HUMAN BEING.

A. The crucial difference between the argument in Book I and the argument in Books II–X which makes the latter in Plato's eyes so much superior to the former (see on 357a–b), is that the latter is based on a substantial investigation into what justice is (see 354a–c, where the previous argument is said to be vitiated by the lack of such an investigation).

B. In reading the *Republic* it is often important to remember that the word "city" is not an entirely accurate translation of the Greek word *"polis."* The translation "city-state" is closer, but it is cumbersome and ugly. What is important to bear in mind is that the term *polis* connotes a certain degree of independence of government and self-sufficiency of economy. These are features that Plato's treatment will emphasize throughout. [Shorey, *Rep.*, I, pp. xxviii-xxix.]

C. Plato says that to help us discover what justice is in an individual, we should first discover what it is in a city. His reasons for proceeding in this way are complex. Fundamentally, they come down to the view that colloquial uses of the word "just" are closer to the use of the term that he thinks applicable to a city than they are to the use that he thinks applicable to a man. (The reason is that the latter use is bound up with his theory of the human soul, a theory that plays no role in colloquial usage.) He therefore thinks that there will be clearer justification for his use of the term in application to individuals if he first exhibits the parallel use in application to cities (cf. 591a–592b, n. D). But this is only a sketch of what is really a very complicated situation (see 442d–443b, n. B).

One particular oversimplification, however, should be guarded against. Frequently, it is asked whether in his discussion of justice Plato argues "from city to individual or from individual to city." The answer is that his argument has too many parts, too intricately interconnected, for either of these characterizations to be anything but misleading.

D. It will help us to understand Plato's procedure if we look closely at the psychological phenomenon he is describing when he talks of our reading of larger and smaller letters (368d). It is the following, which the reader can, with the help of a collaborator, put to the test himself. If you have some letters set out at a distance from you that is just barely too great for them to be read, and you then have larger versions of the same letters set out at the same distance, you will discover that you suddenly can actually *see* what the smaller letters are. (To avoid your relying on an assumption on your part that the letters are the same, have your collaborator deceive you a number of times in the beginning, by setting out larger versions of different letters.) It is not that you *infer* that because the larger letters are, say, "O, A, L, T, P," the smaller letters must be "o, a, l, t, p" (for you cannot *assume* that the smaller are the same as the larger). Rather, once you are presented with larger letters, you can actually *see* the smaller letters, *and*, at the same time, *see* that they are the same as the larger. I do not know the explanation of this phenomenon (though I conjecture that by seeing the larger letters, you suddenly conceive a hypothesis about what features—what projections and curves, *etc.*—to look for in the smaller, a conjecture that turns out to be right when the smaller letters are in fact the same), but it is certainly not an argument or inference from an indentification or description of the larger letters to an indentification or description of the smaller.

Thus understood, Plato's simile in fact turns out to be closely parallel to the procedure that he adopts in discovering what justice is in the city and then in the individual. See further nn. A–B on 441c–442d.

369b–d: THE BEGINNING OF A CITY IS DESCRIBED, AND THE NEEDS THAT PRODUCE IT. THE ESSENTIAL MINIMUM IS A GROUP OF FOUR OR FIVE PEOPLE. THE CITY ARISES BECAUSE INDIVIDUAL HUMAN BEINGS ARE NOT SELF-SUFFICIENT.

A. This passage is the beginning of Plato's explanation of what justice is, which will take him to the end of Book IV, in which we will be given accounts, first, of justice in the city (432b–434c) and, second, of justice in the individual (441c–442d).

B. Plato characteristically packs several crucial ideas into a short passage. All of them will be developed later.

The first is that cities are said to arise because individuals are not self-sufficient and need others in order to remain alive (d2). In the same breath, it is said that they will institute exchanges with each other because it is "better" for them to do so. Plato evidently does not expect his Thrasymachean opponents to claim that a strong man could do without society altogether; even the dictatorial man, who is the most anti-social of the types whom Plato delineates (573c–576b), does not aim to do without other people. Plato's belief is clear: we have needs that only cities can fulfill, and the establishment of cities to meet those needs is a good.

Second, this being so, we must realize that a city is made necessary by certain—as we may put it—unavoidable imperfections in the human constitution. If a man were perfect in the sense of having no needs, then cities would be unnecessary. Plato will later make clear the ways in which the city is an institution suited to deal with human imperfections (see, e.g., 370c–371e, n. B, 371e–373c, n. B, 410a–412a, n. A, 403c–404a, n. C, 502c–504d, n. B, 558c–559d, n. B).

Third, there is an apparently trivial point, but one that will be developed later (see 422e–423d, n. A, 427e–428a, n. B, 484a–d, n. D), that a city is a gathering of *many* men into *one* habitation (c2–3). The idea that will be developed is that of the unity of the city. [Grote, pp. 111ff; Robin, pp. 281–2; Guthrie, *HGP*, pp. 445, 447–9.]

C. It is important to notice that Plato is constructing his city in response to human *need* (*chreia*, 369c10). On the other hand, it is equally important to notice that this does not commit Plato to any particular view about how the city is to be constructed, or about exactly how we are to assess the degree of satisfactoriness of a city, beyond the vague claim that it must serve human needs. In particular, Plato is not hereby committed to the view that whatever measure will increase the total satisfaction of needs of the individual citizens ought to be adopted by or for the city, or that a city is good in the exact proportion that it satisfies such needs. He never maintains that this is the case, nor expresses any interest in, or awareness of, the idea of comparing policies by seeing which will produce the greatest sum of satisfaction of individuals. Moreover, he turns out to have a quite different notion of how the goodness of a city is to be assessed (see 427e–428a, n. B, with 419a–421c, n. D).

369e–370c: THE CITY WILL BE BEST ORGANIZED UNDER THE PRINCIPLE OF THE NATURAL DIVISION OF LABOR, WITH EACH

SINGLE MAN PERFORMING A SINGLE TASK, THE TASK FOR WHICH HE IS NATURALLY SUITED.

A.   A seemingly unobtrusive passage—even a trivial-seeming one; but it provides the underpinnings for almost all of the rest of Plato's description of his city. No understanding of the *Republic* is possible without an awareness of the role that this principle plays. [Grote, pp. 98, 114ff., 187; Shorey, *WPS*, p. 217; Adam, I, p. 95; Vlastos, *JHR*, pp. 76–7.]

B.   The principle that Plato enunciates here differs from notions of the division of labor as they typically figure in modern economic theory. Crucial to Plato's principle is the idea that people should be given tasks for which they are, in some sense, *naturally* suited, and, moreover, the idea that each person has *exactly one* task to which he is naturally suited. Like the theme of the unity of the city (n. B on 369b–d), this theme of unity of task will be developed further (see 397e, 423c–d with 422e–423d, n. B, and 519b–d, n. B).

C.   The present section emphasizes what was implicit in the previous one, that the development of the city is a natural occurrence, rather than one that is imposed on people from outside in some manner. Contrast with this the view expounded by Glaucon about justice, that it is a kind of imposition, established by convention, on those who would otherwise be able to pursue their own gain unmolested (n. A on 358a–362c). Plato is not yet talking about justice, but he is paving the way for saying that justice is not the sort of arbitrary imposition on anyone's natural inclinations that his opponents take it to be (see 357b–358a, n. A, 444a–e, n. A, 590a–c, n. A). Rather, as we have seen already (n. C on 362d–368c), it is independent of strictures which human beings lay down. [Bosanquet, pp. 82–3.]

D.   There is more than one way in which Plato takes his city to exhibit natural tendencies. One is that each person is to perform the task to which he is naturally suited by ability and temperament (370b). Another is that certain types of work demand attention at certain times and cannot wait until one has finished doing something else (370b7 with c4)— a clear example being the fact that crops will decay if not harvested in time. Yet a third involves an assumption that Plato is forced to make. If his city is to operate, each necessary task must have the required number of people on hand to perform it. Plato takes note of this fact later, when he observes that the city's need for only a small number of rulers, and for a large number of people for other forms of labor, fits nicely with the fact that there are, he thinks, only a small number of people naturally suited to rule and a large number suited to less intellectually demanding tasks (see n. B on 428a–429a and n. C on 491b–494a). [Schleiermacher, pp. 359–60.]

E. There are substantial difficulties of a philosophical kind in the notion of "nature" that Plato employs here (370a8–b1, c4). To say that someone has a certain function by nature is to say that that function is not somehow arbitrarily assigned to, or imposed on, him. But this explanation does not take us very far. In particular, it does not give us directions for telling what a person's natural function is, or for distinguishing one's natural function from arbitrarily imposed activities. For reasons such as this, many would find this notion of naturalness philosophically suspect and would expect Plato to provide some substantial explanation of it. Moreover, they will perhaps claim that some of the activities that he regards as natural (notably those involved in the training of the rulers of his city) could equally well be thought to be highly unnatural and to suppress natural tendencies. The fact is, however, that Plato clearly does not find such difficulties in the notion, and thinks it clear enough, at least provisionally, for his purposes in the *Republic*.

Moreover, although he does not develop the argument himself, he must think that he has a defense against the charge that he has been arbitrary or mistaken in his estimation of which are the natural functions or tasks for human beings. For the line of thought that he is following has begun with the claim that a city or *polis* (368c–369b, n. B) is a natural response to human needs (n. C, *supra*). His argument continues by saying that if the city is to provide for human needs satisfactorily, then certain functions must be formed within it. The conclusion drawn is that these required functions must themselves be natural, and, furthermore, that there must be people who are naturally suited to perform them. (This last clause involves the view that human beings are, as a group, naturally suited to perform the tasks that are required for the satisfaction of their needs.) Plato believes that these functions are not generally well performed in actual cities, and that that is why actual cities are not satisfactory. His task, therefore, is to explain how, by breeding and training (374e–376c, n. A), people could be produced who would perform these functions well. Because he is confident that the functions, being necessary for a natural institution, the city, are themselves natural, he tends to be equally confident of the naturalness of the breeding and training which lead to their performance. In addition, he seems to think that when we actually examine the tasks required for the city and the dispositions of human beings, we can tell that the latter are suited to the former in some natural manner. But his readiness to think this is no doubt encouraged by the line of thought just described. [Grote, pp. 173–4.]

F. Plato's notion of a task or function (*ergon*, 369e2, 374d8) has already been introduced in Book I, in 352d–354a (see n. A there), in the view that the excellence of a thing involves its performing its function well. The same view appears again in Book X, in the statement (601d) that the rightness, beauty, and virtue or excellence (*aretē*) of a thing lie in the fulfillment of that use (*chreia*) for which it either was made or arose by nature (*pephykos*, 601d6). This view is closely connected with the notion of goodness which Plato develops in Books VI–VII (see 507a–509c, n. B).

Plato's present use of the notion of a function adds something to what he said about it in Book I. There his account of it did not rule out the possibility that a thing might have more than one function (though he assumed without argument—see 352d–354a, n. B—that the soul has only one function). Here he attempts to give a partial justification for ruling out that possibility, at least so far as concerns human beings, by his contention that a person performs a task far better when he concentrates on that single task alone. (For a difficulty here, see 452e–456b, n. B.)

370c–371e: ON THE BASIS OF THE PRINCIPLE OF THE NATURAL DIVISION OF LABOR, IT IS SEEN THAT THE CITY WILL, AFTER ALL, NEED MORE THAN THE FOUR OR FIVE PEOPLE JUST MENTIONED. FURTHER NECESSARY OCCUPATIONS ARE DESCRIBED, INCLUDING THOSE REQUIRED FOR TRADE WITH OTHER CITIES.

A. Plato is not here going beyond the minimum necessary population for a city. He is saying that if we adhere strictly to the Principle of the Natural Division of Labor, we shall *all along* have needed more than the four or five that we thought were a sufficient minimum (370b–c).

B. The discussion of the positive need for trade with other cities shows that Plato is designing an institution that is meant to function in, and deal with the problems arising in, the physical world as it in fact is. For this reason it can be misleading to call it an "ideal" city. It is indeed ideal in a certain sense (see n. A on 472e–473b), but it is ideal neither in the sense of existing in ideal circumstances, nor in the sense of containing a population of ideally gifted people (see also 369b–d, n. B). [Nettleship, pp. 304–5; Guthrie, HGP, p. 528, n. 4, p. 560; Shorey, Rep., I, p. 345.]

371e–373c: THE CITY IS APPARENTLY COMPLETE. WHERE, THEN, ARE JUSTICE AND INJUSTICE IN IT? PRESUMABLY, IN THE DEALINGS OF PEOPLE WITH EACH OTHER, SO WE MUST LOOK AT HOW THEY LIVE THEIR LIVES. THIS IS BRIEFLY DONE, AND GLAUCON REMARKS THAT FURTHER AMENITIES MIGHT WELL BE ADDED, AND THAT THE CITY AS THUS FAR DESCRIBED SEEMS LIKE A "CITY OF PIGS." SOCRATES' REAC-TION IS THAT ADDING FURTHER AMENITIES WOULD PRODUCE A LUXURIOUS CITY; BUT THEN HE SAYS THAT PERHAPS BY EXAMINING SUCH A CITY THEY WILL BE ABLE TO SEE HOW JUSTICE AND INJUSTICE ARISE. HE THEN ADDS FURTHER OCCUPATIONS AND PURSUITS, GOING BEYOND THE NECESSI-TIES TO WHICH HE HAS THUS FAR CONFINED HIMSELF.

A.   Why does Plato add unnecessary luxuries to his city? Why does he introduce things of which the city will then have to be "purified" (399e)?

The reason, he says (372e4–6), is to enable us to "see how justice and injustice grow in cities." This is neither to imply that the city thus far described is not just (in fact by the standards of 432b–434c it is just), nor yet that it is immune to injustice. It is simply to say that by intro-ducing scope for further imperfections, we shall be able to see more clearly the conditions that constitute justice in a city, because we shall be able to contrast them with the tendencies toward injustice (see 427d, n. B).

B.   But there is a further reason for the introduction of luxuries. Plato wishes to use the notion of justice in the city to help us understand the notion of justice in the individual (368c–369b). He believes, however, that the human soul, at least when embodied, contains an ineliminable stock of appetites of a "bodily" sort which, if they are not controlled, aim at the sort of luxuries here introduced. For Plato, the problem of controlling these appetites is parallel to the problem in a city of con-trolling citizens' appetitive cravings (e.g., 435c–442d), and—what is crucial here—he believes that forms of justice are involved in this control in both cases (441c–442d). We can therefore see that if he is to use his description of the city to help us discover justice in the indivi-

dual, then he will need something in the city that is parallel to the appetites in the individual, and it is for this purpose that luxuries are introduced into the city. If it were not for them, then he would be unable to
draw the analogy between city and individual that he needs.

We can see that in both cases Plato is considering justice as an attribute of things that have a strong tendency to depart from it and become
unjust. So he can regard justice, like the city itself (369b–d, n. B),
as something that is aimed at in order to combat the undesirable tendencies that arise in groups of human beings. [Crombie, *EPD*, p. 90;
Friedländer pp. 83–4.]

C. Even though Plato's purposes in describing a luxurious city are
thus primarily expository, we may ask whether he thought it inevitable
that a city of the sort described before 371e should turn into one of the
sort described thereafter. But this question raises the broader question
whether Plato intended his whole description of the city, from 369b
onward, to describe historically a process that actually took place. In
fact it is probably impossible to establish whether, or in what degree,
he intended his description to be historical. But however we answer
this question, nothing in his subsequent argument depends on the answer.
What is important for him is neither that events of this sort did take
place nor that they did not. What is important is simply that the city as
it is finally constituted should manifest natural human tendencies as he
maintains that it does (see nn. B–D on 369e–370c). (For a further
comment on the irrelevance of historical description to Plato's aims, see
nn. B–C on 545c–547c). [Nettleship, pp. 69–70.]

D. Contrary to one's first impression, the addition of "seasoning" or "sauce" (*opsos*)
to the diet in 372c does not mark the beginning of the description of the luxurious city
(though sauces are certainly in use in that city—373a3, c3). For Plato observes later
that sauces may be necessary to good health and nutrition (559b1, 6). The description
of the luxurious city begins at 372d7.

373d–374e: HAVING GONE BEYOND WHAT IS NECESSARY, THE
CITY WILL BE SUBJECT TO TWO IMPORTANT FURTHER NEEDS:
(1) FOR PHYSICIANS TO CURE ILLS THAT ARISE FROM SUPER-
FLUITY; AND (2) FOR MORE TERRITORY TO SATISFY GREATER
WANTS, AND THEREFORE FOR WAR IN ORDER TO GAIN AND
PROTECT THIS FURTHER TERRITORY, AND SO, IN CONSE-
QUENCE OF THIS, FOR CERTAIN PEOPLE, NAMELY, "GUARD-
IANS," BY WHOM WAR MAY BE WAGED.

A.   By far the most important effect of the alteration in Plato's city is the introduction of the need for "guardians" (374d8), the account of whose role, natural disposition, and education will overwhelmingly dominate the rest of Plato's description of his city.

The appearance of the guardians is motivated by the additional wants that appeared in the previous section, coupled with the Principle of the Natural Division of Labor, which requires that if there is a task to be done in the city, then there must be a group of people who are specially suited to performing it. To show that there is such a group, and that they can perform the task, is one of Plato's main problems in the *Republic*. Later on it turns out that the class of guardians must be divided into two, the rulers and the auxiliaries (412a–414b). Plato must then try to show that it is possible to have a group of people who can adequately perform the task of ruling. This he attempts to show in his discussion of his "philosopher-rulers" in Books V—VII (see esp. 474b–c, 484a–d, 502c–504d), by showing that such people are suited by nature and training to guard and preserve the city.

B.   Physicians are left aside here, and taken up in 405a–410a.

374e–376c: BY THE PRINCIPLE OF THE NATURAL DIVISION OF LABOR, THE GUARDIANS MUST HAVE A PARTICULAR NATURAL APTITUDE FOR THEIR TASK. THEY MUST BE HIGH-SPIRITED, BUT THEY MUST BE GENTLE TO THOSE WHOM THEY ARE GUARDING, BECAUSE OTHERWISE THEY WILL NOT BE GOOD GUARDIANS. WITH THEIR HIGH-SPIRITEDNESS, THEREFORE, THEY MUST COMBINE THE PHILOSOPHICAL TEMPER OF A GOOD GUARD-DOG (WHO IS "PHILOSOPHICAL" IN LIKING THOSE WHOM HE KNOWS).

A.   There are two parts to the idea that the people who are to be guardians must be suited to their task or function (*ergon*, 374d8). One is that they must have a certain natural disposition, which is prior to education but developed by it. The other is that they receive the appropriate education. Plato spends much more time on the latter, not because he thinks it more important, but because he thinks that it is difficult to describe accurately, and because it involves the need for the city to diverge from current educational practices. [Shorey, *Rep.*, I, pp. 100–1.]

B.   Plato emphasizes that there is a kind of conflict between the two tendencies necessary in a guardian, fierceness (toward enemies) and gentleness (toward friends). The harmonization of these two tendencies is one of the main problems confronting his system of education, as he recognizes (see 410a–412a). It is not only that it is difficult to find and train people in whom these two tendencies are appropriately combined. It is also that the very task that they must do itself requires such a combination (see n. B on 369b–d).

C. Plato maintains that dogs are like philosophers, in that dogs like those whom they know. Presumably, this implies that philosophers are like dogs–in liking those whom they know. This, in my experience, is false. One supposes that Plato's comparison is partly whimsical. There is, after all, a difference between liking those persons or things you know, and welcoming a prospective increase in the quantity of what you know. (Moreover dogs, as Plato perhaps did not know, remember with dislike those whom they know as enemies.) But Plato *does* think that guardians, or the best guardians, must be philosophers (473b–474b).

376c–e: THIS BEING THE GUARDIANS' NATURE OR NATURAL DISPOSITION, WE MUST NOW ASK HOW THEY SHOULD BE RAISED AND EDUCATED.

A. The question just posed about the necessary natural disposition for guardians was a question about how they must be naturally disposed *in order to be good guardians*. Likewise, the question now being posed is *not* "What is a good education?" but rather, "What sort of education will induce people with the right natural aptitude for guardianship to turn out to be good guardians?" The question, in other words, is one of how the prospective guardians may be educated so as to perform their task in Plato's city. It is with an eye to this, and nothing else, that the ensuing discussion of education is carried out.

376e: TWO KINDS OF EDUCATION OR TRAINING ARE PERTINENT: (1) PHYSICAL TRAINING OR GYMNASTICS (*GYMNASTIKĒ*), FOR THE BODY; AND (2) TRAINING IN THE ARTS, OR MUSIC (*MOUSIKĒ*), FOR THE SOUL.

A. The translations "gymnastic" and "music" are misleading. "Training in the arts" and "physical training" come much closer to the idea. Notice, however, that although Plato here suggests that physical training is for the sake of the body, it later turns out that it is really as much for the sake of the soul (410a–412a). [Grube, *Rep.*, p. 46, n. 12.]

376e–379b: WE FIRST CONSIDER TRAINING IN THE ARTS, AND IN PARTICULAR THE KINDS OF STORIES THAT CHILDREN ARE TO BE TOLD, WHICH HAVE A STRONG INFLUENCE OVER THEM. THEY MUST NOT BE TOLD FALSE STORIES ABOUT THE GODS, WHICH WILL HAVE BAD EFFECTS ON THEM.

A. Plato's discussion here is not a treatment of arts as such, but a treatment of the kind of training in the arts that will best enable his guardians to fulfill their task as guardians, and it is in this light that it should primarily be read. This is not to deny, of course, that Plato disapproves of many features of the arts, as they were and are pursued. At the moment, however, he is concerned predominantly with their role in the guardians' education. Later, in Book X, he will say more about them in a broader context (see 595a–608b).

B. In this section, Plato insists both that the stories told to children about the gods should be true, and that they should be such as to improve the natural dispositions of the children. Because he believes that the gods are good examples to hold up to children, he believes that in the present case the two aims coincide, that is, that the truth about the gods is educationally salutary. (On occasion, however, he emphasizes that some parts of the population will need to be controlled by telling them falsehoods; see 382c, 389b–d, 414–415, 458b–460b). His complaint about traditional poetry and literature is that they portray the gods inaccurately, as do painters who produce inaccurate images (377e—for further comparison with painters, see also 597e–598d, 602c–605c), and in so doing inculcate bad traits of character. (Cf. 485a–d, n. A.)

C. Plato avoids asking just what stories should be told to future guardians (379a). The reason is that he has not yet put himself in a position to explain the virtues that he wishes to instill. He is, however, willing to insist that the stories should not encourage discord or fighting among the citizens by portraying it among the gods (378c). Presumably, he takes it to be obvious that performance of the guardians' function will be hindered by discord among them; and in fact he makes much of this point later on (see esp. 465b, n. A, 545c–547c, n. A).

379b–380c: ONE FALSEHOOD THAT MUST NOT BE TOLD IS THAT GODS ARE CAUSES OF ANY BUT GOOD THINGS.

A.   Plato argues that because the gods are good, and because what is good cannot be the cause of anything that is not good, the gods cannot be the cause of anything that is not good. One should not overlook the fact that, although he does not explain the notion of goodness here, he is making an approach to his extensive exploration of the notion in Books VI–VII, and his other uses of the notion elsewhere in the *Republic* (see esp. 504d–511e, 519–521b, 531d–534d, and secs. 2–4 of the Introduction). In 380d–383c below, he reveals some aspects of his notion of goodness.

B.   The principle that whatever is good can be the cause of only good things is probably to be associated with the views on causation expressed at *Phaedo* 101a–b, *Parmenides* 131c–d. But there is the potential for conflict between this principle and 509b, which, at least on one interpretation, prompts us to think that something good might be the cause of bad things (see 507a–509c, n.C). (On a god's not being the cause of something bad, see also 617e.)

380d–381e: ANOTHER SORT OF FALSEHOOD THAT MAY NOT BE TOLD ABOUT THE GODS IS THAT THEY CHANGE THEIR SHAPE. GODS, BEING PERFECTLY GOOD, HAVE NO REASON TO CHANGE.

A.   Plato maintains that insofar as a thing is good, it is stable and unalterable. This thesis has roots in his metaphysical theory, his theory of Forms (see Introd., sec. 3), and is later applied in an important way to his city (see 422e–423d, n. A, and 427e–428a, n. B). Plato uses this discussion of the gods to adumbrate his views about goodness; at the same time he is trying to ensure that the future guardians not have a false conception of divinity and so of goodness.

381e–383c: BEING PERFECTLY GOOD, A GOD HAS NO NEED TO BE DECEPTIVE (AND HENCE NO NEED TO CHANGE SHAPE, AS GODS ARE SAID TO DO IN SOME STORIES). GODS ARE NON-COMPLEX OR SIMPLE IN NATURE, AND THEY ARE TRUTHFUL; AND MEN WHO ARE GOD-FEARING OR PIOUS MUST RECOGNIZE THIS FACT.

A.   Another aspect of divinity and of goodness appears. Insofar as the gods are good they are also simple or non-complex (*haploun*, 382e8), and accordingly do not have a plurality of aspects or appearances which they may present to men. For further connections between goodness and simplicity (or unity), see 427e–428a, n. B, and Introd., sec. 3.

B.   The non-deceptiveness of the gods arises in two ways, though both spring ultimately from the sort of goodness that Plato attributes to them. In the first place, the gods will not convey a falsehood to others because they will lack all of the reasons that sometimes induce men to do so, such as ignorance, fear of enemies, and the madness of kinsmen. (One particular way in which the gods are said by poets to be deceptive, namely, by changing their shapes as they appear to men, is already ruled out by the argument of the previous section against the possibility of a god's changing.) In the second place, as we have just seen, the gods lack the plurality of appearances that make deception possible (cf. by contrast what Plato says about sensible objects at 479a–b, 523a–524d, 602c–603b).

C.   The present passage, like some others (especially in Book X), raises questions about how much of traditional Greek theology Plato believed. Did he, for example, believe in a plurality of gods at all (sometimes he speaks of gods in the plural, at other times of god in the singular)? He does not attempt to settle such issues here. But he does, as we have just observed, make clear some of the features that he thinks are entailed by divinity.

Book III

— education of guardians continues - life style
— division of guardian class

Unlike some of the other divisions between books (such as the one between Book I and Book II, and the one between Book IX and Book X), the division between Book II and Book III marks no important break in Plato's argument.

386a–392c: MANY STORIES AND MYTHS ARE TO BE FORBIDDEN BECAUSE THEY DISCOURAGE BRAVERY, ESPECIALLY BY HEIGHTENING THE FEAR OF DEATH. EXCESSIVE TENDENCY TO LAUGHTER MUST ALSO BE DISCOURAGED. TRUTH MUST BE ESTEEMED, AND LIES MAY NOT BE EMPLOYED BY PRIVATE CITIZENS, THOUGH RULERS SOMETIMES MAY HAVE TO USE THEM. LIKE BRAVERY, MODERATION OR TEMPERANCE MUST ALSO BE ENCOURAGED BY THE STORIES WHICH ARE ALLOWED, AND STORIES DISCOURAGING MODERATION MUST BE FORBIDDEN. WE MUST PRESUMABLY FORBID STORIES TEACHING THAT INJUSTICE IS PROFITABLE—BUT WE SHALL HAVE TO SEE ABOUT THIS LATER, WHEN WE DISCOVER WHAT JUSTICE IS.

A. The present section takes up two of the four virtues with which Plato will deal extensively in Book IV, namely, bravery (*andreia*) and moderation or temperance (*sōphrosynē*), and directs that stories discouraging them must be excluded from the education of the guardians. These two virtues are the ones whose conduciveness to the task of guardianship Plato takes to be uncontroversial. The two other virtues are left aside, justice because its desirability in general is what is at issue, and wisdom because its role in the city will not become clear until the discussion of the rulers, which begins only in 412c.

B.   In 389b–c and 390a we have our first explicit mentions of the rulers of the city, but nothing is said until 412c about who they are.

C.   There is a reiteration in 389b–d of Plato's views on truth from 376e–379b, but here the emphasis is not on the need for the stories about the gods to be true, but on the necessity for the trait of truthfulness to be cultivated in the guardians. Although the rulers of the city will on occasion employ falsehoods (382c, 389b–d, 414–415), an esteem for the truth will later turn out to be an important feature of the rulers' character, when Plato comes to explain that his rulers must be philosophers (see 473b–474b, 475e–476d, and cf. 374d–376c).

392c–398b: FROM THE CONTENT OF STORIES SOCRATES TURNS TO THE STYLE AND MANNER OF THEIR TELLING. HE DISTINGUISHES PURE THIRD-PERSON NARRATIVE FROM IMITATIVE TECHNIQUES (*MIMĒTIKĒ*) AND THE GENRES EMPLOYING THEM. ON THE BASIS OF THE PRINCIPLE OF THE NATURAL DIVISION OF LABOR, IMITATION IS CONDEMNED, EXCEPT IN CASES WHERE THE MAN IMITATED IS A GOOD MAN ACTING IN A GOOD MANNER; THE USE OF NARRATIVE IS TO BE FAVORED IN ALL OTHER CASES.

A.   Once again Plato is not discussing literature and the arts on general grounds; he is concerned with how they should figure in an effort to produce people who will be as good guardians as possible, and with what sorts of pursuits are compatible with, and helpful to, the maintenance of a guardianly character (394e1–2, 398e). In Book X he discusses the more general basis for his views about these topics (see 595a–608b).

B.   It is easy to overlook the fact, but Plato makes it clear that his strictures against imitative arts are meant to be derived from the principle with which he began his discussion of his city (369b–370c), the Principle of the Natural Division of Labor. He wishes to raise the guardians to have a certain sort of character, and if they take part in the imitation of other sorts of character, he goes so far as to say that they will be violating the principle (394e, 395b, 397e) and will be "two or more persons at once" (397e1–2). He takes it as incompatible with his principle that those who are being educated should be trained to have a guardianly character but at the same time take part in the imitation of other sorts of character. For this reason, he does not forbid imitation of good actions by good men (396c–d). (The notion that it is undesirable to be "two or more persons at once" is explored and exploited later: see 443b and 554a, with 381e–383c, and 422e–423d, n. A.) [Shorey, *WPS*, p. 219; Bosanquet, p. 99.]

C. Plato extends the idea of the desirability of unity and simplicity to the point of directing that the guardians' education should dispense with instruments of many strings and any kind of elaborate harmony (399c–d). He believes that simple and non-complex music encourages bravery and moderation (399a–c). [Nettleship, pp. 109–112.]

D. In regarding imitation of other characters as a breach of the Principle of the Natural Division of Labor in the present context, Plato shows that he is thinking of the *participation* of the future guardians in performances, not their mere *witnessing* of performances. The question at issue here is not what they should be allowed to watch so much as what arts they should learn to practice themselves. In Book X, at 605c–608b, Plato discusses the influence of dramatic performances on the audience.

E. As before, Plato indicates his belief that in insisting that each person perform one and only one narrowly defined task, he is following human nature (395b4–6).

398c–400c: LYRIC ODES AND SONGS ARE TO OBEY THE SAME PRINCIPLES. MUSICAL MODE AND RHYTHM MUST FIT THE WORDS AND BE SUITABLE TO GOOD CHARACTER, BRAVERY, AND MODERATION. WE CAN NOW SEE THAT WE HAVE BEEN IN THE PROCESS OF PURIFYING THE LUXURIOUS CITY.

A. This passage points back to 372e *sqq.* where luxuries were first introduced into the city, and observes that the effect of the educational provisions so far has been to eliminate some of what was introduced there. But the process of cleansing has only begun and Plato indicates that it must continue (the correct translation of 399e5–6 does not say that we *have cleansed*, but that we *have been cleansing*, the city).

B.   In this passage Plato continues his effort to instill bravery and moderation (399a–b, e–400a) by training in music and the arts, again making the connection with simplicity of style (399c–d; cf. previous n. C).

C.   It should be borne in mind that Plato does believe that, as a matter of observation, the kind of music and poetry with which one is brought up does influence one's character. In urging the salutary effects of music and poetry that are simple, he is pointing to what he takes to be observable facts. But he clearly takes it to be no accident that simplicity and salutariness go together (cf. 381e–383c, n. A).

400d–401d: ONLY POETRY AND MUSIC FITTING THESE SPECIFICATIONS WILL BE ALLOWED IN THE EDUCATION OF THE GUARDIANS, SO THAT THEY WILL BE ABLE TO PERFORM THEIR TASK. THERE IS A CONNECTION BETWEEN BEAUTY AND ORDER IN MUSIC AND THE CORRESPONDING FEATURES OF CHARACTER AND OF SOUL.

A.   This passage makes the connection between the themes just discussed and the notion of order and harmony, directing our attention to the idea of order in the soul, which will be developed further in subsequent sections, especially in Book IV (see, e.g., 441c–442d, 443b–444a).

B.   Notice that Plato is talking of *sung* poetry, which is what Greek poetry of the time was (cf. 598d–601b, n. B).

401d–403c: THE KIND OF CHARACTER BEING INCULCATED HERE IS INCOMPATIBLE WITH EXTREMES OF PLEASURE AND SEXUAL PASSION. THOSE TRAINED IN THE FOREGOING MANNER WILL REGARD MODERATION AND HARMONY AS MORE BEAUTIFUL AND ATTRACTIVE THAN ANYTHING ELSE.

A.   Plato draws out what he takes to be further consequences of the point already established (n. A on 386a–392c), that to fulfill their task as guardians, those being educated must be of brave and moderate character. Part of his point here is negative, that those being educated will not be given to strong passion of a sexual kind (cf. 572b–573c). The other part is positive, that their feelings of love and attraction will be different, and channeled in a different direction, so that they will be attracted by manifestations of beauty of the sort prescribed for the arts in the foregoing discussion. These are the things that Plato claims are in fact the most beautiful (402d).

B.   With characteristic unobtrusiveness, Plato here takes a step that is of some importance to his overall plan, in saying that not only will guardians recognize and esteem orderliness in the arts, they will also recognize and esteem it in each other. From this a very important claim is made to follow—which seems trivial but in fact is not—that those qualified to oversee the future education of guardians will be guardians themselves, because they will be able to recognize the traits that are to be inculcated. What this piece of reasoning allows is an expansion of the formerly narrow task alloted to the guardians, or rather—as Plato views it—a demonstration that the function of guardianship is actually broader and more inclusive than it seemed at first sight. We shall see that later the guardians' task turns out to be even broader, and in fact includes the ruling of the city (see 412a–c, n. A, and 412e–414b, n. B). [Shorey, *Rep.*, II, p. 230.]

403c–404e: SOCRATES TURNS NOW TO PHYSICAL TRAINING, WHICH IS SAID TO BE LIKE TRAINING IN THE ARTS, IN THAT IT REQUIRES SIMPLICITY RATHER THAN VARIETY AND ELABO-RATENESS, AND IN THAT IT PRODUCES A HEALTH IN THE BODY THAT IS ANALOGOUS TO MODERATION IN THE SOUL.

A.   Because Plato believes in a parallelism of effects and techniques between artistic and physical training (404b, e; cf. 444a–e), he is able simply to transfer the basic points about the former to the case of the latter. Notice in particular that the training is not the ordinary training for athletes but is a training specially suited to the requirements of being a guardian (404a).

B.   It will soon emerge, in 410a–412a (note also 410b), that not only is there a strong parallelism between training of body and training of soul, but Plato believes that physical training really is a way of training the soul.

C.   By insisting on the importance of physical training, Plato is once more underlining the fact that his city is not an otherworldly institution designed for beings—gods or disembodied souls—who do not have to worry about the imperfections of the sensible world. Cf. 369b–d, n. B.

405a–410a: THE TASK OF PHYSICIANS AND JURISTS SHOULD BE PRIMARILY TO MAINTAIN HEALTH AND JUSTICE WHERE THEY EXIST, RATHER THAN TO RESTORE OR PRODUCE THEM

WHERE THEY DO NOT. EACH MAN HAS A TASK TO PERFORM, RATHER THAN SPENDING HIS TIME BEING CURED OR RE-FORMED. THE PHYSICIAN SHOULD HAVE PERSONAL ACQUAIN-TANCE WITH ILLNESS, BUT THE JURIST SHOULD NOT KNOW INJUSTICE BY HAVING BEEN UNJUST HIMSELF.

A. It was the introduction of superfluity and luxury at 371e–373c that led to the need for both guardians and physicians in 373d–374e. Since then Plato has been discussing guardians. Now he turns to physicians, and also to jurists, because he wants to make the point about both of them that they have no place in his city as curers of evils but only—insofar as they can adopt this role—as preventers of them. In form, the present passage is a digression, because instead of continuing to describe the education of the guardians, it tells what happens when education is *not* good and a great many physicians and jurists are there-fore necessary (405a).

B. Once again Plato wishes to advance his argument not in an *ad hoc* way, but by reliance on the Principle of the Natural Division of Labor. "Every man in a well-governed community," he says, "has his own prescribed task to fulfill, and no one has the leisure to be ill and under treatment for long periods" (406c; cf. d–407a). The curative tasks of the jurist and the physician will be reduced to a minimum, not because the city is perfect (Plato indicates that there will be some illness and some legal infractions), but because the existence of such tasks would entail a group of people who extensively violated the principle that each man is to spend his time at one task.

C. In 407a and 410a Plato makes claims to the effect that certain of his arrangements are *good* for or to the *benefit* of the city and the people in it. These claims foreshadow further claims, e.g., at 412e, 413c, e (cf. 419a, 420b, 519e) about what is good for the city and its citizens. One important one, to be made shortly, is that the interests of the guardians and the interests of the city will coincide.

It will obviously be of the utmost importance for Plato, in order to explain his meaning, to make clear his notion or notions of goodness, benefit, and interest. The need has been present ever since the beginning of Book II (357b–358a), but passages like the present one make it more pressing. A question that must be addressed with special attention, of course, is the question of the relationship between benefit to the individ-ual in Plato's city and benefit to the city as a whole. Plato begins to attack this question in 412d–415d, and again at the beginning of Book IV. But he makes it clear that a full understanding of the issues involved requires more than this cursory treatment, and that is why he ultimately maintains that the rulers of his city must have a certain kind of thorough knowledge of the Good (504d–506a). In Books VI–VII he explains something of what this knowledge involves and how it is acquired.

D.   In 409c–d Plato briefly introduces the idea that a person maintains his character and regulates his behavior by referring to "a model within himself." This idea of a "model" receives further elaboration in the discussion of Forms in Books V–VII (see esp. 472b–e, n. B, and 592a7).

410a–412a: THE PROBLEM IN TRAINING THE GUARDIANS IS TO PRODUCE A COMBINATION IN THEM OF HARSHNESS AND GENTLENESS, WHICH REQUIRES THE HARMONIZING OF THE SPIRITED AND WISDOM-LOVING (OR PHILOSOPHICAL) PARTS OF THEIR NATURE, SO AS TO PRODUCE MODERATE AND BRAVE SOULS. FOR THIS REASON WE BLEND TRAINING IN THE ARTS WITH PHYSICAL TRAINING, SO THAT THE LATTER TURNS OUT TO BE NOT MERELY TRAINING OF THE BODY.

A.   The need for blending of traits in a guardian's character was already raised in 374e–376c. Contrary to some impressions, Plato certainly does not advocate the maximum possible strengthening in his guardians of the philosophical temperament and the desire to pursue philosophy. Here he suggests that such traits have to be kept from becoming too strong, and that we must produce a balance of philosophical and spirited impulses which will create people well suited to the guardians' task. He emphasizes that the two impulses are contrary to each other, so that it requires careful effort to make them coexist and cooperate—another indication that the establishment of his city requires dealing with recalcitrant features of the material with which one is obliged to work (cf. 369b–d, n. B). When he comes in Book VII to the final point in his description of the task of a ruler in his city, it becomes crucial that the impulse toward pursuing philosophy be capable of being overriden by other motives (519d–521b, nn. D–E).

B.   Plato's language here makes explicit what is already latent in what he is saying, that what is needed in educating guardians is a kind of *harmony* or *fitting* (410e, 412a) of the tendencies in their natural disposition. This idea recurs again when Plato talks about the harmonization of the parts or elements of the soul (see esp. 443b–444a, n. A).

412a–c: WE SHALL NEED THIS SORT OF HARMONIOUSLY DISPOSED MAN AS OVERSEER OF THE CITY, IF IT IS TO BE PRESERVED. THE RULERS OF THE CITY MUST BE THE MOST GUARDIANLY OF ITS GUARDIANS.

A.   This brief passage takes one of the most important steps in the whole description of Plato's city. Suddenly the city has rulers. From where did they come? Not from any source outside what has been discussed so far. For the rulers turn out to be a subclass of the guardians whom we have been educating all along. Indeed, they turn out to be those who perform the function of guardians in the highest degree (the Greek word *phylaki-kōtatos* in c10 means literally "most guardianly"). They are the people regarded by Plato as most crucial to the preservation (a10) of the city. For Plato takes the function of the ruler to be nothing other than preservation of the city which he rules (see 412e–414b, n. B).

B.   The rest of Plato's description of the city takes account of this new revelation about what the function of the guardian really amounts to. In obedience to his construal of the Principle of the Natural Division of Labor, he now introduces further features into the city and into the training of the guardians, which will ensure that the most guardianly of them are able to perform the task of ruling.

412d–e: THE GUARDIANS WHO RULE WILL DO SO BEST IF THEY LOVE THE CITY. BUT BECAUSE ONE LOVES A THING MOST IF ONE BELIEVES THAT ITS BENEFIT AND ONE'S OWN COINCIDE, WE MUST TRAIN THE RULERS TO WISH EAGERLY TO DO THAT WHICH IS BENEFICIAL TO THE CITY, AND TO HOLD STEADFASTLY TO THIS.

A.   The rulers having been identified, Plato now says what their motivation to rule must be and how it should be fostered. This is a crucial matter for him, because if he cannot show that his rulers can be induced to act as the true guardians that he needs, then he will be unable to show how the city can maintain itself (see n. C on 419a–421c). [Bosanquet, pp. 174–5.]

B.   What, then, will their motivation be? At 412d Plato implies that it will be a kind of love for the city, based on the belief that the interests of the whole city coincide with their own. From this it might be inferred that in Plato's view the rulers are always fundamentally motivated by their own self-interest and nothing else, so that the only thing inducing them to help the city is the belief that by doing so they will best further their own interests. From the very fact that Plato is trying to show that being just is advantageous to oneself we know that he considers self-interest to be an important part of one's motivation to be just. But it turns out that he does not think that there is no other motivation working in favor of justice. Indeed, he thinks that being just can involve clear-cut sacrifice of one's own good. This fact begins to emerge shortly, in 419a–421c, and it becomes extremely important in Book VII (see 358a–362c, n. D, and 519d–521b, n. E). Therefore, his statement that the same things benefit (*sympherein*) the city and the guardians, and that both fare well or ill together (412d), is not meant to imply that in all situations a guardian gains from working to the benefit of the city. What it does imply is that by working to benefit the city the guardian is made very well off indeed—a point that is reiterated at 465c–466c. The full situation, however, emerges only when Plato finally comes to his discussion of the Good (see 519d–521b, and nn.).

412e–414b: IN ORDER TO BE ABLE TO GUARD THE CITY, THE GUARDIANS MUST BE ABLE, IN THE FACE OF FORCES THAT MAY TEND TO OVERTHROW IT, TO GUARD IN THEMSELVES THE BELIEF THAT THEY MUST DO WHATEVER THEY THINK TO BE IN THE BEST INTEREST OF THE CITY. THIS BELIEF BEING TRUE THEY WOULD NOT LOSE IT WILLINGLY, BUT THEY MIGHT LOSE IT UNDER THE INFLUENCE OF SUCH THINGS AS FORGETFULNESS, PLEASURE, PAIN AND FEAR. WE MUST THEREFORE TEST PROSPECTIVE RULERS TO SEE THAT THEY CAN PRESERVE THEIR BELIEF AGAINST THESE FORCES. THOSE WHO CAN DO SO WILL BE DEEMED GOOD GUARDIANS OF BOTH THEMSELVES AND THEIR TRAINING. THEY WILL BE THE *RULERS*, AND THE OTHERS OF THOSE WHOM WE HAVE BEEN CALLING GUARDIANS WILL BE MORE PROPERLY CALLED *AUXILIARIES*.

A. Plato here explains the basis of the selection and the education of rulers as distinct from the rest of the guardians. The crucial test is the ability to retain the belief that they must do what is good for the city. Those who have this ability to the fullest will be rulers, and the rest will be auxiliaries. (Sometimes Plato uses the term "guardian" to apply to both rulers and auxiliaries; sometimes he uses it for the rulers alone; usually the context makes his meaning quite clear, and I shall adopt a similar latitude in using the term.)

B. Plato begins here to emphasize another aspect of the role of a guardian, one having to do with the notion of *stability*. As we shall shortly see (424b–e, 422a) he views the guardians (of both groups) as those who will work to keep the city stable, i.e., to *preserve* it in its present condition. But to do this they must also themselves have stability of character, and accordingly Plato speaks of them here as "guardians of themselves" (413e3), referring to the harmony and moderation that they possess (compare the extreme changeability of the democratic man at 559d–562a). In this vein, Plato says that it is the rulers who are fully guardians (414b2), because they preserve the city against both external and internal forces (cf. 415d–e, 417b). Once again the role of guardian has been broadened (cf. n. B on 401d–403c), from that of a military force for defense against other cities (373d–374e) to a force charged with all aspects of the preservation of the city as it is against whatever might alter it. (See also 423d–425b.) [Schleiermacher, pp. 387–8.]

414b–415d: IN ORDER THAT THE REST OF THE CITY MAY BE PERSUADED OF ITS COMMUNITY OF INTEREST, THE RULERS MAY HAVE TO TELL THEM A MYTH, NAMELY, THAT THEY ARE ALL BROTHERS BORN FROM EARTH, AND THAT SOME ARE MADE FROM GOLD, SOME FROM SILVER, AND OTHERS FROM BRONZE OR IRON. THE TYPE OF WORK THAT EACH DOES SHOULD DEPEND, EACH MUST BE TOLD, ON WHICH METAL HE IS MADE OF. THE RULERS MUST BE ON GUARD LEST THIS PRINCIPLE BE VIOLATED, AND ESPECIALLY LEST THE CITY BE RULED BY SOMEONE OF BRONZE OR IRON.

A. The myth is not told in order to convince the rulers (414b–c); but it may be necessary to convince the rest. The rulers will be able themselves to understand the principles that the myth contains, both of the essential community of interest of the city and of the need for the Principle of the Natural Division of Labor.

Plato's statement that a falsehood may be necessary for this purpose harks back to his earlier statement that it is sometimes necessary for men (as opposed to gods) to tell falsehoods (376e–379b).

B. The chief manifestation in the myth of the Principle of the Natural

Division of Labor pertains to the rulers: the city cannot be preserved unless it is ruled by those who are naturally suited to preserve it (415c5–6). But the emphasis on the general principle continues Plato's insistence on it and also foreshadows his later statement at the beginning of Book VIII (545c–547c), that the crucial factor that could lead to the destruction of his city is a neglect of eugenic arrangements, and the consequent breakdown of the system for assigning tasks to those with the natural aptitude for them.

415d–417b: THE GUARDIANS MUST CHOOSE A SITE FOR THE CITY THAT WILL ENABLE THEM TO GUARD IT AGAINST EXTERNAL AND INTERNAL DANGERS. THEIR HOUSES MUST BE SUITABLE FOR THEIR SOLDIERLY OCCUPATION; THEY MUST NOT HAVE PRIVATE PROPERTY, NOR ANYTHING BEYOND WHAT IS NECESSARY TO MAINTAIN THEMSELVES AS GUARDIANS; AND THEY MUST NOT HAVE MONEY. ONLY THUS WILL THEY BE ABLE TO PRESERVE THEMSELVES AND THE CITY.

A. Plato again derives the arrangements for the guardians from the necessity that they perform their assigned task. The military aspect of the guardians' task manifests itself both in the arrangements for the guardians' lives and in the choice of a site for the city.

B. The comparison of the guardians with watchdogs is repeated from 374e–376c. But something new is added: the guardians' gentleness toward those whom they guard is now presented as a manifestation of their willingness to act on the idea, introduced just now, that their interests coincide.

Book IV

— three part soul

419a–421c: WHAT SHALL WE ANSWER IF SOMEONE OBJECTS THAT WE HAVE NOT ALLOWED THE GUARDIANS TO HAVE MUCH HAPPINESS *(EUDAIMONIA)?* WE SHALL ANSWER THAT IT WOULD NOT BE SURPRISING IF THEY ARE INDEED HAPPY, BUT IN ANY CASE OUR AIM IS TO MAKE THE WHOLE CITY AS HAPPY AS POSSIBLE, RATHER THAN ANY PARTICULAR GROUP IN IT. MOREOVER, WE DO NOT WISH THE GUARDIANS TO HAVE ANY SORT OF HAPPINESS THAT WILL MAKE THEM OTHER THAN GUARDIANS, BECAUSE IF THEY DO THE CITY WILL BE RUINED. IF WE DO NOT MAKE THEM GENUINE GUARDIANS, WE SHALL NOT HAVE A CITY BUT SOMETHING ELSE. WE MUST MAKE EACH PERSON PERFORM HIS PROPER TASK, SO THAT WHEN THE CITY IS THUS WELL GOVERNED, NATURE WILL PROVIDE EACH GROUP WITH ITS SHARE OF HAPPINESS.

A.   In stressing the idea of the fulfillment of the guardians' task, Plato is of course continuing to rely on the Principle of the Natural Division of Labor (420c–d, 421a–b). But he connects the idea that they must be genuine guardians with another idea, that if the guardians do not perform their task, then the institution that he is constructing will no longer be a *city*, but will be something other than a city (421b). The way in which Plato puts the matter makes us aware of a point that will emerge more fully later, that the city being described is intended to be, in some sense, a paradigm case of a city (see n. A on 472e–473b and 592a–b).

So we are dealing with something that is paradigmatically a city, guarded by people who are paradigmatically guardians (cf. 428d7, e1). [Bosanquet, pp. 124–125.]

B. The objection by Adeimantus that stimulates this passage touches the nerve of Plato's overall argument. By denying that the guardians will have much happiness, he casts doubt on their motivation to rule as Plato has specified that they should, and therefore, too, on Plato's plans for the whole structure of his city (see esp. 412d–414b).

C. Plato is at this point quite circumspect in his manner of dealing with the objection. In fact, his full reply to it cannot be given until much later, after he has explained the task of the rulers more fully and also made clear a good deal more about his conception of the Good, of which the rulers themselves are required to have knowledge (see 519d–521b and nn. thereon). But his adumbration of the reply which he will eventually give is accurate: that although the guardians will be extremely happy, and indeed happier than any of the other inhabitants of the city or of other cities (465c–466c), there are nevertheless certain sacrifices which will have to be made, in particular, by the rulers (519b–521d, nn. D–E). He emphasizes that his ultimate aim in the construction of the city is not to provide the maximum possible happiness for any one type of person, but to plan for the greatest possible happiness of *the city as a whole*. When this is achieved, he suggests (421c), nature will provide a certain appropriate share of happiness to each type of person in the city.

D. The notion of the happiness of the city as a whole, like the notion of the good of the city as a whole (405a–410a, n. C, 461e–462e), is in need of some explanation. Many will think that happiness and benefit properly attach to individuals primarily and not to groups or institutions. But it does seem uncontroversial that in a secondary or derived sense things like cities can be called happy or benefited. The most natural way would be to say that the happiness, e.g., of a city is a kind of sum of the amounts of happiness possessed by the individuals in it. Thus, increasing the happiness of the city as a whole would simply be a matter of increasing the sum total of net happiness of the individuals, and correspondingly for decrease.

One of the most striking things about Plato's treatment of these notions, however, is that at no point in the *Republic* does he treat the happiness or benefit of the city in this way. We saw earlier that he constructed his city to meet human needs (369b–d, n. C). We also saw, though, that his explanation of this point did not commit him to any more precise claim about how the satisfactoriness of a city in meeting human needs was to be assessed. Moreover, he is certainly not thereby committed to the particular view that the happiness of a city is proportional to the total happiness of its individual citizens. This is not to say that he considered the notion of a sum of amounts of individual happiness and rejected it as an explanation of the happiness of a whole city. It is rather that he seems to regard the happiness of the whole city as a fairly clear notion that requires no immediate explanation in terms of the happiness of individual citizens. At no point whatever in his discussions of the benefit or happiness of the city, or in his descriptions of how it is to be arranged, does he ever make any attempt at all to assess the amounts of happiness of individuals or to say how their sum might be increased. At 421c, rather than saying that if we provide sufficient happiness for the various groups of people in the city we shall make the city as a whole happy, he moves in quite the opposite direction, and says that if we secure the greatest possible happiness for the city, by making the citizens perform their tasks, then we may expect the citizens to have the appropriate amount of happiness. Plato views the city as— to use an expression from modern times—a kind of "organic whole," whose happiness or benefit is not simply the sum of the happiness or benefit of its constituent elements.

As a result, the efforts that Plato makes to show that his city is happy concentrate on other features of it than the degree of its citizens' happiness. This is not to say that Plato believes that its citizens will *not* be happy; rather it is that the *maximizing* of their total happiness is not his chief aim. Rather, as he says in 421c, he concentrates on making the guardians conform to a certain other standard of what it is for them to perform their guardianly task, allowing the appropriate degree of happiness to emerge for each type of person as a byproduct of this arrangement. This is why, in his construction of the city so far, his main preoccupation has been adherence to the Principle of the Natural Division of Labor, rather than to some principle of the maximization of the sum of individual happiness.

For further treatment of his notion of benefit to the city, see 461e–462e, n. B, and 441c–442d, n. E. Parallel to the notion of the benefit and happiness of a city, there is notion of the benefit and happiness of an individual. For problems associated with this latter notion see 441c–442d, n. E.

421c–422a: WE MUST KEEP WEALTH FROM OUR GUARDIANS,

BECAUSE WEALTH MAKES ANY PRACTITIONER OF A TASK WORSE AT IT.

A. Plato alludes to the point made earlier (415d–417b), that the guardians will not have any gold or silver, or indeed any private property, and he links this point to the idea of performance of one's task. For the guardians to be concerned with money would be for them to try to perform another task, that of money-making (cf. 345b–347e, and n. A on 551b–552e), in addition to that of guardianship.

B. Plato wishes the guardians to be in a middle condition between wealth and poverty. He objects to both on the ground of their tendency to produce, among other things, *change (neōterismos*, 422a). Plato has already made the claim that in their capacity of guardians and preservers, the guardians are to prevent change and keep the city stable (412e–414b), and he will make the same claim again (e.g., at 545c–547c).

422a–d: BUT WITHOUT WEALTH HOW WILL THE CITY DEFEND ITSELF? BY BEING BETTER TRAINED AND TOUGHER THAN ANY OF ITS ADVERSARIES, AND BY OFFERING ALL OF THE PLUNDER OF WAR TO POTENTIAL ALLIES TO WIN THEM OVER TO ITS SIDE. (NOT DESIRING WEALTH, THEY WILL NOT WISH TO KEEP THE PLUNDER THEMSELVES.)

A. Plato tries to make the guardians' lack of interest in wealth seem an advantage in foreign and military policy. He does not say that the city will always or inevitably be able to defend itself successfully. But he does think that the training of its guardians is a decided advantage.

422e–423d: WE CANNOT APPLY THE TERM "CITY" TO ANYTHING OTHER THAN THE ONE WE ARE CONSTRUCTING; THE OTHERS ARE REALLY COLLECTIONS OF CITIES RATHER THAN CITIES. TO KEEP OUR CITY A CITY, THE GUARDIANS MUST MAKE SURE THAT IT DOES NOT GROW SO LARGE THAT IT CEASES TO BE ONE SINGLE CITY. AND TO ENSURE THIS END THEY MUST SEE TO IT THAT EACH PERSON PERFORMS THE TASK TO WHICH HE IS NATURALLY SUITED.

A. Plato has already said that only the city which he is constructing should properly be called a city (n. A on 419a–421c). That this is so is viewed as the result of several connected facts. One is that it does not grow too large or lose its cohesiveness and cease to be "one" (422e–423b, b10, c4, d6). A second is that it is not divided into groups whose interest conflict (423a), so that it might break apart or be easy prey to enemies. A third is that each person in it performs his own task or function (*ergon*, d4; cf. n. A on 374e–376c), and that that task be single or one, so that the person performing it must likewise be one (423d), and so that there is no conflict among people over who is to do or have what, and in particular over who is to rule (cf. 414b–415d).

B.   Of these factors, one that should be especially noticed, concerns the notion of unity, and particularly the idea that Plato's city must be one city and not a plurality of cities. This idea has an important place within Plato's scheme of things in the *Republic*. It is connected with the various ways in which Plato tries to make the organization of his city cohesive, constructed according to a uniform plan (by contrast, say, with the variegated and disorganized structure of the democratic city as depicted in 555b–558c; cf. 500b–e, n. C, and 520a). It is also connected, as here, with the idea that unity means lack of internal dissension and strife, on the undesirability of which Plato frequently harps, as at 547a, 462a–b (cf. 519d–521b, n. H). And it is connected too with the idea that the city must be stable and not susceptible to decay, which is itself partly a result of its freedom from strife (see 545c–547c with 465b). (Here there is a particular contrast with the oligarchic city, which is said at 551d to be "not one city but two.")

The idea that the city must be unitary finds its companion in the idea that an individual human being should be, in a certain psychological sense, not a plurality of persons but one, unified, person. In 423d Plato links the unity of the city with the idea that each of its citizens should pursue one single task, and thus be "one person and not many." By contrast once again, the kind of man who dominates an oligarchic city is said to be "in discord with himself," and "not one man but two" (554d–e); and the kind of man who is characteristic of democratic cities is pictured as being just as variegated in his behavior and desires as the city in which he lives, without a unified plan by which to govern his life (559d–562a). But the idea of psychological unity is carried further by Plato, by means of his theory of the parts of the soul, which he begins to expound in 435c–436b and then employs in 441c–442d during his account of justice in the individual. For his theory highlights the desirability of a kind of harmony among the various impulses of the soul, which he characterizes in terms of the notion of unity, saying that when a person produces an accord among the parts of his soul, "he binds them all together, and himself from a plurality becomes a unity, . . . moderate and harmonious" (443d–e, cf. 431d–432a).

The notion of unity and harmony involved here, in both the case of the soul and the case of the city, is a quite straightforward one, resting in the latter case primarily on the idea of the absence of strife and dissension, and in the former case on the idea of a lack of internal psychological conflict. The place where Plato moves beyond the platitudinous, however, is in his claims about what must be the case for these sorts of unity and harmony to obtain. He takes no account of the possibility that someone might object to him by proposing alternative ways in which a city or a soul might be unified or harmonious.

There are in addition connections between the idea of unity in city and individual, and certain important aspects of Plato's metaphysical theory, particularly as it concerns itself with the notion of goodness. On these see Introd., sec. 3. [Grote, pp. 97, 184ff.; Nettleship, pp. 176ff., 169–170, 178; Guthrie, *HGP*, pp. 468, 481; Zeller, p. 905; Gosling, pp. 57–71, 229; Bosanquet, p. 129; Adam, I, pp. 305, 213; Shorey, *Rep.*, I, p. 327; Crombie, *EPD*, pp. 123–4; Cooper, pp. 154–5; Friedländer, pp. 94–5, 124, 127; Krämer, *APA*, p. 112, n. 154, pp. 136, 141–2, 109–10; Diès, pp. xxxv, xxxviii; Robin, p. 284.]

C. In Glaucon's original challenge to Socrates in 358a–362c, it was presupposed that a human being naturally will aim at an unlimited increase of what he has (see n. E there). In 371e–373c, Plato allowed his city to fall prey to a similar tendency toward potentially unlimited acquisition and expansion beyond what is necessary (373a, c, d). What the present passage maintains, however, is that so long as we adhere to the principles that he has enunciated, there *is* a natural limit to the growth of the city, namely that point at which the city can no longer be one city, but becomes a collection of cities. As regards the individual, Plato does agree that certain desires and impulses are indeed unlimited in a sense, but he also maintains that there are others, arising out of reason, that do have both a natural limit themselves and an ability to limit the other desires, in such a way that all of the desires are capable of receiving a sufficient degree of satisfaction. This idea is gradually developed throughout the work, particularly at 430c–432a, 443b–444a, 587a–b, 588b–590a, 590c–591a.

423d–425b: BUT TO ENSURE ALL OF THESE ENDS THE GUARDIANS MUST KEEP TO THE MOST IMPORTANT INJUNCTION THAT

WE LAY UPON THEM. THIS IS THAT THEY MUST MAINTAIN GOOD EDUCATION AND UPBRINGING, WHICH ENABLES THEM TO KEEP TO THE PROVERB THAT THE POSSESSIONS OF FRIENDS ARE HELD IN COMMON. FOR THEM TO DO THIS IT IS ESSENTIAL THAT THERE BE NO INNOVATION IN ARTISTIC AND PHYSICAL TRAINING, AND THAT YOUNG PEOPLE BE TRAINED SO THAT THEY ADHERE CLOSELY TO LAWS AND CUSTOMS.

A.   Once again we encounter the theme of stability and the undesirability of change (n. B on 412e–414b and n. B on 421c–422a), especially with emphasis in 424b on the importance of stability in the system of education which was established in Books II–III.

425b–427c: WE SHALL NOT ATTEMPT FURTHER TO SPECIFY LAWS, BECAUSE THE GUARDIANS WILL DISCOVER THEMSELVES WHAT LAWS ARE NECESSARY. BUT EDUCATION, NOT LAW, IS THE CRUCIAL THING, BECAUSE IF EDUCATION IS NOT WELL MAINTAINED, LAWS ARE OF ONLY LIMITED USE AND CANNOT CAUSE ANY BASIC IMPROVEMENT IN A CITY (NOTWITHSTANDING THE CLAIMS OF ORDINARY POLITICIANS, WHO OPPOSE THOROUGHGOING REFORM).

A.   Plato really makes two distinct points here. One is that a specification of the best possible city cannot be given by giving a specification of its laws, because other aspects of its organization are more important. The other is that the thorough reform of an actual city cannot be accomplished by tinkering with its laws, but only by a basic reform of the educational system (cf. 540d–541b).

B.   Some have taken the present passage to show a belief on Plato's part that it is impossible to specify completely the duties by which we are bound if we are to be just. But whether or not Plato did hold this belief, he does not express it here.

C.   Notice that 424a6 shows that Plato does not always use the term *physis,* "nature," to stand for something inborn as opposed to something inculcated (the Greek says literally, "Good education and upbringing, if preserved, put good natures into [*sc.* people] ..."). But sometimes he does use the word in this way (457e–458b, n. B). [Dover, pp. 84ff.]

427d: OUR CITY MIGHT BE SAID TO BE ESTABLISHED NOW, AND SO WE MUST LOOK IN IT AND SEE WHERE JUSTICE AND

INJUSTICE ARE, HOW THEY DIFFER FROM EACH OTHER, AND
WHICH ONE A PERSON MUST HAVE IF HE IS TO BE HAPPY,
WHETHER OR NOT HE ELUDES DETECTION BY GODS AND MEN.

A.   This passage marks an important transition in the *Republic*. Plato
has now finished the basic outline of his city (a further stage of the
description is given in Books V–VIII). The original purpose of giving it
(368c–369b) was to aid us in our effort to discover what justice is, and
to this task he now turns. It will occupy him to the end of this book.
Although he now begins to refer frequently to his view that justice is
beneficial to its possessor, it is important to realize that his official presentation of that view, and his official arguments for it, do not begin
until Book IX (see n. A on 576b–578b).

B.   Although Plato wishes to explain what justice is, he makes clear that
he is equally anxious to explain what injustice is. For he must compare
the life of the perfectly just man with that of the perfectly unjust man
(see 358a–362c, n. B, and 580a–c, n. B). One of the defects of the original
city which Plato sketched (see n. A on 371e–373c), for his expository
purposes, was that it did not offer an easy way in which to explain
injustice, because it did not offer fertile enough ground for injustice
to take root, so that we could understand clearly the contrast between
injustice and justice as he now begins to present it (see 432b–434c and
443b–444e).

427e–428a: OUR CITY AS WE HAVE ESTABLISHED IT IS COM-
PLETELY GOOD. IT MUST THEREFORE BE WISE, BRAVE, MOD-
ERATE, AND JUST. WE CAN FIND JUSTICE BY FIRST INDENTIFY-
ING THE OTHER THREE AND RECOGNIZING JUSTICE AS THE
ONE THAT REMAINS.

A.   The crucial first step in Plato's attempt to find justice in his city is
to maintain that the city as he has established it is good, and indeed
perfectly good *(teleōs agathēn,* 427e7). By saying that it is perfectly
good he implies that it has all virtues or excellences, *i.e.*, all attributes
(appropriate to a city) which make it good *(cf.* n. E). One of these, it
emerges, is justice (see n. C).

B.   What is Plato's argument for the contention that his city is perfectly
good? Evidently, it must lie in what has gone before, because at 427e he
plainly takes it to be already established and makes no effort here to

support it further. (He makes the same claim elsewhere, e.g., at 433c, d, 472d–e, 501d.)

One argument for the goodness of the city, an argument that will occur readily to the modern reader, is conspicuous by its absence. I have already remarked that when Plato calls his city happy, he does not take its happiness to consist simply in the happiness of its citizens (419a–421c, n. D, 369b–d, n. C). The companion point to this one is that when he calls his city good, he nowhere suggests that the goodness of the city consists in, or can be demonstrated by citing, nothing but the happiness or welfare of its citizens. This does not mean that the goodness of the city is completely unconnected with its ability in one way or another to minister to human needs (369b–d, n. C). It does mean, however, that once Plato has satisfied himself that the city does to some extent perform this function, as he does in 369ff., he does not feel at all obliged to test the goodness of his city by showing how great an aggregate of welfare it provides for its citizens (Nor—another possibility—does he test the goodness of the city simply by showing how good its citizens are). Instead, the argument for the goodness of the city with which he has provided himself proceeds here in independence of such considerations.

His argument for the goodness of the city must, as we have seen, be based on the notions that he has already used in explaining and justifying his construction of the city. It must therefore lie in the fact that in the city each person performs his own single task, so that the city is itself unified, without internal conflict or the possibility of being easily destroyed either from without or within. For these are the features that Plato has just used to contrast his city with other institutions pretending to the title of "city" (see n. A on 422e–423d, n. A on 419a–421c, and n. C. on 500b–e). It would be wrong to say that the city's being good simply *consists in* its possession of these features. For neither here nor later, in his treatment of the good (see 504d–534d), does he suggest that goodness can simply be identified with any such attributes as these. Rather, it is that the possession of these attributes supplies, so far as he has thus far undertaken to explain it, the ground for his attribution of goodness to the city. (Using some modern jargon again, without claiming any explanatory force for it, we can say that they are "good-making" attributes.)

C.   From the claim that it is good, Plato infers that the city has four particular excellences or virtues (*aretai*), namely, wisdom, bravery (courage), moderation (temperance), and justice. He indicates that our search for justice will lead us to identify the other three first, allowing us to recognize justice subsequently (432b–434c) as the one that remains. He evidently expects no one to dispute that wisdom, bravery, and moderation are excellences or virtues. Nor does he seem to expect strong argument that beside justice, there are any other additional virtues of the city (cf. n. D). What he does have to reckon with, however, is the objection, from people like Thrasymachus, that justice itself is not an excellence or virtue. On this matter see esp. 432b–434c, nn. B–C.

D.   It is often remarked that Plato here omits from his list of virtues or excellences of the city the traditional Greek virtue of piety. He does so because piety does not seem to him to perform a role comparable to the others in preserving the unity and stability of the city (cf. n. B). But some account has been taken of piety earlier, in the discussion of the proper conception of divinity at the end of Book II (379b–383c).

E.   A word is necessary at this point about the Greek term *aretē* (plural, *aretai*), which is translated by either "virtue" or "excellence," and which I often render here by the phrase "virtue or excellence" to take account of the fact that its meaning can often cover the territory of both of these English words. In the context of the present argument, the crucial thing about an *aretē* is simply that it is, so to speak, a "goodness" of a thing, i.e., an attribute that is part of the thing's being *good*, and it is so indicated by Plato (see 432b4, 433c5 with d7). Of course, at this point we must ask, "Good in what way?" or "Good in what sense?" But this question cannot be answered until we see more of Plato's treatment of the notion of goodness (see 504d–506a, n. C). [Shorey, *Rep.*, I, pp. 100–1.]

428a–429a: WISDOM IN THE CITY: THE CITY IS WISE BY VIRTUE OF ITS SOUND JUDGMENT, WHICH IS ITS KNOWLEDGE OF GUARDIANSHIP. IT IS THEREFORE WISE BY VIRTUE OF A VERY SMALL PART OF ITSELF, CONSISTING OF THOSE WHO HAVE THIS KNOWLEDGE, NAMELY, THE RULERS.

A.   Notice that Plato's identification of this feature of his city as wisdom is not given any formal argument but simply left to rest on its natural plausibility. It is obvious, Plato thinks, that this feature of the city is one of its virtues or excellences, and it is equally obvious that the term "wisdom" is appropriately used to stand for it. The identifications of bravery and moderation rest on the same kind of grounds. Matters become more difficult, however, when he comes to justice.

B. In 428e–429a Plato gives voice to an idea on which we remarked earlier (n. D on 369e–370c), that there must be a correspondence between the number of people needed to perform a given task and the number of people able to perform it. He indicates here that he thinks that, at least in the case of guardianship, such a correspondence is established by nature. And he appears to think that because there are by nature only a small number of people naturally suited to be rulers, we therein have further ground for thinking that the arrangement of his city is a natural one (see nn. C–D on 369e–370c and n. C on 491b–494a).

C. In using the term "knowledge" (*epistēmē*) here in application to artisans such as carpenters, Plato is not contradicting his contention later on (see 476d–480a) that there is, to speak strictly, no knowledge of the sensible world but only of Forms. But he has not yet drawn the distinctions nor made the epistemological claims that would render it feasible to make that point here. He therefore deals here instead with the simple, colloquial distinction between *epistēmē* and *amathia* (ignorance, 428b7). (One should always bear in mind that his distinction between *epistēmē* and *doxa* (belief or opinion) was not intended as an attempt to reflect ordinary or actual usage of those terms. It is therefore possible for him to use ordinary terms, such as *epistēmē*, in ordinary ways different from those that he introduces for his own philosophical purposes, without thereby casting any doubt on the propriety of the latter.)

429a–430c: BRAVERY IN THE CITY: THE BRAVERY OF THE CITY LIES IN ITS SOLDIER OR AUXILIARY CLASS. IT IS THE ABILITY TO PRESERVE CORRECT BELIEF, ARRIVED AT THROUGH EDUCATION AND TRAINING, ABOUT WHAT IS TO BE FEARED.

A. In his account of bravery, Plato has in mind (429e8–430a2) his earlier discussion in 412d–415b of the training that the rulers will receive and the myth that the others will be told, which will foster their retention of the belief that their benefit and that of the city coincide. It is this sort of disposition, linked as it is to the construction of the city and the education in it, rather than mere "animal courage" (430b), that he wishes to call genuine bravery, which makes the city good (nn. C, E, on 369e–370c).

B. By saying in 430c3 that he is talking of "political" or "civic" bravery, Plato looks forward to 441c–442d, where he will explain the bravery of an individual in terms of his theory of the tripartite soul.

430c–432a: MODERATION IN THE CITY: MODERATION IS NOT

IN ONE PART OF THE CITY, BUT IN THE CITY AS A WHOLE. IT
CONSISTS IN A NATURAL HARMONY AND AGREEMENT ABOUT
WHO SHOULD RULE, WHICH CORRESPONDS TO THE COMMON
NOTION OF SELF-CONTROL (WHICH REALLY MEANS THE RULE
OF THE WORSE BY THE BETTER).

A. Plato's contention that moderation or temperance is a kind of
harmony (430e, 432a) echoes his earlier claim that the city will be
unified and free from internal strife (see 422e–423d, n. A). But something
else is added here that has so far not been much attended to, namely, the
idea that there will be agreement among *all* of the parts of the city
about who should rule. This idea has not been attended to because he
has not said much about people other than the guardians, and in particular, except for saying that the guardians will manage the city and
keep it unified and stable, he has said little or nothing about the inclinations of others in the city to abide, or not to abide, by this arrangement. So the question naturally arises (particularly in a reader living in
any sort of democratic political system) to what extent Plato thinks that
his arrangements must run counter to the desires and motivations of
other parts of the population, and how he thinks any contrary desires
and motivations are to be prevented from subverting his system.

At the start it should be said that Plato's response to this problem is
not as thoroughgoing as the modern reader will feel that it ought to be,
and one must conclude that he did not consider it one of the most urgent
of the problems facing him or the one with the strongest claim on his
attention. His overall position seems to be that once it is granted that his
guardians are genuinely bred and raised to perform their function of
guarding the city against external and internal forces, then they will,
somehow, be able to deal with whatever disruptive motivations the inhabitants of the city may harbor. Sometimes, as here, he appears to
think that disruptive motivation will be absent and all will agree on his
arrangements. (In 421c he suggests that when the city is well governed,
each group will have its share of happiness.) At other times (e.g., at
410a, 590c–591a), he indicates that the use of force will be necessary to
keep the city running. Perhaps he does not regard these two claims as
mutually incompatible, but they raise questions which most readers will
think pressing.

B. To understand Plato's views on this matter one must distinguish
two questions. One concerns the extent to which his arrangements for
the city are supposed to run counter to certain *immediate desires and*

inclinations of people in the lower classes. The other concerns the extent
to which those arrangements require some sacrifice by members of the
lower classes of their *good* or *interests*. From the passages just cited in
n. A, it appears, in regard to the former question, that sometimes their
immediate desires and inclinations are to be thwarted to some extent.
(The only person seemingly not subject to much thwarting of desire is
the democratic man in a democratic city, to judge by 559d–562a.) In
regard to the latter question Plato says very little, either here or in the
rest of the work. But the drift of the present passage is clearly that sacrifice of interest will be required by members of all classes, including the
lowest. The difference between rulers and others, however, is that the
former will understand and approve the rationale for their own sacrifices (519d–521b, n. E), whereas the members of the other two classes,
and particularly the members of the lowest class, will not do so, and
will have to have their sacrifices in some degree enforced from outside
(this is made plain in 590c–591a—see nn. B–D there).

But the question then arises how, if this is so, Plato can say that
there is *agreement* among all classes about who should rule. The answer
must be that, in his view, agreement on the part of the lower classes
about *who* should rule is compatible with a certain degree of dissatisfaction with those measures taken by the rulers which thwart their desires. But Plato does not here attempt to explain how the agreement
comes about or how it can override conflicting motivation. For further
discussion of this matter see 590c–591a, n. D.

C. In 431b Plato distinguishes between those in the city who are
"better" and those who are "worse." He does not yet, however, explain
the basis of this distinction until 444a–e. (see n. B there). At the beginning of Book V it is regarded as demonstrated that the rulers of his city
are good (449a). Just notice for now that their desires and appetites are
said to be "simple" (*haplas*) rather than many and various (431b–c).
Compare such passages as 399a–c, 382e, along with n. B on 422e–423d,
and 519b–c, where it is said that one ought to have a single aim or goal
at which one aims in all one's actions.

432b–434c: JUSTICE IN THE CITY: WE HAVE ALREADY SEEN IT,
AT LEAST TO SOME DEGREE. FOR WE HAVE BEEN SPEAKING
OF THE FACT THAT IN THE CITY EACH PERSON PERFORMS
THAT ONE TASK FOR WHICH HE IS NATURALLY SUITED; AND
MOREOVER WE HAVE OFTEN HEARD IT SAID IN OTHER CON-
TEXTS THAT JUSTICE CONSISTS IN THE PERFORMANCE OF

ONE'S TASK AND NOT MEDDLING IN OTHERS. IT IS REASON-
ABLE, THEN, TO SAY THAT THIS FEATURE OF OUR CITY, WHICH
IS THE ONE REMAINING FACTOR THAT MAKES THE CITY
GOOD, IS JUSTICE. THAT IS, JUSTICE IS THE PERFORMANCE OF
ONE'S OWN TASK BY EACH OF THE THREE PARTS OF THE
CITY, NAMELY, THE RULERS, THE AUXILIARIES, AND THE
OTHERS, WHOM WE SHALL CALL THE MONEY-MAKERS. IN-
JUSTICE IS CORRESPONDINGLY THE MEDDLING BY THESE
GROUPS IN EACH OTHER'S TASKS.

A. Justice in the city turns out to be precisely its accord, taken as a
group of three classes, with the Principle of the Natural Division of
Labor which has all along been the basis for Plato's construction of
the city (see 369e–370c). It is therefore no surprise that this accord
should turn out in his view (433b) to be what makes possible the presence
of the other three virtues or excellences in the city. [Adam, I, p. 242.]

B. What grounds does Plato give for accepting his account of justice
in the city, and for saying that the notion developed here is properly
labeled by the word "justice"? Several considerations complicate the
situation, making the line of argument not entirely clear.
   At the outset, we must realize that he must here pay at least some
attention to the ordinary use of the term "justice" (*dikaiosyne*), because
he is, after all, asking us to accept that word as an appropriate one to
attach to the notion that he has developed, of the performance of its
task by each of the classes in the city. (On this matter see further 442d–
443b, n. B.)
   The second thing we must realize is that in his argument Plato must
convince a certain kind of opponent, represented by people like Thrasymachus in Book I, who have advanced claims that Plato hopes to dis-
prove. One of these claims is that justice, at least when it attaches to individual human beings, is not a good for them and is also not a virtue or
excellence of them (337d–339b, 347e–349a). From this fact there arises
a particular difficulty confronting Plato. An examination of 427e–428a
and 432b–434c stimulates one to believe, at least on first reflection,
that in his argument for his identification of justice in the city (i.e., for
his claim that justice in the city is the performance of its task by each
element in the city), Plato is *assuming*, without argument, that justice is
a virtue or excellence of the city, and then, on the basis of that assumption, arguing for his claim about what justice in the city is. This, however, would obviously be an illegitimate procedure, if we are to think

that Thrasymachus and those like him would not allow Plato to assume that justice is a virtue or excellence of a city. The question is, does Plato here proceed in such an illegitimate way?

In response to this question, and to the points made in the previous two paragraphs, let us first notice an important fact to which we shall return later. It appears that a crucial part of Plato's argument for his identification of justice seems to rest on his claim that justice, as he explains it, obviously resembles a notion that most people associate with justice, namely, the idea of "doing one's own" (443c–d, 433a–b with Shorey, *Rep.*, *ad loc.*, and 332c, 550a). For in 432d–433a, he depicts Socrates' situation, once he has identified justice, as one of finding something close at hand which he would have found earlier had he not been looking in the wrong direction.

Before we deal fully with this point, however, let us consider three arguments that Plato gives for his identification of justice and see what their flaws are.

One argument is given in 433e3–434a2. It seems quite weak, depending as it does on an unargued assimilation of *having* one's own, which Plato says that judges must enforce as just, and *doing* one's own, which is what is involved in Plato's own notion of justice in the city. Still, this argument may be thought of as showing a certain rough resemblance between Plato's conception of justice and the ordinary one.

A second argument is given in 434a–c. It rests on the assumption that justice is the greatest good for the city and injustice is the greatest evil. We have seen, however, that Plato's opponents might well not allow him this assumption.

A third argument (433b–e) has been adumbrated by the way in which Plato sets up his search for justice in 427e–428a (see n. C there). It involves the contentions that there are four virtues or excellences of the city, that we have already identified three of them, and that the one remaining must accordingly be justice. Commentators have frequently expressed dissatisfaction with the obvious looseness of this argument. (How, for example, do we know that there are only four virtues of the city?) Even more important, however, is the fact that the argument seems to rely on the unargued assumption that justice is a virtue of the city.

None of these arguments seems very strong, and the main weakness of the latter two is that they rest on assumptions that we have reason to doubt Plato would be granted by his opponents. But perhaps the latter two arguments can be defended. Perhaps Plato thinks of his opponents as having denied that justice is a good for *individuals* or a virtue of

them but not as having denied that it is a good for, or a virtue of, *cities.*
So perhaps Plato could think himself entitled to assume, as he does in
these arguments, that justice is good for cities and a virtue of them.
Unfortunately for this line of defense, however, Thrasymachus in 351b
identified the best city with the most completely unjust city, and this
fact certainly makes it unlikely that he would allow Plato to make the
assumptions that he needs for these arguments. Thus, it may be that
Plato has allowed himself to rely on assumptions that his opponents
would reasonably refuse to allow him, so that his argument for his identification of justice would be undercut.

There is, however, a further defense for Plato's argument, one of
which he may well have been aware and have wished to rely on. Before
I described the three arguments given above, I mentioned that his argument might make significant use of his claim that his notion of justice
obviously resembles the ordinary idea, associated with the ordinary conception of justice, of "doing one's own." If we think that this is the case,
then we can perhaps free his overall argument of its dependence on the
cripplingly controversial assumptions in which it has seemed thus far to
be involved. We would take him to be reasoning as follows. He has
argued that his city is perfectly good and so has all excellences or
virtues of a city (427e–428a); and he has shown that one thing responsible for the goodness of the city is that each of its parts performs its
own task, which is to say that he has shown that being in this condition is a virtue or excellence of the city. He may then contend that the
resemblance between this condition and the notion of "doing one's own,"
taken as identical with the ordinary notion of justice, is strong enough
to justify our identification of the two. One result would be that this
condition in the city is identified with justice in the city. The other
would be that, given this identification and the fact that this condition
of a city is shown to be responsible for its being good, justice would be
shown to be a virtue or excellence of a city. Thus, Plato would not have
assumed that justice is a virtue or excellence of a city; he would have
argued that it is, by showing it identical with a condition of a city that
is a virtue or excellence of it. The whole argument would, of course,
depend on the alleged resemblance of this condition of a city to the
notion of "doing one's own," and on the identification of this notion
with the ordinary notion of justice; and these claims might be disputed.
But the argument would, on this interpretation, be free of the charge of
question-begging against Thrasymachus.

I think it unclear whether or not Plato intended to rely heavily on this
line of argument. The view that he did is recommended by the fact that

in 432d–433a, before any of the other arguments described above have been advanced, he announces his identification of justice and even seems to treat it as established. (Translations sometimes make the third argument that I described, the one in 433b–e, into a "proof" of the identification; but the verb used at 433b5, *tekmairomai*, does not strictly mean "prove" but is a relatively weak word, meaning something more like "take as an indication".) On the other hand, Plato gives the other, defective, arguments more prominence than he should if he means this one to be his chief support and the others to be merely ancillary, designed for those who, unlike Thrasymachus, were already willing to concede justice to be a virtue even though they did not yet know what virtue it was. The result is that how charitable we wish to be in our interpretation must determine whether or not we regard Plato as having illegitimately assumed what his opponents here would deny. [Adam, I, pp. 224–5; Grote, pp. 99–106; Sachs; Vlastos, *JHR*, esp. pp. 75–6.]

434d–435c: BUT LET US NOT TAKE ANY CONCLUSION AS FINAL YET, UNTIL WE LOOK AT THE INDIVIDUAL MAN AND SEE WHETHER JUSTICE IS THE SAME THING THERE. A JUST MAN AND A JUST CITY OUGHT TO RESEMBLE EACH OTHER IN THE WAY IN WHICH THEY ARE BOTH JUST, AND SO WE SHALL EXPECT THE JUST MAN ALSO TO HAVE IN HIS SOUL THE SAME PARTS THAT THE CITY HAS.

A. Plato makes clear his belief that his account of justice requires further confirmation, in the form of an assurance that the same feature that he has identified in the city can also be found in the individual. But it is also true that from the beginning it was the nature of justice in an individual man that he wished to discover, and it was for this purpose that he broached the idéa of justice in the city in the first place (368c–369b).

B. Plato lays down a very strong condition that he says must be satisfied if his account of justice is to be confirmed. Rather than simply showing, for example, that an individual's soul has *some* plurality of parts, he insists that the individual must have precisely the same three parts that the city has. That it does so he now attempts to establish, on grounds independent of those that he used to establish the tripartite nature of his city.

435c–436b: WE MUST THEREFORE SEE WHETHER A MAN IS

DIVIDED INTO THE SAME THREE PARTS AS THE CITY, NAMELY, A PART WITH WHICH WE LEARN, A PART WITH WHICH WE GET ANGRY, AND A PART CONTAINING THE APPETITES FOR FOOD, SEX, AND OTHER SUCH THINGS. WE SHOULD EXPECT THIS TO BE SO, BECAUSE WE SHOULD EXPECT THAT THE CITY WOULD GET ITS ATTRIBUTES FROM ITS INHABITANTS. OUR PRESENT METHODS MAY NOT YIELD A FULLY ACCURATE RESULT (TO WHICH A LONGER ROAD MAY BE EXPECTED TO LEAD), BUT PERHAPS THEY WILL BE SUFFICIENT FOR PRESENT PURPOSES.

A. Plato here introduces his famous notion of the soul that has three parts: reason (that by which we learn, know, and calculate), spirit (that by which we are angry and indignant, and are motivated to self-defense), and other appetites. (This third part is a motley collection of various desires and impulses, rather than being a genuinely unitary part as the others are; see 554a–555a, n. C, 580c–581e, n. C.)

It emerges later that the members of each class in Plato's city are dominated by the desires and satisfactions of one part of their soul: the rulers, by reason; the auxiliaries, by spirit; and the rest by various other desires grouped together in the third part of the soul (580c–581e).

B. A briefly formulated reason is given here for expecting the soul to have the same parts as the city. It is that this supposition will help account for the existence of different characteristics of the city as a whole. But this idea is only a prelude to the main argument, running from 436b to 441c, and is not intended to have strong probative force of its own. [Shorey, *Rep.*, I, p. 379, n. *c*; Cooper, p. 153, n. 7; Vlastos, *JHR*, p. 79.]

C. Plato indicates in this section and the following one that there is something merely provisional about the argument that he is about to give, though he suggests at 504b that the full education given to the rulers, culminating in a knowledge of the good (see 531d–534d, 506b–509c), would supply a more satisfactory argument on the issue. See n. A on the following section, and 502c–504d, n. C.

436b–437a: WE BEGIN WITH THE ASSUMPTION OR HYPOTHESIS, ON WHICH THE REST OF THE ARGUMENT DEPENDS, THAT ONE AND THE SAME OBJECT CANNOT DO OR SUFFER CONTRARY THINGS AT THE SAME TIME IN THE SAME PART OF ITSELF IN RELATION TO THE SAME OBJECT.

A. The principle on which Plato's argument is based is expressly said to be a hypothesis that can be questioned. He applies to it the same expression *(hypothemenoi,* 437a6) that he uses later in his discussion of the role of hypotheses in the sciences, when he criticizes geometers and others for not seeing that the statements on which they base their inferences are merely hypotheses that are themselves in need of demonstration (see 509d–511e, n. A). It is because he sees this principle as merely a hypothesis that he voices reservations (in 435c–436b) about the finality of his argument for asserting the soul to be tripartite.

Offhand, one might well think that Plato has chosen one of the most certain propositions in the whole *Republic* about which to express uncertainty, and one can easily wonder why he singled it out to be the focus of special caution. The answer, which does not much affect the progress of his argument here (as he rightly says in 435d), does not emerge until much later, in Book X (see n. A on 611a–612a).

B. The principle here presented is not a fully general principle, on a par with the Law of Contradiction or the like. It deals, for the most part, only with the "doing" and "suffering" of contraries of a fairly specific kind. [Robinson, *SRD,* pp. 38–40.]

437b–439b: DESIRES CAN BE CONTRARIES IN THE SENSE OF THE PRINCIPLE JUST ENUNCIATED; FOR EXAMPLE, THIRST AND THE DISINCLINATION TO DRINK ARE LIKE TWO MOVEMENTS IN CONTRARY DIRECTIONS. FURTHERMORE, THIRST IS NOT THIRST FOR DRINK OF SOME PARTICULAR KIND (E.G., HOT OR COLD OR GOOD OR BAD), BUT SIMPLY FOR DRINK. IN LIKE MANNER GENERALLY, IF *X* IS SOMEHOW RELATED TO *Y*, THEN WHAT IS THUS RELATED TO *Y*-OF-A-PARTICULAR-SORT IS NOT SIMPLY *X* (WHICH IS ONLY THUS RELATED TO *Y*), BUT RATHER *X*-OF-A-CORRESPONDING-PARTICULAR-SORT (THOUGH NOT NECESSARILY *X*-OF-THAT-SAME-SORT).

A. Why does Plato spend so much energy arguing for this principle concerning relations? The answer appears if we consider his denial that thirst is (a desire or appetite) for *good* drink, and his assertion that it is (a desire or appetite) for drink *simpliciter.* For he wishes to show that thirst can be opposed by the contrary action of the reason (439c–d), which is portrayed as looking out for the benefit or *good* of a person (e.g., 442c). But if thirst were identified with the appetite for good drink (construed as drink that is good for the person); then it would be difficult, he thinks, to represent reason as acting contrary to it.

B.   Considered in this light, Plato's principle of correlates has an important consequence for his views about the good and the way in which we desire it. At 505d, he says that *we* all desire things that are good. But the present passage shows that he does not believe that all of *our desires* or appetites are themselves desires or appetites for the good. Thirst, for example, is simply an appetite for drink, without any consideration of whether drink (let alone any particular kind of drink) is in any way good. One must accordingly think of these appetites (or at least those of the appetitive part of the soul) as *cravings*, or *urges* to pursue things (cf. 437b–c and 572b–573c, n. C), and not as having in any way as part of their content an awareness of good or benefit to be gained. On Plato's view, it is only the reason that considers good or benefit (see 504a–511e, 521d–534d, with 441c–442d, n. D, 588b–590a, n. C, and 590c–591a, nn. D–E). [Bosanquet, p. 154; Adam, I, p. 250; Irwin, *PMT*, pp. 192–5.]

C.   The term translated by "appetite" or "desire," and sometimes here by "appetite or desire," is *epithymia*. Plato often speaks of the third part of the soul as the *epithymētikon*. But the *epithymētikon* is not the only seat of *epithymiai:* Plato makes plain that the reason and the spirited part of the soul may also have *epithymiai* (see 580c–581e, n. B). It is characteristic of the *epithymiai* of the reason that they do aim at, or in some manner take account of, the good (cf. n. B above).

439c–d: BECAUSE THERE ARE CASES IN WHICH WE ARE THIRSTY BUT ARE NEVERTHELESS UNWILLING TO DRINK, AND SO REFRAIN FROM DRINKING UNDER THE INFLUENCE OF REASON, IT FOLLOWS THAT OUR SOULS CONTAIN AT LEAST TWO PARTS, A REASONING PART AND AN UNREASONING, APPETITIVE PART.

A.   Plato now begins to apply the principles for which he has been arguing in 436b–437a and 437b–439b, to distinguish between the reason and the appetitive part of the soul. In what sense we are to think of the soul as having "parts" is unclear (Plato's word is frequently *eidos*, as at 435c5 and e2, which does not literally mean "part"). [Robinson, *SRD*, pp. 44–7.]

439e–440c: OTHER CASES SHOW US THAT THE SPIRITED PART OF THE SOUL CAN TEND IN A DIRECTION CONTRARY TO THAT OF APPETITE, SO THAT THEY CANNOT BE IDENTICAL. IN A CONFLICT BETWEEN REASON AND APPETITE, THE SPIRITED

PART IS NEVER ALLIED WITH THE APPETITE ONCE REASON HAS DETERMINED THAT IT SHOULD NOT BE OPPOSED.

A. Plato has in mind cases in which we have an appetite or craving, and simultaneously a feeling of anger and indignation with ourselves concerning what the appetite is directed toward, anger and indignation that counteract our tendency to try to satisfy the appetite.

B. Contrary to some translations, Plato does not appear to think that anger is never capable of allying itself with appetite. If he thought this, there would be no need for him to speak, as he does in 441e–442a, of the need to soothe the spirit and keep it obedient to reason. Moreover, to take the political analogy, he does not seem to think (to judge by his sketch of the timocratic city at 547c–548d) that the auxiliaries will necessarily follow the dictates of reasonable rulers. What he means here is, rather, that anger never takes sides against reason when reason has fully and resolutely decided on the proper course in a given situation. (We must thus follow Jowett and Burnet against Shorey in not reading a comma after *dein* in 440b5.)

440c–441c: BUT IF THE SPIRITED PART NEVER CONFLICTS WITH THE REASON, IS THERE GROUND FOR SAYING THAT THE TWO ARE DISTINCT? YES, BECAUSE CHILDREN AND SOME ANIMALS HAVE THE FORMER BUT NOT THE LATTER, AND BECAUSE SOMETIMES WE HAVE THE FEELING THAT OUR REASON IS ADVISING AND EXHORTING OUR SPIRIT.

A. Plato's argument for the distinctness of reason and spirit is quite different from his arguments for the distinctness of appetite from the other two parts, which rely on the principle laid down in 436b–437a. The reason is of course that, as he has just said, he does not think that reason and spirit ever pull in contrary directions.

B. It is not entirely clear just what Plato thinks occurs when reason advises and exhorts spirit. Are we to think of spirit as in some way *understanding* the thoughts or words of reason? To do so might seem to threaten to assign to spirit a kind of "rationality," of a kind that Plato might intend to attribute to the reasoning part of the soul alone. See further n. D on the following section. [Robinson, *SRD*, pp. 44–7; Penner.]

441c–442d: THE INDIVIDUAL'S SOUL THEREFORE HAS THE

SAME PARTS THAT THE CITY HAS; SO IT WILL BE WISE AND BRAVE AND JUST IN THE SAME WAY THAT THE CITY IS. WE MUST REMEMBER THAT A PERSON WHOSE SOUL'S PARTS ARE PERFORMING THEIR OWN TASKS WILL HIMSELF BE PERFORM-ING HIS OWN TASK. AND THE MIXTURE OF ARTISTIC AND PHYSICAL TRAINING THAT WE HAVE PRESCRIBED WILL BRING ABOUT THIS STATE OF AFFAIRS. *BRAVERY IN THE SOUL* IS, THEN, THE ABILITY OF THE SPIRIT TO PRESERVE, AMID PLEASURES AND PAINS, THE DECLARATION OF REASON ABOUT WHAT IS TO BE FEARED AND WHAT IS NOT. *WISDOM IN THE SOUL* IS THE KNOWLEDGE IN THE REASONING PART OF THIS AND ALSO OF WHAT IS BENEFICIAL TO EACH PART AND TO ALL THREE IN COMMON. *MODERATION IN THE SOUL* IS THE LOVE AND HARMONY OF ALL THREE WHEN THE RULING PART AND THE RULED PARTS ALL AGREE THAT THE REASON SHOULD RULE AND ARE SUBJECT TO NO DISSENSION. *JUSTICE IN THE SOUL* IS THE PERFORMANCE BY EACH PART OF ITS OWN TASK.

A.   Plato has now finally arrived both at the confirmation that he said in 434d–435c was needed for the account of justice as it was found in the city, and simultaneously at the account of justice in the soul that he has been seeking since 368c–369b, and for the sake of which he investi-gated justice in the city in the first place.

B.   The interpretation of this passage brings with it certain severe diffi-culties, arising from the complex dialectical situation into which Plato has put himself because of the dual role of his account of justice in the soul, remarked on in n. A. On the one hand, it is meant to serve as a confirmation of his account of justice in the city. On the other hand, he had earlier said, in 368c–369d, that the account of justice would be an aid to us in identifying justice in the individual. These two roles are not, it is true, formally incompatible; for it is possible for the account of jus-tice in the city to help us know *where to look* for an account of justice in the soul, in accordance with 368c–369d (see n. D there), and at the same time be confirmed by that latter account once it is found. What is essential, however, if this line of thought is to be followed successfully, is scrupulously to avoid taking for granted the account of justice in the city in the argument for the account of justice in the soul. For if this is done, the account of justice in the city will be a premise in the very argument that is supposed to confirm it. On the other hand, if the account of justice in the city is supposed to help us know where to look for an account of justice in the soul, it will be perilously easy to slip into treating the former thus illegitimately as a premise in the argument for the latter. In this complex situation, it is not surprising that Plato has allowed the lines of argument to become somewhat blurred.

For the present passage does not seem to supply us with an argument for the identification of justice in the soul that is entirely independent of the assumption that the account of justice in the city is correct. In particular, the line followed in 441c–d seems to involve this assumption, as does also the material in d–e. (Moreover, certain of the inferential steps, if that is what they are, are left ambiguous, such as the one to 441d8, which makes it unclear whether what follows is intended as an argument for, an inference from, or simply a continuation of, what precedes it.)

It is perhaps because of his sense of this problem that Plato presents us in the following passage with a further argument for his identification of justice in the soul, an argument that is quite separate from his discussion of justice in the city. [Irwin, *PMT*, pp. 204–6; Adam, I, p. 261.]

C. In 441d–e Plato draws an important connection between justice in the city and his newly-arrived-at-identification of justice in the soul. He says that we must remember that a person in whose soul each part performs its own task is a person who himself performs his task in Plato's city. But why does he say "remember"? Where has he shown this? The next few lines show what he has in mind. He explains that the effect of his recommended education was precisely to train each individual in such a way that each part of his soul performed its own task. That is, he maintains, the effect of the mixture of physical and artistic training is to develop the reason, to soothe the spirit so that it will be obedient to reason (441e9–442a2), and to establish both of them as overseers of the appetites (442a4–b3) so that the appetites will be unable to rule. This blend of the two kinds of training was described in Books II–III, and its effects were particularly highlighted in 412–414, where it was explained how that education would help to ensure that each ruler and auxiliary performed his own task. (As often, the members of the third class are left out of account; see 590c–591a, n. C, 499a–500b, n. B.) Plato accordingly thinks it clear that the training by which a person comes to perform his own task in the city is just the same as that by which a person comes to have a soul whose parts all perform their own tasks; so that (given that, as Plato appears to believe, there is no education producing the former effect without producing the latter or vice versa) those who perform their own tasks are precisely those in whose souls the parts perform their tasks.

This result is very important, because it means that justice in the individual, as Plato explains it, is thus argued by him to be coextensive with what he regards as its characteristic manifestation within his city, namely, the performance by the individual, and by the group of which he is a part, of his tasks. [Vlastos, *JHR*, pp. 79–95, esp. p. 82; Sachs; Cooper, pp. 152–3.]

D. Plato's treatment of the soul, especially in his discussions of bravery and moderation, has a tendency to personify the parts of the soul, as though each of us were inhabited by three persons (cf. 588b–590a). Among the products of this tendency is the fact that he tends to treat the lower two parts of the soul as much like creatures with a kind of rationality (cf. 440c–441d, n. B). For he speaks of the spirit as retaining "declarations" of reason (442c2), and of all of the parts as holding a "common belief" (d1) concerning who should rule (cf. 432a8). We should presumably take these phrases as mere manners of speaking, but it is unclear what more literal way Plato has of expressing the state of affairs. See 588b–590a, n. C, and 590c–591a, n. E. [Penner.]

E. Another important byproduct of Plato's quasi-personification of the parts of the soul is a strong tendency to speak as though they have *interests*, as though it is appropriate to talk of their respective *benefits*, and, further, as though the interest of the person as a whole is a kind of *common interest* of the several parts. Moreover, in making it seem that the interest of the person is a kind of common interest of the parts of the soul, Plato raises the question how this common interest is to be construed. Is the benefit of the person to be thought of as the *sum* total of the net benefits of the parts? Or is the benefit of the person regarded as like an "organic whole," which is not simply the sum of the benefits of the parts? (Is the *arrangement* or *distribution* of the benefits, for example, a factor in the person's benefit over and above the sum or quantity?) The reader will notice that this question is analogous to the question that we asked earlier about the relation between the benefit of the city and the benefits of its components (419a–421c, n. D). For further discussion of it see 576b–578b, n. C, 588b–590a, n. C.

F. According to Plato, the soul is in the best possible condition if it is ruled by reason, that is, by the "calculative" part of the soul (*to logistikon*, 442c11). It is important for the modern reader, however, not to confuse this thesis with a quite different one which frequently crops up in ethical writings in the present day. This other thesis is to the effect that what is rational to do is, *eo ipso*, the thing to do, *simpliciter*. In other words, this view is that by showing that something is the rational course of action (or the rational way in which to be) is to say *the last word* which can be said to recommend it, beyond which there is no further argument or court of appeal. On this view, for example, what is good is *defined* as what would be rational, all things considered, to choose; what *makes* it good, so to speak, is that it is rational to choose. Therefore, on this view, it is simply a truism that reason should preside over the soul.

Plato does not adopt this view—though those who do adopt it will probably maintain that he can in the end be forced to accept it. He does not adopt it because he believes that a further reason can be offered to explain *why* the rule of the soul by reason is best, and does not speak as though this explanation is to be accepted simply because it is accepted by reason. The rule of reason is best, he thinks, because it can be seen to put the soul in the best condition that it can be in, a condition in which there is as little conflict as possible, and in which all of the parts of the soul gain satisfaction in an orderly manner (see 573c–576b, n. B, 588b–590a, n. B). By the same token, the rule of the city by rulers dominated by reason is argued for not simply on the ground that they are reason-dominated, but on the ground that such an arrangement results in a city that is good, as shown by its unity and its obedience to the principle of the Natural Division of Labor (422e–423d, n. B). In addition, the discussion of the good that Plato presents in Books VI–VII makes no suggestion that the *criterion* of what is good is simply its being declared choice-worthy by reason. Rather, the criterion of the satisfactory functioning of reason is that it accurately apprehends the good (see Introd., sec. 4).

Opponents of Plato on this matter will, as I have said, think that he cannot maintain his position. In brief, their line of argument will be that we must have some way in which *we* can tell what is good—that is, whether we have actually apprehended the good correctly—and that we can tell this only by telling whether our conclusions about the matter have been rationally arrived. (How we can tell *this* may well, of course, be argued to be a further problem, which we must let pass here.) Moreover, they will say, Plato himself recognizes this fact in one of his arguments in Book IX for the superiority of the life of justice over the life of injustice (580c–583a). For in that argument he seems to take as the criterion of superiority the mere fact that such a life will be chosen by the man who is ruled by his reason. I waive the question whether Plato *ought* to accept the view of his opponents. He does not, however, *in fact* accept it. The important thing to notice is that the argument cited is not the only argument that Plato presents in Book IX for the superiority of the just life. It is one of three distinct arguments for that claim (576b–578b, n. A), and it is not singled out as having any special status. It therefore cannot be taken to provide the single criterion that Plato adopts for determining goodness.

What criterion, then, does he adopt? How does he think that one can tell that one is right about one's view of the good? The *Republic* does not make his answer to this question clear. For some remarks about this matter, see 531d–534d, n. D.

442d–443b: IF WE CONSIDER PEOPLE'S ORDINARY NOTION OF JUSTICE, WE SEE THAT IT CONFIRMS OUR VIEW OF WHAT JUSTICE IS IN THE INDIVIDUAL. FOR A MAN WITH THE NATURE AND EDUCATION THAT WE HAVE DESCRIBED WILL NOT COMMIT SUCH CRIMES AS THEFT AND THE LIKE, AND THE REASON FOR THIS IS THAT EACH PART OF HIS SOUL PERFORMS ITS OWN TASK.

A.   Plato maintains that a man educated as he has prescribed will not commit what are commonly regarded as crimes. And he further maintains that this fact provides further confirmation that justice in the soul is the same as the justice that we earlier saw in the city (442d10–e1).

B.   In making the first of these claims Plato is attempting to forge a link between the notions of justice that he has introduced in connection with the city and the soul, and the notion of justice as it figures in ordinary uses of the term "just" in application to action. And he is trying to show that if a person is just in the sense that he has commended to us, then that person will also be just in the sense in which that term is ordinarily used (i.e., in the sense of refraining from what are ordinarily thought of as crimes).

It has been noticed (see Grote and Sachs) that there is an urgent need for Plato to forge this link. For he is in the midst of an argument over whether or not justice is beneficial to the person possessing it, which began when Thrasymachus maintained, using the ordinary sense of "justice," something to the effect of "Justice is not beneficial." But if Plato now replies, "No, justice *is* beneficial," and then suddenly turns out to be using a completely *new* sense of the word "justice", having no connection with the one in which Thrasymachus was using it, then obviously Plato cannot be said to have disproved, or even to have denied, what Thrasymachus was asserting. Yet Plato does indeed seem to be in danger of using a sense of "justice" different from that of Thrasymachus and thus of making a reply to Thrasymachus that is irrelevant to what he had asserted. For the reader will now have seen from Plato's accounts of justice in the city and in the soul that the meaning he attaches to the term appears to be quite different from the one that Thrasymachus had attached to it. For Thrasymachus' sense of "justice" had to do with refraining from what are ordinarily thought of as crimes, whereas Plato's sense of the term, as we have seen, is explained in terms of his complex and non-ordinary theory of the parts of the soul.

If it could be shown that Plato's sense of "justice" as applied to the individual is equivalent to the ordinary sense (i.e., if precisely the same people were necessarily just in both senses), then there would be no difficulty in regarding Plato's argument as a legitimate effort to refute what Thrasymachus had maintained. For if this equivalence held, then in a very real way the shift from one sense of "justice" to the other would make no difference to the argument. But matters do not turn out to be this simple, as we shall now see. [Grote, pp. 99–110, with Aristotle, *Nicomachean Ethics* 1129a26ff.; Sachs; Demos; Vlastos, *JHR*; Kraut, *RJR*; Kahn, pp. 570–5; Irwin, *PMT*, pp. 204–12; Shorey, *Rep.*, I, pp. 410–11; Zeller, pp. 886–92.]

C. Plato contends here that a person who is just in the same manner as the city is just will not commit such crimes as embezzling, temple-robbing, and so forth. (The crime of temple-robbing is not as quaint as it may sound: temples in Greece often served as public treasuries; cf. 568d.) He gives no argument for this contention, except to say that such a person will refrain from these acts because each part of his soul performs its own task, in particular, the task of ruling or of being ruled. Plato's implication here is that if this condition of soul prevails, then the motivations that a person might otherwise have to perform such crimes would be removed or counteracted. He must think that this idea is made plausible by his description of the guardians' education, with its measures to foster control of the appetites (cf. 441c–442d, n. C). The assumption that he is making is that the cause of such crimes is always the excessive power of the appetites. Given this assumption, he can feel entitled to conclude that a person educated according to his instructions, which are designed to moderate the appetites, will necessarily refrain from those crimes.

In Books VIII–IX, when Plato comes to discuss various types of people who are less than perfectly just, he will carry out an elaborate description of their condition in terms of his theory of the soul. At that time, he will present more clearly his ideas about how it is that crimes of the sort mentioned here are caused by deviations from justice in his sense (see 590a–c, n. B).

For the present, notice that all that Plato maintains here is that if a person is just in Plato's sense, then he will be just—or at least refrain from unjust actions—in the ordinary sense. He does not here maintain the converse, that if a person is just in the ordinary sense, then he must be just in Plato's sense. To say this would be to say that the *only* cause of a person's refraining from crimes would be the presence in him of justice in Plato's sense. But it is not at all clear even here that Plato would be willing to say this, and later on it becomes even clearer that he would not be (see *ibid.* with 619c–d).

D. In our discussion of the previous section, we observed the problems that afflicted Plato in his attempt to establish that the features that he had isolated in the city and the soul really were appropriately called justice (see n. B there). It is obvious that because of those problems, the present passage bears much of the weight of his effort to show that his notion of justice is not a complete departure from the ordinary one.

443b–444a: WHEN WE EARLIER CONSIDERED THE IDEA THAT EACH PERSON SHOULD PERFORM HIS OWN TASK, AND THE PRINCIPLE OF THE NATURAL DIVISION OF LABOR, WE WERE SEEING AN IMAGE OF JUSTICE. FOR JUSTICE DOES NOT PRIMARILY CONCERN A PERSON'S EXTERNAL ACTION, BUT IS THE CONDITION OF SOUL IN WHICH EACH PART PERFORMS ITS OWN TASK, SO THAT THE SOUL IS BOUND HARMONIOUSLY INTO A UNITY. JUST ACTIONS ARE THOSE THAT PRODUCE OR PRESERVE SUCH A CONDITION. WISDOM IS THE KNOWLEDGE OVERSEEING SUCH ACTIONS. UNJUST ACTIONS ARE THOSE THAT UNDO SUCH A CONDITION OF SOUL, AND IGNORANCE OVERSEES THEM.

A. Plato indicates that his account of justice is now complete (443b7). He maintains that the idea that each person must perform his own task (*to hautou prattein*) is an image of justice but not the complete explanation of it. Rather, an individual's justice does not attach primarily to his actions but rather to his soul. It involves a *harmony* among the parts of his soul, the analogue of the harmony that Plato has already claimed to be present in his city (e.g., at 431e–432a; cf. 422e–423d, n. B, 410a–412a, nn. A–B, 400d–401d, n. A). As before (see *ibid.*) this notion of harmony is linked with the notion of unity, Plato's contention being that a person with a harmonious soul will be "one" or unified in the way in which a well-governed city is also "one" or unified (see also 427c–428a, n. B). [See, e.g., Vlastos, *JHR*, p. 69, n. 11, p. 70, n. 14.]

B.   Although Plato says that doing one's own task is not all that justice in the individual comes to, the connection between this notion and Plato's final account of justice in the soul is plainly intended to show further, beyond what was done in the previous section (n. B there), that his account of justice is not a complete departure from the ordinary notion of justice (cf. n. B on 432b–434c). He hopes we can see that given that we ordinarily associate justice with a person's performing his own task, minding his own business, and not interfering with others, and given his theory of the soul, it is reasonable to say that justice in the soul is the condition in which each part performs its own task without meddling. [Shorey, *Rep.*, I, p. 368.]

C.   The foregoing is Plato's sense of "just" as that word is applied to individuals. From it he allows us to derive a secondary sense, which is applied to actions. An action may be called just, he says, provided that it tends to the establishment or preservation of justice, as explained, in the soul of the person performing the action. (It is possible to ask why Plato did not say "establishment of preservation of justice in the souls of people in general"; see 591a–592b, n. C.) Both of these senses of "just" (and "justice") are to be distinguished from the sense in which it is applied to cities: a city is just provided that the members of the classes in it perform their respective functions (432b–434c). It is easy to see that Plato might have said that there is accordingly another sense of "just" as applied to individuals, according to which a person would be said to be just provided that he performed his task in Plato's city. One reason might be that such a sense of "just" would be irrelevant to people not in Plato's city or one like it. In any case, although Plato certainly uses the concept of a person who performs his function in such a city (cf. 441c–442d, n. C), he does not build thereon a sense of the word "just".

   (It should be noticed that my talk here of different senses, or even uses, of the term "just" is somewhat loose. Plato does not talk as though there is anything involved that *he* would readily call a difference of sense or meaning, and he plainly links all of his applications of the word to a single entity, the Form of Justice—see nn. on 476d–480a and Introd., sec. 3. And indeed he has emphasized that justice in the city and justice in the soul must be the same thing [434d–435c, esp. 435a–c, and 442d; cf. 444a].)

D.   From Plato's statement that justice in the soul is prior to justice in an individual's actions, it becomes still clearer than it was (see 362d–368c, n. C) that in his view, whether or not a person is just is not simply a matter of his following the standards that happen to be in force in a particular community. To be sure, Plato does believe that many of the actions that are forbidden by communities are unjust; what he says in the previous section makes this fact clear. But he does not believe that such actions are unjust simply because they are called so by any particular community (here he differs from the account of justice embodied in Glaucon's speech at 357b–358a and Adeimantus' speech at 362d–368c —see n. B on the latter). Rather, actions acquire their justice or injustice, independently of these facts about human communities, from their effect on the condition of one's soul. (There is a sense in which this notion of justice can be thought of as egoistic; see further n. C on 591a–592b.) [On Plato's responses to various problems arising from his epistemological realism, or anti-conventionalism, see White.]

E.   Plato's views on justice in the soul are in an important way uncongenial to philosophers with behavioristic tendencies. He never even hints at how claims about the state of a person's soul might be confirmed by his behavior to the outside observer, nor suggests that this must be so if the notion of states of the soul are to make sense. Nor, for that matter, does he comment explicitly on the role of introspection in our ability to ascertain psychic states. Indifference toward such issues is connected with his general lack of inclination to adopt any sort of verificationism whatever. [White, pp. 212–213.]

F.   In another way, too, Plato's account of justice in actions is likely to seem odd to the contemporary philosopher. Nowadays, we are probably more inclined to think of a just action as one that *proceeds from* the justice of the person who performs it, than as one that brings about or strengthens justice in the person who performs it. There is no doubt, however, that in the present passage Plato sees things differently from the way in which we do, and never offers an account of just action that makes it proceed from a just condition of soul. In 590a–c, however, he does say things that suggest the idea that, at least by and large, the actions proceeding from a just condition of soul are the same actions that strengthen such a condition (see n. B there).

444a–e: INJUSTICE IS ACCORDINGLY STRIFE AMONG THE PARTS AND MEDDLING IN EACH OTHER'S TASKS. JUST AND UNJUST ACTIONS ARE THEREFORE LIKE HEALTHFUL AND DISEASED ACTIONS, PRODUCING RESPECTIVELY HEALTH AND DISEASE IN THE SOUL. BECAUSE A HEALTHY CONDITION IS ONE IN ACCORD WITH NATURE AND A DISEASED CONDITION IS CONTRARY TO NATURE, A JUST SOUL HAS PARTS THAT RULE

AND ARE RULED ACCORDING TO NATURE, AND AN UNJUST
SOUL HAS PARTS THAT RULE AND ARE RULED CONTRARY TO
NATURE. SO EXCELLENCE OR VIRTUE (*ARETĒ*) IS A KIND OF
HEALTH, AND DEFICIENCY OR VICE (*KAKIA*) IS A KIND OF
DISEASE. FINE PURSUITS, ACCORDINGLY, LEAD ONE TO AC-
QUIRE VIRTUE, AND BASE ONES LEAD TO THE ACQUISITION
OF VICE.

A. Plato now presents, briefly, his account of injustice. He then maintains that justice is in accord with nature, and is analogous to health in
the body, and that injustice is contrary to nature and analogous to
disease in the body (cf. 403c–404e).

   The analogy between justice and health appeals to a theory, current
at the time, according to which bodily health depends on a balance and
harmony among various bodily constituents. Acceptance of that theory
would naturally make someone tend to think of justice as a desirable
characteristic, once it has been explained as Plato explains it. Because
we no longer accept the theory, it has no probative force for us. But although Plato does believe that analogy is important, because it is revelatory of a uniformity holding in both bodily and psychic matters, he
fortunately places little or none of the weight of his argument on it.

   Much more important is his claim that justice is in accord with nature
and injustice is contrary to it. Although there are great obscurities surrounding the notion of accord with nature (see 369e–370c, n. E), we can
easily see how this claim fits with his line of argument thus far (quite
apart from the analogy between justice and health with which it is here
linked). For the city that he has constructed has been based, as we have
seen (369e–370c), on the Principle of the Natural Division of Labor. By
adhering to this principle, he has hoped to establish a city in which the
activities of each person accord with nature to the maximum extent possible, and in which the activities of the parts of the rulers' souls do likewise (on the parts of the others' souls, see 590c–591a, nn. C–D). But
adherence to this principle has turned out to be what makes the city just
(432b–434c), and it is this fact that enables Plato to say that in this
sense justice is in accord with nature. [Bosanquet, pp. 169–70.]

B. Unobtrusively, Plato inserts into this passage some important contentions about excellence or virtue (*aretē*—see n. E on 427e–428a). First,
there is an analogy between virtue and health (cf. n. A). More important,
there is the plain indication that he takes himself to have established
that the kind of man whom his educational system has produced, and

who is to rule in his city, has virtue and is accordingly (as 449a treats as demonstrated) good. (On the connection between *aretē* and being good, see again n. E on 427e–428a.) Although Plato has not explicitly presented an argument for saying that such a man is good, it is plain enough why he thinks himself entitled to that conclusion. For one thing, the man has the same kind of unity and stability that Plato took as ground for calling the city good (see 427e–428a, n. B, on the city, and, on the man, 422e–423d, n. B, with 591a–592b, n. D). For another, Plato takes it as established that such a man has all of the relevant excellences or virtues to make him good (441c–442d). Henceforth, beginning at the outset of Book V, Plato will treat the goodness of such a man as proved.

444e–445b: WE MUST NOW INVESTIGATE WHETHER OR NOT IT IS ADVANTAGEOUS TO ACT JUSTLY AND TO BE JUST.

A. It is *most* important to bear in mind that the argument thus far has not been intended to settle whether and how far it is beneficial to be just (and, now that Plato has explicitly distinguished the two in 443b–444a, to perform just actions), even though Plato has repeatedly voiced his belief that it is. Forgetfulness of this fact has probably caused more misinterpretation of the *Republic* in recent times than any other factor. What has been accomplished so far is simply an account of what justice and injustice are, along with descriptions of the good man and the good city (see the previous n. B, and 427e–428a, n. B). The account of what justice is, of course, is the necessary preliminary, which was demanded at the end of Book I (354b–c), to the investigation of whether or not justice is beneficial. The way for that investigation is now prepared (cf. 465c–466c, n. A).

445c–e: WE MUST NOW EXAMINE THE DEFECTIVE OR VICIOUS SOULS AND CITIES. THERE ARE INDEFINITELY MANY TYPES OF THEM, BUT ONLY FOUR THAT ARE WORTHY OF NOTICE HERE. THE ONE VIRTUOUS OR EXCELLENT TYPE OF CITY, WHICH WE HAVE EXAMINED, IS EITHER KINGSHIP OR ARISTOCRACY, DEPENDING ON WHETHER THERE IS ONE RULER OR SEVERAL; ITS RULER IS THE KINGLY MAN.

A. The first part of Plato's strategy is announced for showing that justice is beneficial to its possessor. It is to show various ways in which cities and men can be worse and less just than his city and its rulers, so as to be able to compare his city and its rulers with others, particularly

with the least just city and the least just man, to see which is better off.
But this strategy is interrupted by Books V–VII, to be continued again
in subsequent books.

B.   For Plato the number of rulers in the city is unimportant. What
matters is rather the structure of the city and the principles on which it
is organized. So Plato's city can be either a kingship or monarchy, or
an aristocracy with a committee of rulers. Nevertheless he tends to presuppose a plurality of rulers (e.g., at 540a–b, where rulers take turns
at various parts of their task), even while insisting, however, that the
task of rulership is a unitary task, in the sense that a man is naturally
suited, and educated, either to the whole of it or to none of it (see esp.
484a–d, n. A).

Summary of the *REPUBLIC*

Book V

— education of guardians - women
  ↳ communal loving arrangements
— one & many
— philosopher-king — → knowledge & Form

449a–550c: SOCRATES IS ABOUT TO CONTINUE WITH HIS DESCRIPTION OF THE FOUR DEFECTIVE CITIES, WHEN HE IS INTERRUPTED BY A DEMAND THAT HE EXPLAIN WHAT HE MEANT WHEN HE SAID THAT WITHIN THE CLASS OF GUARDIANS WIVES AND CHILDREN SHOULD BE HELD IN COMMON.

A.   The discussion of defective cities, announced by Socrates at the end of Book IV, is deferred to the beginning of Book VIII. The whole of Books V–VII is devoted to a response to the questions raised here by his interlocutors.

Plato begins the response in a deceptively casual manner, using Polemarchus' surprise at the evidently shocking institution of "holding wives and children in common" (cf. 423e–424a) to motivate a discussion that is really far more general and wide-reaching. In fact, the discussion is a further investigation of the theme that the guardians will hold all things in common, because each will regard his own benefit as coinciding with that of the city as a whole (see 412d–e, nn., 412e–414b, n. A). This continuing investigation is focused on the notion of having and doing things "in common" (i.e., on the notion of *koinōnia*, e.g., in 450c1, 451e1; cf. 350c–352c). The particular questions raised are whether the kind of community of interests and activities which Plato advocates is really best (e.g., 456c), and whether it is possible (e.g., 450c, 466d). The examination of whether the arrangements are possible leads Plato to say that they could be carried out, provided that philosophers came to be rulers

139

of a city (473c–474b). The mention of philosophers, however, requires him to explain that by this term he does not mean those to whom people ordinarily apply it, but genuine philosophers. But this explanation requires in turn an explanation of whom he takes to be the genuine philosophers (474b–c), an explanation that takes up most of Books VI–VII. If the argument of Books V–VII is viewed as a whole, then, we can see it as an explanation of the sense in which guardians hold all things in common, designed to show that such an arrangement is both best and possible, with an argument explaining how this possibility might be made actual by the rule of genuine philosophers.

The idea of the community of the benefits and activities of the guardians is obviously related to Plato's intention that the city as a whole be as unified and cohesive as possible (422e–423d, n. B). But it is important to notice that for the overwhelming bulk of Books V–VII Plato is concerned only with the guardians (and sometimes only with the rulers; cf. 412e–414b, n. A), and not with the rest of the population. The connection between the unity of the city and the unity and cohesiveness of the class of guardians is made at 465b, where Plato says that as long as the guardians remain united, the city as a whole will remain so as well (cf. 545c–547c). [Bosanquet, pp. 171–2.]

B. Plato begins this part of the argument with a reiteration of the claim that the city he has established is good (cf. 427e–428a, n. B), and that the man of the corresponding sort is likewise good (444a–e, n. B).

450c–451c: SOCRATES EXPLAINS THAT THIS DEMAND RAISES THE DIFFICULT TASK OF SHOWING THAT THE ARRANGEMENTS HE PROPOSES ARE POSSIBLE AND FOR THE BEST. BUT HE ACCEDES TO THE DEMAND AND BEGINS TO DISCUSS THE TASKS OF WOMEN.

A. As indicated in the previous note A, Plato intends to treat a much broader issue than Polemarchus actually broaches. But there is a rationale for his procedure. One of his aims in Book V is to show that his arrangements for the city are good for it (461e–462e, n. B; his other aim, on which see 472e–473b, n. A, being to show that the establishment of his city is in a certain sense possible). A major part of this demonstration invokes a system of eugenics involving the training and selection of both male and female guardians, who will be seen to be the best to produce future guardians as offspring (458b–460b). But the operation of this system requires that women be subject to the same process of upbringing and selection as men, and hence requires that they share with men the role of guardians. Therefore, Plato's response to Polemarchus is a necessary preliminary to the rest of the argument in Book V.

451c–452e: IF WOMEN ARE TO PERFORM THE TASK OF BEING GUARDIANS, THEN THEY MUST HAVE THE SAME UPBRINGING AND EDUCATION AS THAT ALREADY DESCRIBED. TO THE OBJECTION THAT THIS WILL REQUIRE THINGS THAT ARE RIDICULOUS, ESPECIALLY THE PARTICIPATION TOGETHER BY WOMEN AND MEN IN PHYSICAL TRAINING, THE APPROPRIATE RESPONSE IS THAT IF THE ARRANGEMENT IS GOOD, IT CANNOT BE TRULY RIDICULOUS.

A. In keeping with his attitude toward his whole scheme of education, Plato does not care about the fact that his arrangements for physical training conflict with what is conventionally regarded as acceptable or proper. (Cf. 362d–368c, n. B.)

B. Here and elsewhere (457b, 473c, 518a–b) Plato shows concern with the notion of the ridiculous and laughable (*geloion*). This concern has already manifested itself in his provision that the guardians be trained not to indulge in excessive laughter (388e–389a; cf. 606c). The point underlying this concern is that there should not be an independent standard of etiquette which rivals the standard of what is good and bad (cf. Introd., sec. 4). [Bosanquet, p. 96; Adam, I, p. 283; Shorey, *Rep.*, I, p. 211.]

452e–456b: SOCRATES AGAIN CONSIDERS THE OBJECTION THAT HIS PROPOSALS COULD NOT POSSIBLY BE CARRIED OUT. HE ALSO CONSIDERS THE OBJECTION THAT, BECAUSE WOMEN DIFFER IN NATURE FROM MEN, AND BECAUSE ON HIS OWN PRINCIPLE DIFFERENT NATURES SHOULD BE ASSIGNED DIFFERENT TASKS, WOMEN SHOULD THEREFORE NOT HAVE THE SAME TASKS AS MEN. HIS REPLY IS THAT NOT EVERY DIFFERENCE IN NATURE IS PERTINENT TO ONE'S TASK.

A. Adhering to his basic strategy in the construction of his city, Plato here refers to his Principle of the Natural Division of Labor and insists that women are in fact as naturally suited to the task of guardianship as men are (though he says that their abilities may be somewhat less, 455c).

He has no choice but to allot to women the task of childbirth, but he does not give them the task of bringing up the children, because he regards that as part of the task of the guardians in general, as it pertains so directly to the preservation of the city (see 401d–403c, n. B).

B. Plato's manner of dividing the work of the city into different discrete tasks or functions raises the question what principle governs this division. How do we tell when we have one task or two? Plato does not believe that his division is merely arbitrary; he thinks that it follows lines that are in some sense laid down by nature (369e–370c). In 454d he expresses the opinion that differences of soul, rather than differences of body, are the most important determinants of one's task, though plainly bodily endowments are also relevant (455b9–c1). But he does not attempt to say in general how single tasks are to be marked off and recognized (cf. 474b–c, n. C).

456b–c: THAT MALE AND FEMALE GUARDIANS HAVE A COMMON EDUCATION IS THEREFORE IN ACCORD WITH NATURE AND NOT CONTRARY TO IT. SO THE ARRANGEMENT IS POSSIBLE.

A. From the contention that the arrangement governing education is natural, Plato concludes that it is possible. The underlying assumption, which he does not spell out or examine, is that in general what is in accord with nature must be possible.

456c–457a: HAVING SEEN THAT THE ARRANGEMENT IS POSSIBLE, WE MUST ALSO SEE THAT IT IS BEST. CLEARLY IT IS, BECAUSE THE SYSTEM OF EDUCATION THUS ESTABLISHED MAKES PEOPLE BETTER, AND MAKES THE GUARDIANS THE BEST OF ALL CITIZENS. ALL THAT THE PRESENT SUGGESTION ADDS IS THAT THE CLASS OF GUARDIANS INCLUDES THE BEST POSSIBLE WOMEN AS WELL AS THE BEST POSSIBLE MEN.

A. Plato has already argued that people educated according to his scheme will be good and have all of the relevant virtues or excellences (see 444a–e, n. B). Here he simply applies that claim to women.

B. In addition, he tacitly asserts something that has not been made explicit, that it is to the good of the city to have men and women as guardians who are as good men and women as possible (456e6–7). In other words, he is now thoroughly committed to the proposition that the best guardians are the best people. Once again, however, it is pertinent to remark that the force of this contention awaits further clarification when he comes to explain his views on the good (see 504d–534d, *passim*).

457a–c: THAT WAS THE *FIRST WAVE* OF CRITICISM THAT FACED US, DIRECTED AGAINST THE IDEA THAT MEN AND WOMEN SHOULD SHARE TASKS IN COMMON.

A.   Book V is in fact taken up with three "waves" that Plato sees threatening to engulf his argument. The first is the foregoing. The second is the one to follow immediately, which has to do with the idea that wives (and, as is clear, husbands) and children are to be held in common, in the sense that the guardian (ruler and auxiliary) class will contain no families in the conventional sense of the word but will be organized to resemble something more like one single large family. The discussion of this wave lasts until 466d, where the third wave first appears. The third wave concerns the question whether the city that he describes is possible, that is, could actually be established on earth. The effort to answer this question leads him to explain who he thinks are genuine philosophers (cf. 449a–450c, n. A). This explanation, beginning at 471c (cf. 472a, 473c), extends to the end of Book VII, and so it can be said that the third wave really extends to that point too.

457c–e: THE *SECOND WAVE* CONSISTS OF OBJECTIONS AGAINST THE IDEA THAT WIVES AND CHILDREN SHOULD BE HELD IN COMMON, AND THE IDEA THAT PARENTS SHOULD NOT KNOW THEIR OWN CHILDREN AND CHILDREN SHOULD NOT KNOW THEIR OWN PARENTS. DOUBTS ARISE BOTH ABOUT THE POSSIBILITY OF THIS ARRANGEMENT AND ABOUT ITS ADVANTAGEOUSNESS.

A.   Socrates suggests that it is already obvious that his proposals here are beneficial to the city, and that therefore he will have to argue only their possibility, but he is brought up short by Glaucon, who insists that he will have to argue both points. The result is that there is further explanation of the notion of what is beneficial to the city, coming to a head at 461e–462e.

457e–458b: SOCRATES ASKS TO BE ALLOWED TO TAKE THE

"LAZY" WAY OF ASSUMING THAT THE ARRANGEMENT IS POS-
SIBLE, AND SHOWING THAT IF IT WERE PUT INTO EFFECT, IT
WOULD BE BEST.

A.   What is "lazy" about the procedure that Plato adopts? It is the fact
that he supposes, before he has demonstrated it, that his arrangement
of family life is really a coherent possibility (see 472e–473b, n. A). Making this supposition, he discusses the advantages of the arrangement in
458b–471c. (The form of the argument is not entirely straightforward;
see 461e–462e, n. A. In addition, there is at 466d a brief allusion to the
question of possibility, but the question is postponed, and the description
of advantages is continued to 471c.) The result is that the whole question
of possibility is shunted into the discussion of the third wave, begun at
471c (see 471c–472b, n. A). However, what the third wave concerns is
really broader than what is postponed here. For the third wave involves
the question of the possibility of *all* of the arrangements for Plato's city,
not merely the ones affecting family life and procreation. Plato believes
that the possibility of the latter should be treated in the context of a
full-scale account of the possibility of the whole system.

458b–460b: BECAUSE MEN AND WOMEN WILL BE TOGETHER
IN ALL ACTIVITIES, THEY WILL NECESSARILY HAVE SEXUAL
INTERCOURSE. BUT WE WANT THIS TO BE AS BENEFICIAL AS
POSSIBLE, AND SO WE SHALL HAVE TO ARRANGE AND CON-
TROL IT. AS IN THE BREEDING OF ANIMALS GENERALLY, WE
WANT TO BREED THE BEST PARENTS IN ORDER TO PRODUCE
THE BEST OFFSPRING. THIS WILL BE ARRANGED BY THE RUL-
ERS, WHO, HOWEVER, WILL PROPOUND THE FICTION THAT
MARRIAGES ARE ARRANGED BY LOT, SO AS TO AVOID STIRRING
UP DISSENSION. IN ARRANGING BREEDING, THE RULERS WILL
TRY TO KEEP THE POPULATION STABLE, ALLOWING FOR WARS
AND OTHER CONTINGENCIES.

A.   The use of a falsehood to deceive most of the guardians about the
arrangements for sexual intercourse recalls what Plato said earlier about
the need for falsehood among men (see 376e–379b, n. B). The justification of its use here is the avoidance of dissension (*stasis*, 461e3), and the
theme of the unity of the city is also recalled at 460a5–6, where Plato
reminds us that the city must be neither too large nor too small (422e–
423d, n. B).

B.   As we can see, Plato believes that most of the human characteristics important to his city are inherited, though he allows for exceptions (see 425b–427c, n. C).

460b–461e: CHILDREN WILL BE PLACED IN A NURSERY AND CARED FOR BY NURSES. PARENTS AND CHILDREN WILL THUS NOT KNOW EACH OTHER. INCEST WILL BE AVOIDED BY PROHIBITING INTERCOURSE BETWEEN PEOPLE WHO COULD, UNDER THE RULERS' ARRANGEMENTS, BE RELATED AS PARENT TO CHILD OR GRANDPARENT TO GRANDCHILD. OTHERWISE, INTERCOURSE BETWEEN PEOPLE OF CHILDBEARING AGE WILL BE ALLOWED ONLY IN ACCORDANCE WITH THE RULERS' PLANS TO PRODUCE THE BEST OFFSPRING. CHILDREN OF UNIONS NOT THUS SANCTIONED WILL BE EXPOSED TO DIE.

A.   Plato sets up strict rules to achieve his main aim of making the guardians think of their own interests as coinciding with those of each other (449a–450c, n. A, 412d–e, nn.). The proximate aim here, which leads to that result, is to avoid the emergence of any other attachments and loyalties which might conflict with it (as special attachments to the members of one's family might do). [On infanticide, see Adam, I, pp. 357–60.]

B.   Obviously, Plato's rulers are faced with a difficult and complicated task. It is made somewhat less difficult by the fact that incest is defined quite narrowly. (Notice that he sees even the prohibition of incest as in its way making for unity in the city.·For it is initially the effort to avoid incest that forces him to have people treat as children, parents, and siblings, people who are not actually thus related to them.)

461e–462e: WE MUST CONFIRM THAT THIS ARRANGEMENT IS BEST AND THAT IT FITS WITH THE REST OF OUR DESCRIPTION OF THE CITY. THE GREATEST GOOD FOR A CITY IS WHAT BINDS IT TOGETHER AND MAKES IT ONE, AND THE GREATEST EVIL IS WHAT PULLS IT APART AND TURNS IT INTO MANY. UNITY IS FOSTERED WHEN EACH PERSON FEELS PLEASURE AND PAIN AT THE SAME THINGS AS THE OTHERS, AND WHEN THE GROUP FUNCTIONS LIKE A SINGLE ORGANISM, WHICH GRIEVES AS A WHOLE WHEN ONE PART IS DAMAGED, AND WHEN NO ONE DISTINGUISHES BETWEEN WHAT IS HIS AND WHAT IS SOMEONE ELSE'S.

A.   We must be careful here to follow a slight twist that the argument takes. Plato briefly suspends his description of the city and turns instead to a specification of what in general engenders what is good for a city. At 462e he again returns to his city and asks whether it has what fits this specification (he responds that it does).

B.   Plato says that the greatest good for a city is what makes it one, and the worst thing for it is what pulls it apart and makes it many. This contention is obviously meant to recall to us his earlier insistence that the city must be one and not many (422e–423d), and his connection of the unity of the city with its being good (427e–428a, n. B).

There is, however, a difference between these two ideas. In the earlier passage, Plato was concerned with what it is for the city to *be good*; here, on the other hand, he is dealing with the question what is *good for* the city, in the sense of what is *beneficial* to it. He does not draw an explicit distinction between these two ideas, and in fact it will turn out that in a sense he thinks it ultimately wrong to distinguish them (see 519d–521b, n. E). However, we can see already that he thinks that what makes for a good city is the same as what makes for benefit for the city: in both cases it is the unity of the city.

It cannot be said that Plato argues explicitly either for the proposition that a good city is a unitary city, or for the proposition that what is good for the city is to be unitary. Rather, he tries to make these propositions plausible *ambulando* in the course of his description of the city. But it should not be inferred that he has no argument to make, and still less that he thinks that the propositions are evident with no further discussion. For he later makes clear that there is a great deal to be explained about the notion of goodness that he does not explain here (506b–507a); and if we examine his metaphysical theory, we can see some of the considerations that made him believe in the connection between unity and goodness which he here presupposes (see 519d–521b, n. E, and Introd., sec. 3, with 419a–421c, n. D).

462e–464d: DOES OUR CITY HAVE THE FEATURES THAT PRODUCE THIS GOOD? IT DOES, AND THE REASON IS THE HOLDING OF WIVES AND CHILDREN IN COMMON AMONG THE GUARDIANS. BECAUSE OF THIS THEY DO NOT SPEAK OF DIFFERENT THINGS AS "MINE." IN VIRTUE OF THIS FACT THEY ARE MORE GENUINELY GUARDIANS AND MORE ABLE TO PREVENT THE CITY FROM SPLITTING APART.

A.   Plato returns to his city and argues that it does satisfy the specification laid down in the previous section (n. A there). He emphasizes once again the connection between his arrangements for family and children and the fulfilling of the role of guardians (463b, 464c). He also reiterates the connection between being a guardian (or preserver, 463b1) and avoiding the tearing apart (*diaspan*, 464c7; cf. 462b1) of the city (cf. 422e–423d, n. B, and 412e–414b, n. B).

464d–465b: THERE WILL BE NO DISSENSION AMONG THE GUARDIANS, BECAUSE NONE OF THEM WILL HAVE ANYTHING PRIVATE TO HIMSELF, EXCEPT HIS OWN BODY. NOR WILL THERE BE ANY LAWSUITS FOR ASSAULT, AND THE YOUNGER GUARDIANS WILL BE PREVENTED BY SHAME FROM STRIKING THE ELDER, EXCEPT WHEN THE RULERS COMMAND IT. THERE WILL BE AN ELDER MAN IN CHARGE OF THE PUNISHMENT OF THOSE WHO ARE YOUNGER.

A.   Although Plato believes that the lack of dissension will mitigate the kind of violent behavior that engenders lawsuits, he does not claim to be able to eliminate all fighting among (young) guardians, but only to avoid letting them come to litigation (cf. 405a–410a, n. A, on Plato's desire to limit the necessity for the remedial function of law courts) or go out of control. For he suggests that guardians will sometimes have to defend themselves against each other, and that this roughhousing will help to keep them in good physical condition and will enable them to let off steam (recall that the guardians are to be of a partly ferocious, guard-dog-like disposition; cf. 374e–376c, 410a–412a).

B.   Plato's contention that there will be no dissension (*stasis*; cf. 458b–460b, n. A) among the guardians is connected both with his desire for the unity of the city (see the following section), and with his belief that the conduct of guardians will not generally depart from what is acceptable under ordinary standards of behavior (see 442d–443b, n. B). [See esp. Grote, pp. 169–70, 186–7, *et passim*.]

465b: IF THE GUARDIANS HAVE NO DISSENSION AMONG THEMSELVES, THEN THERE IS NO FEAR THAT THE REST OF THE CITY WILL SPLIT INTO FACTIONS, EITHER AGAINST THE GUARDIANS OR AGAINST EACH OTHER.

A.   This vitally important step in Plato's argument seems to him to require little defense in the light of what he has already said. He believes it clear that the unity of the class of guardians will ensure the unity of the city as a whole (cf. 545c–547c, n. A, and 376e–379b, n. C). This is one of the things that makes it possible for him to spend so little time talking about the organization of the rest of the city, and so much time on the guardians (recall that virtually all of the foregoing discussion of the city, including the education of its citizens, deals exclusively with the guardians).

His certainty on this point, it should be noticed, rests on his belief in the Principle of the Natural Division of Labor, and on a particular application of it. Believing that the guardians are those who excel in the qualities necessary for defending the city (374e–376c), he believes also that they must excel in the qualities that make good fighters. For this reason, he thinks, they will be able to quell any threat of an uprising from the rest of the population, who are dominated by appetites and not by spirit (580c–581e) and are furthermore untrained in warfare. In addition, the guardians, and particularly the rulers, are those who are expert in education, i.e., in recognizing and fostering the attributes necessary for someone to be a good guardian (401d–403c, n. B). That is, the process of recruitment to the guardian class is carried out expertly. It therefore appears plausible to Plato, on both of these counts, to hold that if the guardians are united, then they can keep the city united.

465c–466c: OUR GUARDIANS SEEM INDEED TO BE PROVIDED WITH MANY BENEFITS, EVEN MORE THAN OLYMPIC VICTORS. WHEN ADEIMANTUS SAID EARLIER (419a) THAT WE DID NOT SEEM TO BE MAKING OUR GUARDIANS HAPPY, WE SAID THAT THAT WAS NOT OUR PURPOSE, BUT RATHER TO MAKE THE CITY AS HAPPY AS POSSIBLE. BUT SURELY AN AUXILIARY'S LIFE IS BETTER THAN A COBBLER'S OR ANY OTHER CRAFTS-MAN'S. IF A GUARDIAN ADOPTS SOME FOOLISH IDEA OF HAP-PINESS, OF A SORT THAT MAKES HIM CEASE TO BE A GUARD-IAN, THEN HE WILL REGRET IT.

A.   Plato states his belief that the life of a guardian is happy, and indeed is the best life (466b7). But that it is best is not something that he regards as proved yet, until the full-scale argument in the latter part of Book IX (see 576b–578b, n. A). (That it is at least fairly happy, and happier than the life of a craftsman in his city, he regards as already plain, but the question whether it is the happiest is mentioned in 544d–545c as still not finally settled.)

466c–d: IT IS AGREED, THEN, THAT IF THERE IS A COMMUNITY

BETWEEN MEN AND WOMEN, BOTH IN THE MATTER OF
CHILD-BEARING AND IN THE SHARING OF TASKS, THEN THEY
WILL BE DOING WHAT IS BEST AND WHAT IS IN ACCORDANCE
WITH THE NATURAL RELATIONSHIP BETWEEN THEM.

A. Plato sums up the results of the argument since 449b, when Socrates was confronted with the first two "waves" (see 457a–c, n. A,
457e–458b, n. A). He has argued that it is both best and possible for
women to share in the task of guarding (456c–457a and 456b–c); and
he has argued that it is best that children and spouses be held in common (see 457e–458b).

466d: WE MUST NOW DISCOVER WHETHER THIS KIND OF
COMMUNITY IS POSSIBLE AMONG HUMAN BEINGS.

A. As we saw (457e–458b, n. A), Plato postponed the question whether
his arrangements governing family life were possible, in order to include
it in the investigation of whether his whole system for the city is possible.
This investigation he now takes up. Here we have, then, the beginning
of the third wave, which is pressed on Socrates at this point, but which
he resists confronting until 471c, though he there delays it once again
until he finally responds to it directly at 473c.

466e–467e: MEN AND WOMEN GUARDIANS WILL ALSO HAVE
IN COMMON THE TASK OF WAGING WAR. CHILDREN SHOULD
OBSERVE WARFARE (FROM THE SAFETY OF HORSEBACK) BE-
CAUSE EXPERIENCE AND OBSERVATION ARE AN IMPORTANT
PART OF EDUCATION.

A. Clearly, Plato does not deny the importance of what the guardians
gain from experience, even though he later emphasizes the privileged
status of information gained not by experience but by the use of a largely
independent rational faculty (475e–476d, 476d–480a).

B. Plato's continued delaying of his response to the third wave, by
dealing with issues such as this, serves to highlight the importance of
that response. But he does not make clear what its importance is until
he finally presents it, in 471c and then in 473c (see previous note A).

468a–469b: SOLDIERS WHO EXHIBIT COWARDICE IN BATTLE
WILL BE REDUCED TO FARMERS AND CRAFTSMEN. THOSE

WHO EXCEL IN BRAVERY WILL BE GRANTED HONORS AND
PRIVILEGES AND BE GIVEN DISTINGUISHED BURIALS AT
DEATH.

A. Plato clearly contemplates that there will be imperfections in his
system for producing, selecting, and training guardians (cf. 545c–547c).
As before, we see that the city is not a completely ideal one with a completely ideal population (see 370c–371e, n. B).

469b–471c: CERTAIN STANDARDS SHOULD BE ADHERED TO IN
WARFARE, HAVING TO DO WITH THE TREATMENT OF THE
ENEMY. THE CITY THAT WE ARE FOUNDING IS GREEK, AND IT
WILL TREAT GREEKS AS AKIN TO IT, WHEREAS IT WILL TREAT
BARBARIANS AS STRANGERS AND NATURAL ENEMIES. IT WILL
NOT TAKE GREEKS AS SLAVES, NOR RAVAGE THEIR LANDS,
AND IT WILL TREAT ITS DISPUTES WITH GREEKS AS BEING
LIKE CIVIL DISSENSION. BARBARIANS, ON THE OTHER HAND,
WILL BE TREATED AS GREEKS ARE NOW TREATED BY ONE
ANOTHER.

A. Plato here eschews an obvious opportunity to develop a notion of
justice, and other virtues, which would make them extend beyond the
bounds of a single city, except in a rudimentary way (see 350c–352c).
But he does make a move toward such an extension, by speaking of the
relationship among Greeks in some of the same ways as those that hold
among citizens of the same city. Thus, war between Greek cities is described as "civil dissension" (*stasis*, 470c–d), just as strife within a city
was described (458b–460b, n. A, 464d–465b, n. B). Similarly, Greeks are
described as "akin" and "related" (470c2), just as fellow-citizens in
Plato's city were (414b–415d). So he sees a kind of kinship between
Greek and Greek comparable to the kinship that holds among the citizens of a fully unified city, though in the latter case the unity and the
kinship are both stronger. It is presumably because the degree of unity
is weaker, without the full degree of harmony and coordination that
exists within Plato's city, that Plato thinks that genuine justice cannot
exist within Greece as a whole, let alone the inhabited world as a whole.
[Crombie, *EPD*, p. 89; Vlastos, *JHR*, p. 86, n. 55.]

471c–472b: BUT THE QUESTION IS AGAIN RAISED WHETHER
IT IS POSSIBLE FOR THIS CITY TO EXIST—THIS IS THE *THIRD
WAVE*—THOUGH IT IS AGREED THAT IF IT DID EXIST, THEN

ALL OF THE ARRANGEMENTS THUS FAR DESCRIBED WOULD BE GOOD FOR IT.

A.   The third wave is now brought in again, in earnest. But Socrates is made to delay again and to give a summary of the present state of the argument. The direct response to the third wave does not begin until 473c (see 466d, n. A).

472b–e: BUT OUR ORIGINAL PURPOSE IN DESCRIBING THE CITY WAS NOT TO SHOW THAT SUCH A CITY IS POSSIBLE. RATHER, WE UNDERTOOK OUR DESCRIPTION OF IT, OF THE PERFECTLY JUST MAN, AND OF JUSTICE, FOR THE PURPOSE OF FINDING OUT WHAT JUSTICE IS LIKE, AND FOR THE SAKE OF HAVING MODELS OR PARADIGMS.

A.   Plato makes clear that his chief aims would not be thwarted even if it should not turn out to be possible to establish a city like the one that he has described. On the status of his description, see 472e–473b, n. A.

B.   Plato's language in this section contains terms that he often uses in expounding his epistemological and metaphysical theory of Forms, of which we shall see more in 476ff. and in Books VI–VII. In particular, his use of the term "model" or "paradigm" (*paradeigma*, 472c4, d5, 9) is meant to be suggestive of his view that there are Forms, which are non-sensible, intellectually apprehensible paradigms to which sensible objects only imperfectly approximate (see 475e–476d, n. B). Justice is plainly one of the Forms in whose existence he believes (479a, e). But although his language here is meant to be suggestive of his theory of Forms, it does not follow that all of the things that he discusses in this connection are believed by him to be Forms. In particular, the city that he has described, though it in certain respects plays the role of a Form (472e–473b, n. B, and 591a–592b, n. D), is too clearly bound up in the sensible world to be thought by him to be a Form (see 369b–d, n. B, 370c–371e, n. B, and Introd., sec. 3).

472e–473b: NEVERTHELESS, WE SHALL SUCCEED SUFFI-CIENTLY IN SHOWING THE POSSIBILITY OF THE THINGS THAT WE HAVE DESCRIBED, IF WE SHOW HOW WE MIGHT COME AS CLOSE AS WE CAN TO APPROXIMATING THEM.

A.   What matters, Plato has just said, is not that it be possible to establish a city such as he has portrayed. What matters is that his description present to us what one might call a *coherent goal*, in the sense that we can clearly·understand what it would be for an actual city to approximate it more or less closely, and how we might make a city approximate it more closely than it does, without any specifiable limit on the degree of closeness. For showing this would help show that, as Plato has often claimed, his arrangements are not contrary to nature but in accord with it (see 369e–370c, nn. B–D). For he wishes to maintain that his city is constructed by exploiting certain tendencies that are exhibited by human nature in the sensible world. In particular, he believes that the Principle of the Natural Division of Labor rests on the fact that each human being does in fact have a single natural capacity to perform some one task well (*ibid.*). And he believes further that a community in which each person's natural capacity is made use of will, as he has explained, be as much without dissension as a human institution can be. If it should turn out, however, that there is *no way* of turning a group of human beings, as they are found in the sensible world, into an organization that more closely approximates the city that he has been describing, then serious doubt would be cast on his claim that his city is simply what one gets by exploiting the natural capacities and tendencies already existing in people. Accordingly, he must make plain just how natural human tendencies might manifest themselves in such a way as to make actual communities more like the city that he has described. [Zeller, pp. 915–6; Guthrie, *HGP*, pp. 483–6, 544; Friedländer, p. 140.]

B. By being something to which we can and should make something in the sensible world approximate, Plato's city resembles one of the Forms that he describes in expounding his metaphysical theory (see the previous n. B). But the city is not itself a Form (*ibid.*, and 591a–592b, n. D).

C. Why does Plato say in 473a that practice has a lesser grip on truth than theory (to paraphrase one translation), or, more literally, that action (*praxis*) touches truth less than speech (*lexis*)? The *Republic* contains a number of such *obiter dicta*, dealing with philosophical issues with which Plato is not directly concerned, and which are not fully developed or explained. Here the idea seems to be that a word has a somewhat better chance of putting us unambiguously in mind of a Form or combination of Forms than any sensible action in the sensible world does. Why should this be? Because although sensible objects and actions always exhibit a plurality of attributes, including contrary attributes (see 479a–b), a word is an attempt to pick out only one of these attributes; and when language is properly used it corresponds to one and only one Form rather than to a pair of contrary Forms or a set of distinct Forms (see 472b–e, n. B, and

White, pp. 66–69, 74–75, 137–148). (But this does not entail, nor does Plato here say, that language *is* in fact always used in this way and with this effect.)

473b–474b: THERE IS ONE SMALL CHANGE THAT WOULD BE SUFFICIENT TO LEAD TO THE ESTABLISHMENT OF A CITY LIKE THE ONE THAT WE HAVE DESCRIBED. IT WOULD OCCUR IF PHILOSOPHERS CAME TO RULE, OR IF A RULER BECAME A PHILOSOPHER—I.E., IF POWER IN A CITY AND PHILOSOPHY SHOULD BE COMBINED INTO ONE. BUT THIS NOTION WILL SEEM ABSURD TO MANY.

A.   This is, at last, Plato's response to the third "wave" (see 471c–472b, n. A). The explanation of the response, including an explanation of who he thinks the genuine philosophers are and how they must be educated to rule, takes him until the end of Book VII (see 457a–c, n. A; the discussion of their education begins at 502c–504d, where see n. A).

474b–c: TO DEFEND OURSELVES AGAINST THIS REACTION, WE SHALL NEED TO EXPLAIN WHOM WE MEAN WHEN WE SPEAK OF "PHILOSOPHERS." WE MEAN THOSE WHO ARE BY NATURE SUITED TO PHILOSOPHY AND TO RULING.

A.   Plato does not mean by "philosophers" those who are ordinarily so called. He begins his attempt to say who he does think they are by recurring, characteristically, to the Principle of the Natural Division of Labor and the idea that each person has a natural aptitude for a single task. That the same people are naturally both philosophers and rulers is his contention, which he will try in the ensuing discussion to justify (see 484a–d, nn. and 519d–521b, n. B).

B.   It is important to be aware of the place of this discussion within Plato's whole argument. From this point to the end of Book VII, it is part of an argument that Plato's city is possible in the sense of being a coherent goal (472e–473b, n. A). It is accordingly (see *ibid.*) an effort to show that the capacity to rule and the capacity to philosophize, *as we see them manifested* (though imperfectly, and separated from one another) *in the world as it is,* can be seen to go together in some sense naturally. This means that if you let a natural philosopher pursue his natural bent without interference, then he will tend to become a ruler; and if you let a natural ruler pursue his natural bent without interference, then he will tend to become a philosopher.

C. The notion of a natural bent or capacity is philosophically prob-
lematical. Moreover, we have already seen that it can be difficult to tell
when we have a single capacity and when we have more than one, because it is often difficult to tell when we have a single task and when we
have more than one (452e–456b, n. B). But there is a special difficulty
in the present case. For it turns out that at a certain point, the pursuits
of philosophizing and ruling actually seem to come into conflict (519d–
521b, 536d–540c), and so it becomes questionable whether Plato can
easily maintain that they are really two parts of a single task, and that
the capacities for them are really two parts of a single capacity. He does,
however, continue to maintain this (see 519d–521b, nn. B–E).

474c–475c: TO UNDERSTAND THIS IDEA, WE MUST REMEMBER
THAT SOMEONE WHO IS PROPERLY CALLED A LOVER-OF-*X* IS
NOT SOMEONE WHO LOVES ONLY *X*-OF-A-CERTAIN-SORT, BUT
SOMEONE WHO LOVES ANY AND ALL *X*. THEREFORE A PHIL-
OSOPHER, OR LOVER-OF-WISDOM, IS SOMEONE WHO LOVES
ALL WISDOM AND LEARNING, NOT MERELY WISDOM AND
LEARNING OF A CERTAIN KIND.

A. Plato uses this principle to focus our attention on what the genuine
philosopher is concerned with. The principle was laid down in 437d–
438b (see n. A on 437b–439b) and is here applied to the notion *lover-of.*
(It is because he is appealing to something already laid down that he
uses the word "remember" in 474c–d.) (Plato's view might be disputed,
e.g., by claiming that a true wine-lover not only does not love, but
actually despises, wine of certain sorts. But if we wish to say this, it is
probably because we think that a wine-lover ought to love only wine
that attains a certain standard, and that what he really loves is (at least
fairly) *good* wine. But Plato has already indicated his opposition to this
view (see *ibid.*)

475d–e: GLAUCON OBJECTS TO THIS IDEA, ON THE GROUND
THAT IT WOULD INCLUDE AS PHILOSOPHERS MANY STRANGE
PEOPLE, INCLUDING LOVERS OF SIGHTS AND SOUNDS.

A. Glaucon here makes a somewhat complex mistake, which Socrates
then endeavors to combat. Part of his mistake is to take the term "philosopher" in Plato's sense as including people with various specialized
enthusiasms, such as those who ignore "serious discussions" in order to
attend festivals. The other part of his mistake, which is much more im-

portant from Plato's viewpoint, is to think that the love of wisdom or learning or knowledge involves the love of information and experience of *sensible* matters rather than intelligible ones (see the following sections).

475e–476d: TRUE PHILOSOPHERS, HOWEVER, ARE LOVERS OF TRUTH. WE MUST DISTINGUISH, E.G., JUSTICE AND INJUSTICE FROM EACH OTHER, AND FROM THE VARIOUS BODIES THAT MAY PARTAKE OF THEM. (IT IS BECAUSE OF THIS PARTICIPA- TION IN JUSTICE BY ACTIONS AND BODIES THAT ALTHOUGH JUSTICE IS ONE, IT CAN APPEAR TO BE MANY.) A LOVER OF SIGHTS OR OF SOUNDS IS SOMEONE WHO LOVES THE SENSIBLE INSTANCES OF FORMS SUCH AS THE FORM OF JUSTICE. THE PHILOSOPHER, ON THE OTHER HAND, IS SOMEONE WHO LOVES THE FORMS THEMSELVES. A MAN WHO DOES NOT BE- LIEVE IN THE EXISTENCE OF FORMS IS LIKE SOMEONE WHO IS DREAMING, IN THE SENSE THAT HE MISTAKES ONE THING FOR ANOTHER. BUT A MAN WHO DOES BELIEVE IN THE FORMS AND CAN APPREHEND THEM IS LIKE SOMEONE WHO IS AWAKE, BECAUSE HE CAN SEE THE FORMS AND THE THINGS THAT PARTAKE OF THEM, AND NOT MISTAKE THE ONE FOR THE OTHER. THE LATTER SORT OF MAN HAS KNOWLEDGE, WHEREAS THE FORMER HAS ONLY OPINION OR BELIEF.

A. Plato lays out in summary form a large piece of his theory of knowledge and metaphysics. In the next section he tries to support by argument some of the things that he says in this one. As I have empha- sized in sec. 3 of the Introduction, however, Plato is not aiming here to give a complete exposition of his theory. Instead, he is giving us a more or less general idea of the metaphysical and epistemological support he believes ought to be placed under the political and ethical doctrines which are the main subject-matter of the *Republic*. (We should there- fore be aware that a person accepting major portions of Plato's ethics is not thereby committed to his metaphysics and epistemology.) [Shorey, *WPS*, pp. 226, 234.]

B. His major contention here is that when he says that philosophers should rule in his city, and that their coming to rule could bring it to actuality, he does not intend to speak of philosophers customarily so- called (474b–c). His main line of distinction between genuine philoso- phers and those who are *called* philosophers is expressed by saying that the former have and aim to have "knowledge" (*gnōmē* at 476d5 and *epistēmē* at 477b5), whereas the others only have, and can only aim to have, "belief" or "opinion" (*doxa*). This distinction between the words for "knowledge" and "opinion" is not meant by Plato to reflect in any especially faithful manner the distinction between the Greek words involved (let alone their English translations). It is instead meant to signal a distinction between different cognitive states which Plato thinks are, ordinary usage apart, important to distinguish, and two different kinds of things with which these cognitive states have to do. The things with which "knowledge" has to do are what Plato calls "Forms" or "Ideas" (*eidē* or *ideai*—the term "Form" will be used here exclusively); opinion, on the other hand, has to do with sensible objects.

Plato's view on the proper use of the terms "knowledge" and "opinion" leaves him quite free to endorse experiments and efforts to gather information about sensibles, without, however, treating this information as entirely reliable, or bestowing on it that title "knowledge". See 484a–d, n. D, with 485a–d, 514a–517d, n. C, and 603b–605c, n. F. [Shorey, *WPS*, p. 236; Cross and Woozley, Ch. 8; Crombie, *PMA*, p. 30.]

Plato has a continuing problem in the need to say in a clear and satisfactory manner just what the relationships between sensible objects and Forms are. Normally, he uses the term *metechein* (476d–e), meaning "share" or "partake" or "participate," to express the relation that we might try to express by such terms as "exemplify" or "instantiate" or the like; and he will say that a sensible object or action that is just "shares" or "participates" or "partakes" in the Form of Justice. This term itself is not intended to be fully, or even partially, revelatory of the nature of the relationship: Plato knows that what is in question is not literally a kind of sharing, as we think of the sharing of a pie or even an umbrella. Furthermore, he makes considerable attempts (e.g., in the first part of the *Parmenides*) to explore the problem of what the relationship might be. However, one idea that he finds consistently attractive (at least in the *Republic* and in works written around the same time) is that the relationship can reasonably be expressed, at least by way of approximation, by such terms as "imitate" or "copy," so that a just thing in the sensible world can be said to imitate or copy (be a copy of) the Form of Justice. It is in connection with this idea that it becomes apt for him to use the word "paradigm" to apply to Forms (see 472b–e, n. B) and to think of sensible objects as imperfect approximations of Forms. This manner of looking at the matter plays an important role in various aspects of his thought (see 476d–480a, n. C, fifth point). [Shorey, *WPS*, *passim*; Ross, *passim*; Owen, *PPI*; Vlastos, *DRP*.]

C. Just as Plato has earlier described his city as the only thing strictly deserving the title "city" (or better, *polis*), and its rulers as the only people who strictly deserve the title "guardian" (419a–421c, n. A), so too he is now describing those who strictly deserve the title "philosopher" (476b1–2, 475e3). (Although none of these things is a Form, what I have just said shows them to be analogous to Forms in a manner additional to the manner indicated in 472b–e, n. B, and 472e–473b, n. A. For Plato regards Forms as the strictly proper bearers of the predicates that are respectively associated with them.) [See, e.g., White, pp. 74–75.]

476d–480a: SOCRATES ADVANCES AN ELABORATE ARGUMENT FOR THE CONTENTION THAT THOSE WHO LOVE SIGHTS AND SOUNDS ARE NOT PHILOSOPHERS OR LOVERS OF WISDOM BUT ARE INSTEAD LOVERS OF OPINION. GENUINE PHILOSOPHERS, ON THE OTHER HAND, ARE THOSE WHO LOVE GENUINE KNOWLEDGE, WHICH IS CONCERNED NOT WITH SENSIBLES BUT WITH "BEING," I.E., WITH FORMS.

A. The structure of this argument is complicated, so it will be well to give a summary of it (a less complete one, perforce, than a full treatment of all the issues it poses would involve).

Plato's aim in the argument is to show that Glaucon was wrong in his belief (475d–e) that we would have to count lovers of sights, sounds, and the like, as lovers of wisdom and knowledge. He wishes to show that by virtue of being a lover of sights and sounds one is excluded from being a genuine philosopher (the Greek word *philosophos* means literally "lover of wisdom") and must be a lover of opinion instead (476d5–9, 479e4–8).

The argument has two stages, divided from each other at 478e6. The first part is an attempt to show that knowledge and opinion have to do with different objects, and that because opinion is "between" knowledge and ignorance (*amathia*), and because knowledge has to do with "what is" or "being" while ignorance has to do with "what is not" or "non-being," therefore opinion ought to have to do with something that is "between"—in some sense—"what is" and "what is not." In 478e, Plato says that if we can find something between "what is" and "what is not," then we may conclude that it is what opinion is concerned with. The second part of the argument, running to the end of Book V, is an attempt to show that there is indeed something of this sort, and that it is precisely the sensible things with which the lover of sights, sounds, and the like, is concerned. From the result of the first part of the argument it is inferred that these things must be what opinion, rather than knowledge, has to do with. The conclusion then is that the lover of sights, sounds, and the like, is merely a lover of opinion and not a genuine lover of wisdom or a philosopher. Rather, the philosopher is one who aims to acquire knowledge, not opinion, and so is concerned not with sensibles, which are "between what is and what is not," but with "what is" or "being," namely Forms.

B.   Various points in this argument call for comment. Let us take up a few of them briefly here.

First, Plato takes it to be clear with little argument that knowledge and opinion (*epistēmē* or *gnōsis*, and *doxa*; cf. 475e–476d, n. B) are distinct capacities or "faculties" (*dynameis*), on the ground that the former is infallible and the latter is not (477d–e). By this he means at the minimum, that there is no such thing as knowing mistakenly, whereas there is such a thing as believing mistakenly (477e6–7). He evidently expects agreement that knowledge and opinion are in this way distinct, in advance of any treatment of what objects they respectively have to do with.

At 478c8, it appears at first sight that he is arguing that knowledge and opinion are distinct on quite different grounds, namely, on the ground that knowledge has to do with "what is" whereas opinion does not. But the argument obviously depends on the assumption already made in 477d–e, that knowledge and opinion are distinct because the former is infallible and the latter is not. What makes the line of thought in 478c confusing is that there he is using a quite different sort of argument to show the distinctness of opinion and *ignorance*: that is, he is arguing there that *they* cannot be the same because ignorance has to do with "what is not" (477a4, 478c3), whereas this cannot be what opinion has to do with. Why is his argument in 477d–e for the distinctness of opinion and knowledge of a different type from his argument in 478c for the distinctness of opinion and ignorance? Because his main concern is to *prove* the claim that opinion and knowledge have to do with different objects, so that he does not want to take this claim for granted in his argument for the prior claim that opinion and knowledge are distinct; but he thinks that the distinctness of the objects of opinion and ignorance is plausible initially and so can be used in an argument for the distinctness of opinion and ignorance themselves.

Second, the principle adopted in 477c–d is obviously crucial to Plato's argument that opinion and knowledge are distinct, but the principle appears to be faultily construed so as to allow Plato to draw his conclusion without fully arguing it. Capacities are said to be the same just in case they have to do with (or, are directed to) the same things and have the same effect or result. Plato then argues that because knowledge and opinion do not have the same result (the one being infallible and the other not), they cannot be the same capacity, and he then concludes from this (478a3–b2) that they must have to do with different things. But this is evidently a mistake, because he has given us no reason to rule out the possibility that two capacities might be distinct in virtue of having different effects while nevertheless having to do with the same objects—i.e., in this case the possibility that (if we grant him the rest of his argument) knowledge is infallible and opinion not so, though both have to do with the same things.

Third, it will be noticed that Plato's use of the word "between" asks for some explanation. His argument relies on the contention that because opinion is "between" knowledge and ignorance in respect of "clarity" and "obscurity" (also notions that require explanation), it is therefore reasonable to take opinion to have to do with objects that are "between what is and what is not." But it is not clear that this contention does not trade on an ambiguity in the term "between" as Plato uses it; and even if there is no ambiguity, the contention itself is not clearly true. In fact, pending further explanation of "between," it is not truly clear.

Fourth, the notions of "ignorance" and "what is not" (or "not-being or "non-being") as they appear here are left without explanation. "What is not" here plays the role of an abbreviation for "what in no way is" (477a7) or "what completely is not" (478d7), just as "what is" abbreviates "what purely is" (477a7, 478d6). But it is puzzling what the notion of "what in no way is" can amount to, even granted the further explanation of "what (purely) is" to be given below (n. C). (Some scholars believe that Plato's discussion of "what is not" in the *Sophist* elucidates matters here, or is meant to.)

The incompleteness and compressed quality of Plato's argument makes it appear likely that he regards it as a summary of a more complete argument that it would be possible to give. (Indeed, his remark at 477a2 that more argument would confirm what he says there makes the point evident.)

C. We turn now to a treatment—again a summary treatment—of some matters that are more directly linked to Plato's conception of Forms and the role that they play in the broader argument of the *Republic*. On these matters see further Introd., sec. 3.

First, Plato's main concern here is not to argue for the existence of Forms, and he does so only very indirectly and briefly. In the passage in which he might appear to be giving an argument for their existence, 479a–b, his aim is really to show instead that sensible objects—i.e., what the lovers of sights and sounds are concerned with—are "between what is and what is not," and not to prove that *there is* such a thing as "what is" (i.e., Forms). In effect, therefore, the passage is supposed to show only the *distinctness* of sensibles from "what is," whereas it assumes that *there are* such things as "what is." (This problem raises a host of questions that may be raised about many other passages and dialogues. My own view, however, is as follows: that Plato regarded it as obvious, even a truism of sorts, that knowledge *must* have to do with "what is" (477b10–11, 478a6); that he thought it equally truistic that "what is" must "be"; and that because he did not recognize a distinction between the notion of existence and the notion of "being" which figures in the phrase "what is," the conclusion that "what is" must "be" seemed to him tantamount to the conclusion that "what is" must—as we would put it—exist. This would explain why, here and in other passages, he felt little need for separate, assiduous argumentation for the existence of "what is.")

Second, we must ask how the notion of "what is" is connected with Plato's view, manifest in 479a–b and elsewhere, that there are distinct Forms of the Beautiful, the Just, and so forth. For, as is plain from 479d3–5, b9–10, the phrase "what is" is used by Plato to apply to all Forms collectively. The reason for this usage is clear from 479a–b. Whereas a sensible object may both *be* beautiful and *not be* beautiful, and thus be said both to *be* and *not be* (b9–10), Plato conceives of the Form of the Beautiful as something that *is* beautiful *without* in any way *not being* beautiful. It is because in general the Form of *F is F* without *not being F* in any way that Plato is willing to say that it "purely" *is* (477a3, 7, 478d6).

But, third, what is the contrast between sensible objects that both *are* and *are not F*, and that Form of *F* that purely *is F?* And does it not contradict Plato's earlier claim that an object may not do or suffer contrary things at the same time in the same part of itself in relation to the same object (436b–437a)? The answer to the latter question is that there is no contradiction, because Plato's view is that when, for example, a sensible object both is and is not beautiful, this is so because it is beautiful in certain respects, relations, or aspects, or at certain times, while being not beautiful (i.e., ugly) in certain *other* respects, relations, or aspects, or at other times. A sensible object bears an attribute only, so to speak, *with qualification*, and under another qualification specifying different respects, relations, or whatever, it bears the contrary attribute. A Form, on the other hand, bears its attribute without the need for qualification because it does not also bear the contrary attribute: the Form of *F* is not *F* with qualification or contrary. The Form of the Beautiful is not also, in some manner or other, also ugly or not beautiful; it is "purely" beautiful. And analogously for other Forms.

Fourth, what is Plato's reason for thinking that sensible objects all bear their attributes only with qualification and along with their contraries? The claim is made in 479a–b as though it were fairly obvious, but the passage contains a somewhat puzzling shift of wording. Plato begins by saying that a beautiful sensible object will always also *appear* ugly, and likewise in other cases. But by 479b6–7 he is saying that things that are big will also have "small" applied to them, and then in the next lines maintains that each such thing will also *be* the contrary. In other words, he has gone from saying that each beautiful sensible thing must also *appear* ugly in some respects, to saying that it will also *be* ugly in some respects. What is the justification for this move? The answer, if indeed it can be unambiguously gleaned from what Plato says in this passage (and in 523a–524d, concerned with similar matters), is too long and detached from our main concerns to be expounded here. What is important here, however, is that the move is made, and that Plato holds to the claim that results from making it.

Fifth, while saying that the Form of *F* is unqualifiedly *F* and that sensible objects are both *F* and non-*F* (in different respects, etc.), Plato is also willing to say that sensible *F*s are *imitations* or *approximations* or *copies*, in some sense, of the Form of *F* (see 475e–476d, n. B). Moreover, Plato takes it to be permissible, in accordance with this conception, to allow for *degrees* to which a sensible *F* may approximate or imitate the Form of *F*. This fact is important in places, such as 540a, where he wishes to say that the rulers of his city treat certain Forms, such as the Form of the Good, as *paradigms* after which they try to pattern the city, to make it resemble them as closely as they can. In general, for Plato, the effort to improve something in the sensible world is an effort to make it resemble more closely some Form.

But—sixth—are all Forms things that we would want to make sensible objects resemble? Does not Plato suggest clearly in 479a that there is a Form of the Ugly and a Form of Injustice every bit as much as there is a Form of the Beautiful and a Form of Justice? And do not other passages, such as 523e–524c, suggest equally clearly that Plato believes that Forms come in contrary pairs? If this is so, then are there not some Forms that are "bad," to which we would not want to try to produce close approximations? This too is a difficult and controversial matter, and a complete answer cannot be given here (see Introd., sec. 3). It must suffice to say that the main line of argument in the *Republic* steers clear of the possibility that there might be "bad" Forms. For example, when in Book VII the education of the rulers is surveyed, and it is said that they must come to have knowledge of Forms (531d–534d), there is no warning given that they must be selective in applying such knowledge.

The seventh and final point: the upshot of this passage is that Forms are, so to speak, the objects of knowledge and sensible objects are the objects of opinion or belief. This means that the things about which we can have knowledge are the things that "are," or "beings," in the sense explained above, whereas the things about which we have only opinion or belief are the things that both "are and are not," or are "between being and not being." Why this is a result acceptable to Plato is perhaps not too difficult to see, but it is a complicated matter and the details of it cannot be explored here. [Nettleship, pp. 193–4, 265–6; Owen, PNB, *PPI*; Vlastos, *DRP*; Kahn, p. 579; Bosanquet, pp. 213–4, 281–2; Nehamas, pp. 108–9.]

Summary of the *REPUBLIC*

Book VI

- philosopher-king continued
- Form of the Good "offspring of the sun"
- Divided Line

484a–d: NOW THAT WE KNOW TO SOME EXTENT WHO THE GENUINE PHILOSOPHERS ARE, IT IS CLEAR ENOUGH THAT SUCH PEOPLE SHOULD BE GUARDIANS AND RULERS. FOR THEY HAVE A MODEL TO LOOK TO WHEN ESTABLISHING AND PRESERVING LAWS CONCERNING THE BEAUTIFUL, THE JUST, AND THE GOOD. OUR RULERS MUST THEREFORE BE THOSE WHO KNOW EACH REALITY AND ALSO ARE NOT INFERIOR TO THE OTHERS IN EXPERIENCE OR IN ANY VIRTUE OR EXCELLENCE.

A.   Plato has now explained, in a preliminary manner, who the genuine philosophers are (475e–480a). He must now attempt to prove his claim (473c–474b) that it is they who should rule.

  To do this, he must show that it is philosophers who, strictly, fulfill the function of guardians in his sense. For he has already said that those who rule the city must be those who can best perform the task of guarding and preserving (see 412a–c, nn. A–B). Plato thus continues his reliance, in the construction of his argument, on the Principle of the Natural Division of Labor with which he began it (369e–370c).

B.   The present phase of Plato's argument lasts until 502c, where he says that it has been sufficiently shown that his city is possible and could be brought about by the rule of philosophers (see *ad loc.*). That philosophers should rule is supported by two arguments, one here, and one initiated in 485a–487a (see n. C here). In 487b–497a, Plato tries to meet the objections of those who find it simply too implausible to think of philosophers—even given Plato's explanation of who they are—as rulers. He attempts to meet these objections by showing why in the present state of society the thought should seem so implausible. In 497a, he begins to show why the ability of philosophers to rule would become apparent in a city of the sort that he has described, and he continues in this vein until 502c.

C. Plato's first argument for attributing to philosophers the natural ability to rule is that philosophers will be able to apprehend the paradigms or models after which the city is to be patterned so that it is as good as possible (these paradigms being Forms—see 484d6 with 480a11, 500e–502c, and n. C on 476d–480a). That philosophers will have this ability is argued throughout Books VI–VII, to the conclusion in 531d–534d.

Plato also paves the way here for another argument on the same point, to be begun in 485a–487a. In 484d he says that the guardians must be those who have every excellence or virtue (*aretē*—cf. 427e–428a, n. E). This is something for which he has already argued in 444a–e (see n. B there, and 449a–450c, n. B), on the basis of his theory of the soul. But now he will argue that genuine philosophers, because of the disposition that they will have by virtue of being genuine philosophers, must be precisely those who have all of these virtues; and so he will conclude (487e) that philosophers must be the rulers of the city.

D. It is entirely consistent with Plato's line of thought that he should insist that rulers not only be able to apprehend the Forms, but must also have experience in dealing with the world apprehended by the senses. (Cf. 475e–476d, n. B.) For every one of the excellences or virtues involved in the argument of 485a–487a is a virtue of people living in the sensible world; and we have seen how Plato's city is itself an institution of the sensible world (369b–d, n. B). [Shorey, *Rep.*, II, p. 228, nn. *b*, *d*.]

485a–d: LET US, THEN, SEE HOW MEN CAN HAVE BOTH KNOWLEDGE AND EXPERIENCE. PEOPLE WITH PHILOSOPHICAL NATURES LOVE ALL TRUTH AND HATE UNTRUTH. THEY MUST THEREFORE LOVE EVERYTHING AKIN TO TRUTH, INCLUDING WISDOM.

A. Plato begins his argument—for the proposition that philosophers should rule—with a discussion of the natural disposition or temperament of genuine philosophers (see 485c1, 11, 486a1, b3), as opposed to the developed personality (see the following section, n. A). His aim here is to show that natural disposition will tend toward producing a person who will be suited to rule (cf. 517c–518d, n. A).

He recurs to the principle of 437b–438b and 474c–475c, that one who is in the strict sense a lover of *X* is one who loves *X* of all sorts. He extends the principle, however, to maintain that a lover of *X* will love all things that manifest, and are "akin" to, *X*. So he concludes that lovers of truth will be lovers of wisdom. His idea is evidently to cement the connection between someone's being a philosopher, in the literal sense (*philosophos*—cf. 476d–480a, n. A) of a lover of wisdom, and his being a lover of truth. (But he is not yet claiming that such a person will *be wise*, because he is only here talking about natural temperaments, as noted, not developed traits.)

(When Plato says in 485b that a philosopher will not "accept" (*pros-dechesthai*) untruth, he means that he will not wish to allow *himself* to believe untruth. There is no conflict here with the belief that rulers must sometimes tell falsehoods to the ruled (see n. B on 376e–379b). But the contention here that the lover of truth will love everything "akin" to truth does raise the question of such a conflict.)

B.   At 485b Plato contrasts Forms and sensible objects by saying that the former "are forever" or "always are" whereas the latter "wander in generation and decay." This is a seemingly somewhat different manner of expressing the contrast from the one employed in 479–480, which did not (except very tangentially at 479e7–8) involve any explicit discussion of change or stability or related notions.

It is not, however, very difficult to see how Plato connects the contrast between Forms as stable and sensibles as changeable, and the contrast between Forms as bearers of attributes without qualification and sensibles as bearers of attributes only with qualification (see 476d–480a, n. C, and 585a–e, nn. B–D). The idea is that sensible *F*s are not permanently and invariably *F*, but only *F* at certain times but not at others; only the Form of *F* is *F* no matter what time you may choose. Thus, the Form of *F* is *F* without *temporal* qualification, whereas the sensible *F* objects are *F* only with such qualification. (This view naturally raises questions about how Plato regards statements about objects that no longer exist, but he never explores this matter. My own view (476d–480a, n. C, first point) is that he did not because he did not employ the notion of existence as we do, and so was not confronted with questions about "objects that no longer exist." But he nevertheless held the view that any sensible object that is *F* will stop being *F* at some time, without, however, asking how one is to treat those cases in which *we* would say that the object no longer existed once it stopped being *F*.)

485d–487a: ONE WHOSE DESIRE IS DIRECTED TOWARD TRUTH MUST BE LESS AFFECTED THAN OTHERS BY BODILY DESIRES. SUCH A MAN WILL THEREFORE BE MODERATE. MOREOVER, ONE WHO CONTEMPLATES ALL BEING WILL NOT THINK THAT HUMAN LIFE IS OF GREAT IMPORTANCE AND WILL THERE-FORE NOT BE COWARDLY OR FEARFUL OF DEATH. NOR WILL HE HAVE ANY MOTIVATION THAT PREVENTS HIM FROM BEING JUST. HE WILL ALSO BE QUICK TO LEARN AND HAVE A GOOD MEMORY. AND HE WILL BE GENEROUS AND GRACIOUS.

A. Plato tries to make good on his promise to show that the philosopher will have every excellence or virtue (484d), by arguing that the person with a philosophical nature will by nature tend to be moderate, brave, and just. So far, he is merely treating natural dispositions (485c, 486a; cf. 494a–b) rather than developed traits, and saying that the person with a philosophical nature is one who is by nature disposed to have the virtues argued in 444a–e to be possessed by those with the personali-ties of rulers. What he must now do, as he indicates in 487a, is to show that when a naturally philosophical person is *educated* in a way appro-priate to developing his *philosophical* capacity, he will turn out to be precisely the sort of person who was described in Books II–IV (especially 410a–414b), namely, the person who is by nature and education the appropriate ruler of the city, and thus the person who can best perform the task of a guardian in the strict sense. The description of the philo-sophical education, i.e., the education designed to develop natural phil-osophical capacity, begins at 502c.

487b–489c: ADEIMANTUS OBJECTS THAT SOCRATES' INTER-LOCUTORS FEEL TRAPPED IN A POSITION THAT SEEMS TO THEM PARADOXICAL, IN BEING APPARENTLY FORCED TO AD-MIT ON THE BASIS OF THE FOREGOING ARGUMENT THAT PHILOSOPHERS SHOULD RULE. FOR IT SEEMS, AS MOST PEOPLE THINK, THAT THOSE WHO STUDY PHILOSOPHY A GREAT DEAL ARE EITHER BAD OR USELESS. SOCRATES AGREES THAT THERE IS A CERTAIN TRUTH IN THE CHARGE OF USELESSNESS, BUT SAYS THAT THIS SITUATION ARISES FROM THE FACT THAT TRUE PHILOSOPHERS ARE NOT RECOGNIZED BY MOST PEOPLE

AND SO ARE THOUGHT USELESS. HE PRESENTS THE SIMILE OF THE SHIP, TO SUGGEST THAT THE PHILOSOPHER IS LIKE THE MAN WHO IS THOUGHT USELESS BECAUSE HE KNOWS THAT ONE MUST LOOK AT THE STARS TO NAVIGATE WELL. HIS USE-LESSNESS IS TO BE BLAMED NOT ON HIM BUT ON THOSE WHO DO NOT MAKE USE OF HIM. MOREOVER, THE PHILOSOPHER IS NOT ONE TO BEG OTHERS TO ALLOW THEMSELVES TO BE RULED BY HIM.

A.   Adeimantus objects to the idea that philosophers should rule, in ef-fect continuing the third wave and rejecting Plato's response to it so far. (The third wave—473b–474b, n. A—was that Plato's city. could not be established; Plato's response was that it could be if philosophers came to rule.) The popular and plausible view, Adeimantus says, is that philos-ophers are either bad or else useless. Plato responds to the former claim in the next section, to the latter one here.

B.   In 489b–c Plato introduces without fanfare or explanation the idea that true philosophers will not naturally be inclined to beg to be allowed to rule. This seemingly unimportant statement (which within the simile reinforces the picture of the navigator as aloof from the foolishness of his companions) looks forward to Plato's very important contention, at 519d–521b (see nn. B, D there), that in order to fulfill the function of rulers properly, a person must have something more desirable to do than rule and must not in fact wish to rule. What Plato is saying here is that the tendency to adopt this attitude is part of the philosopher's natural temperament.

489d–491a: WE MUST NOW RESPOND TO THE OTHER CHARGE, THE CHARGE THAT PHILOSOPHERS ARE BAD MEN, BY SHOW-ING THAT PHILOSOPHY IS NOT RESPONSIBLE FOR IT. WHEN ONE LOVES AND ASSOCIATES WITH TRUTH, ONE WILL BE OF GOOD CHARACTER. WE MUST, HOWEVER, SHOW WHAT IT IS THAT RENDERS WICKED THOSE WHO TAKE UP PHILOSOPHY BUT ARE THEN CORRUPTED; AND WE MUST ALSO EXAMINE THOSE NATURES THAT IMITATE THE PHILOSOPHICAL NATURE.

A.   This section announces the discussion that will be carried out in 491b–496a. Plato is continuing with his treatment of the naturally phil-osophical temperament by showing how things can go wrong in the present state of society and its educational system. He begins in 496b to show how things may go right, so that the temperament is properly developed (see 484a–d, n. B).

B. When Plato says (490b–c) that someone who loves truth and associates with it will have a good character, he is of course relying on the point made in 485d–487a, according to which someone with a natural capacity for philosophy will tend to have all of the virtues or excellences. The present passages merely state the same point, by suggesting that when the capacity is developed, a person of good character will result. (The kind of capacity involved here is not a mere disposition in the sense in which some modern philosophers employ that term, but a kind of "tendency," which may or may not be developed—for Plato the presence of the correct type of upbringing is crucial—but is still regarded as, so to speak, pushing toward a certain result.)

491b–494a: A PHILOSOPHICAL NATURE IS CORRUPTED PRIMARILY BY THE INFLUENCE OF THE MULTITUDE, WHO FORCES ITS VIEWS AND PREFERENCES ON IT BY CENSURE AND PUNISHMENT AND PRAISE. BY CONTRAST TO THE EFFECT OF THE MULTITUDE ON SUCH A PERSON, THE INFLUENCE OF PRIVATE TRAINING BY SOPHISTS IS SMALL. SOPHISTS MERELY TRAIN ONE TO CATER TO THE MULTITUDE, WHICH IS TO BE COMPARED TO A GREAT BEAST. THE MULTITUDE CAN NEVER BELIEVE IN THE TRUE BEINGS, I.E., THE FORMS, OR BE PHILOSOPHICAL, AND THOSE WHO FOLLOW IT SIMPLY TREAT WHAT IT PREFERS AND DEMANDS AS GOOD AND BEAUTIFUL AND JUST.

A. The influence of the multitude takes most of the blame for the corruption of philosophical natures. Plato maintains that whatever bad influence sophists (494a–496a, n. A) may have is subordinate to the bad influence of the multitude, and indeed arises out of it, in the sense that the sophists could not exercise their influence if it were not for the bad judgment of the multitude.

B. The chief mistake of the multitude, through which philosophical natures are corrupted, is a mistake about what the good is. The potential philosopher is misled into following the multitude in its view of the good, and in expending his energies in an attempt to please it. Once more Plato shows his conviction that correct standards for action are independent of what most people happen to think (cf. 362d–368c, n. C, concerned with justice; here the same point is seen to apply to the good).

The present passage looks forward to 504d–506a, where Plato begins his own discussion of the good and its role in the education of the rulers. [Ritter, *EPP*, pp. 82–3; Shorey, *UPT*, pp. 29–30.]

C. Plato's contention that the multitude *cannot* be philosophical (494a) —and that it is not merely because of the defects of the present educational system that they are not so—reinforces his earlier claim (428e– 429a) that only a few people are naturally suited to be rulers.

494a–496a: AN INTELLIGENT, ABLE, AND PHILOSOPHICAL PERSON WILL BE THE OBJECT OF SPECIAL ATTEMPTS BY OTHERS TO INFLUENCE HIM AWAY FROM PHILOSOPHY FOR THEIR OWN PURPOSES. THUS HIS PHILOSOPHICAL NATURE IS ITSELF, IN A WAY, THE CAUSE OF HIS FALLING AWAY FROM PHILOSOPHY. THIS FALLING AWAY LEAVES ROOM FOR UN-WORTHY AND PETTY MEN TO MOVE IN AND CLAIM TO BE PHILOSOPHERS. THESE PEOPLE ARE MOST PROPERLY CALLED SOPHISTS, WITHOUT GENUINE WISDOM.

A. People who typically call themselves philosophers, Plato says, are more properly called sophists (Plato uses this—in his mouth—often disparaging term which was frequently applied to such teachers as Protagoras and Gorgias, who had been active in the time of Socrates, and to their successors). The genuine philosopher, as noted (485a), is one who loves the truth and is not concerned to follow mistaken views for gain (cf. on 519d–521b, n. E).

B. Plato intends some paradox in the idea that being a philosopher by nature can be the cause of turning away from philosophy, this idea being at variance with his normal way of viewing causation (cf. n. B on 379b–380c).

496a–497a: THERE REMAINS ONLY A SMALL GROUP WHO ARE SUITED FOR PHILOSOPHY AND GENUINELY ENGAGE IN IT. IN THE PRESENT STATE OF THINGS THIS IS THE RESULT OF SOME HAPPY ACCIDENT OR OTHER, WHICH ENABLES A MAN TO TAKE REFUGE FROM THE AFFAIRS OF HIS CITY, MIND HIS OWN BUS-INESS, AND OCCUPY HIMSELF WITH PHILOSOPHY.

A. In cities as they actually are, Plato believes, philosophers are unable to exercise a part of their natural role, namely, the part that consists in ruling. They must therefore retire and exercise the other part of their role, the part consisting in the search for wisdom. Plato will later compare this sort of life with the life of the philosophic man who is actually a ruler in his city (519d–521b). At that point, it will become important to understand which sort of life Plato thinks is better or happier. Notice now, however, that although Plato says that existing cities are not congenial to or suitable for the philosopher (497a with 497b), and that in a suitable city—Plato's city—he would attain his full stature (to use Shorey's translation of *auxēsetai*, 497a4) and would show that his nature is truly godlike (497c), Plato does not say that the philosopher would there be happier or better off. In fact, it will turn out that Plato thinks the philosophic man is making a sacrifice of his welfare by ruling rather than merely philosophizing (see 519d–521b, n. E).

497a–499a: NO TYPE OF CITY OR CONSTITUTION IS CONGENIAL TO A PHILOSOPHICAL NATURE, EXCEPT THE CITY THAT WE HAVE DESCRIBED, WHICH, AS WE HAVE SAID (484c–d), NEEDS TO CONTAIN SOME PEOPLE WHO UNDERSTAND THE PRINCIPLE ON WHICH IT IS BASED. BUT ONE CANNOT EASILY SAY HOW IT IS POSSIBLE FOR A CITY TO ENCOURAGE PHILOSOPHY AND NOT DESTROY IT. THERE MUST BE A CORRECT ASSESSMENT OF THE AGES AT WHICH PHILOSOPHY SHOULD BE STUDIED AND PURSUED. AND THERE MUST BE ENCOURAGEMENT OF THE DISPOSITION TO SEEK TRUTH FOR THE SAKE OF KNOWING IT, AND NOT TO BE SIMPLY DISPUTATIOUS.

A.   Plato maintains that his city is the only one that is congenial to the development of philosophical natures (cf. previous note). This contention rests on the proposition, which he is in the process of defending, that his city will be ruled by philosopher-rulers, and that the establishment of a city ruled in this way is indeed possible. (Recall that we are still in the midst of Socrates' reply to Adeimantus' objection in 487b–489c and to the general claim that it is implausible that philosophers should rule, which constituted the third wave; cf. 484a–d, n. B.)

B.   At 497c–d Plato says that someone in the city must understand the rational principle (*logos*) on which the city is being constructed. He thus harks back to his statement in 484c–d that the rulers must have clear models to consult when ordering the affairs of the city (see n. C there). But he also indicates that this principle is the one that is now being employed in the description of the city, involving preeminently the Principle of the Natural Division of Labor and the unifying, ordering, and stabilizing effect that it has on the city.

499a–500b: NO PERFECT MAN OR CITY WILL ARISE UNTIL EI-THER TRUE PHILOSOPHERS ARE COMPELLED TO TAKE CHARGE OF AND RULE A CITY, AND THE CITY IS COMPELLED TO OBEY THEM, OR ELSE THE RULERS OF A CITY BECOME TRUE PHIL-OSOPHERS. WHETHER OR NOT THIS HAS EVER HAPPENED OR IS HAPPENING OR WILL EVER HAPPEN, WE MUST MAINTAIN THAT IF IT DID HAPPEN, AND ONLY IF IT DID HAPPEN, WOULD THE CITY THAT WE ARE DESCRIBING ARISE. SO WE HAVE NOT BEEN DESCRIBING AN IMPOSSIBILITY. HOSTILITY TO PHILOS-OPHERS, AND THE INITIAL IMPLAUSIBILITY OF THE IDEA THAT THEY SHOULD RULE, HAS BEEN BROUGHT ABOUT BY IM-POSTERS.

A. Plato reiterates the connection between the present discussion and the third "wave" (473b–474b, n. A), his response to that objection being that there *is* something that *would* lead to the establishment of his city, namely, the rule of philosophers, and that the apparent paradoxicality of this response is due simply to explicable misapprehensions about the true nature of philosophy.

B. This passage contains a seeming conflict of some interest, between the statement in 499d–500b that most people can be persuaded that rule by philosophers is a good idea, and the statement in 499b that if philosophers come to rule a city, the rest of the city must be "compelled" to obey them (on the idea that philosophers must also be "compelled" to rule the city, see 519d–521b, n. E, 540a–b). The nature of the compul-sion is unclear (the idea is that of being in some sense "compelled by chance," but that too is unclear), so the degree and nature of the con-flict here is uncertain.

This is not the only point at which Plato leaves us uncertain of the extent to which the ruled in a city will willingly acquiesce in being ruled as he prescribes (cf. 430c–432a, n. A, 590c–591a, nn. C–D). Evi-dently, he believes that some degree of force will have to be exerted on them (see *ibid.*). On the other hand, the present passage shows that he cannot regard the resistance of people to rule by philosophers as over-whelmingly strong. For to the extent that he did, it would be correspond-ingly more difficult for him to say that there really was a way of estab-lishing the city in the first place. So it is not an insignificant part of his response to the third wave to take a conciliatory attitude toward the multitude at this particular point, and to hold that their hostility toward philosopher-rulers is not wholly ineradicable. [Shorey, *Rep.*, II. p. 66.]

500b–e: A GENUINE PHILOSOPHER, WHO APPREHENDS AND CONTEMPLATES THE RATIONAL ORDER OF THE FORMS, WILL ATTEMPT TO ORDER HIMSELF AND ALSO TO MAKE THE CITY ORDERLY, AND SO TO MAKE IT MODERATE, JUST, AND IN GENERAL EXCELLENT. GIVEN THIS EXPLANATION, THE MANY WILL ACCORDINGLY NOT DISTRUST THE CLAIM THAT A CITY CAN NEVER BE HAPPY UNLESS PHILOSOPHERS RULE.

A. The reconciliation of the multitude to rule by philosophers is said to be possible when the multitude sees that philosopher-rulers will institute order in the city, and therefore the sort of moderation and justice that are ordinarily regarded as excellences or virtues (*dēmotikē aretē*, d8). This, Plato says (d–e), will convince the multitude that rule by philosophers is necessary for their happiness (*eudaimonēseie*, e2).

Plato is obviously concerned here to show that the multitude in the city need not fear that the rulers will behave in an openly bandit-like way. That this is so he believes he has shown, by showing that the rulers will have the four main virtues or excellences, and therefore will accordingly not have the motive to perform what would customarily be regarded as crimes against the rest of the populace (444a–e, n. B, 442d–443b, nn. B–D, 485d–487a, n. A). No doubt this assurance can plausibly be thought to quiet certain fears which the multitude might have. But, of course, it does not follow that it would remove *all* of their motivation to dislike, or even to resist, the system of rule that Plato recommends (cf. 430c–432a, n. A).

B. Plato's explanation of the multitude's acquiescence requires some understanding, but far less than a perfect understanding, on their part of the system of governing the city. They are portrayed as seeing that it is carried out with moderation and justice in something like a conventional sense. But they apparently do not understand the workings of the system which produce this effect. If they did, of course, then they would have the requisite intelligence to be rulers, which Plato believes they could not have. See further 590c–591a, nn. C–D.

C. As he does so often, Plato emphasizes the connection between the excellence and happiness of the city on the one hand, and its orderliness on the other (422e–423d, n. B, and 427e–428a, n. B).

D.   In 500c it is said that a person observing the orderliness of the Forms will wish to make both himself and the city orderly in a like manner. This statement reveals an important aspect of Plato's views about the motives of his rulers, and indeed of anyone who is able to apprehend the Forms. The desire to imitate Forms, both in conducting oneself and in acting on other things, is not presented as derivative from some other desire, but seems to be regarded by Plato as itself basic (cf. Introd., sec. 4, and 519d–521b, n. E). This fact will have important consequences when he fills in his account of the behavior and state of mind of the philosopher-rulers (see 519d–521b, n. E).

E.   When Plato says at 500c4–5 that the Forms manifest a rational order, he does not attempt to make clear whether they do so singly or as a group. That they should be *dis*orderly as a group seems ruled out, but whether their orderliness as a group should be what Plato has primarily in mind is not made evident. I am inclined to think that it is, but even if it is, we must equally notice that he does not see any need to explore the matter here.

500e–502c: SUCH PHILOSOPHER-RULERS WOULD INSIST ON STARTING WITH PEOPLE WHO ARE LIKE CLEAN SLATES, AND MODELING THEIR CITIZENS AFTER JUSTICE, MODERATION, BEAUTY, AND SO FORTH. THIS FACT WILL HELP FURTHER TO CONVINCE THOSE WHO HAVE DOUBTED THE POSSIBILITY OF OUR CITY. WE EARLIER SHOWED THAT IF SUCH A CITY IS POS-SIBLE, THEN IT IS BEST. NOW WE CAN SEE THAT IT IS NOT IMPOSSIBLE.

A.   This section marks the end of the main part of Plato's answer to the third wave, which began in 473, with preludes in 466d and 471c–472b (see 457a–c, n. A). In fact, however, the passage extending from here to the end of Book VII is in an important way a part of the response to the third wave too, because it is designed to make clearer who the phi-losophers are to whom Plato entrusts his city (see 449a–450c, n. A).
   The goodness of the city has already been asserted, especially at 427e–428a (see n. B there, and 500b–e, n. C).

B.   The idea that the rulers would start with clean slates is pursued a bit further at 540d–541b (see n. B there).

502c–504d: LET US DECLARE, THEN, THAT THE RULERS OF OUR CITY MUST BE PHILOSOPHERS. WE HAVE SEEN HOW THE RULERS ARE TO BE TESTED AND SELECTED FROM CHILDHOOD ON, AND THAT THEY MUST COMBINE A DEGREE OF QUICKNESS WITH A DEGREE OF STABILITY IN ORDER TO BE WELL EDUCABLE. WE MUST NOW SEE HOW THE RULERS MUST BE TESTED AND EXERCISED IN MANY KINDS OF STUDIES. THUS, THEY MUST TAKE THE LONGER WAY, OF WHICH WE SPOKE EARLIER (435d).

A. Plato now begins to explain how the education designed to develop a philosophical temperament should be added to the education already laid down for guardians from 376 to the end of Book III. As just observed, this explanation contributes to his attempt to show that the system of rule that he advocates is possible.

B. In 503b–d, Plato says that the system of education must select those who combine quick-wittedness with stability of mind. This need for a blending of opposed tendencies recalls the expression of a similar need for blending in 410a–412a, where future rulers had to combine spirited and philosophical tendencies, and reminds us that the construction of the city requires working with material that is in certain ways recalcitrant (see 369b–d, n. B).

C. When Plato says in 504b that the rulers must travel the longer route which was mentioned in 435d, he does not mean that he himself is traveling this way in the *Republic*, or even that he knows exactly what its course is. He explains (in 504a) that he means the rulers must thoroughly know the principles on the basis of which one might tell with certainty whether or not the soul is tripartite, which was earlier argued for in what he said was a merely provisional way (see 435c–436b, n. C). All of the arguments that the rulers ultimately learn, by contrast, will be entirely polished and satisfactory. In the following pages he goes on to explain that this means that their knowledge will somehow be based on knowledge of the Form of the Good. But he himself gives us only a rough idea about the nature of this proceeding. [Shorey, *Rep.*, I, p. 378, n. *b*.]

504d–506a: THE MOST IMPORTANT STUDY, AND THE ONE THAT THE RULERS MUST ENGAGE IN, HAS TO DO WITH THE FORM OF THE GOOD. IT IS ONLY BY THEIR RELATION TO THE

GOOD THAT OTHER THINGS BECOME USEFUL OR BENEFICIAL OR GOOD. AND IT IS ONLY BY KNOWING THE GOOD THAT ONE CAN GAIN ANYTHING FROM KNOWLEDGE OF OTHER THINGS. IT IS VERY DIFFICULT TO KNOW WHAT THE GOOD IS. SOME THINK THAT IT IS PLEASURE; OTHERS THINK THAT IT IS KNOWLEDGE; BUT NEITHER OF THESE VIEWS IS TRUE. EVERY SOUL PURSUES THE GOOD, NEVER SATISFIED WITH WHAT MERELY SEEMS GOOD, BUT ONLY WITH WHAT REALLY IS GOOD. BUT WITHOUT KNOWLEDGE OF THE GOOD ONE MISSES THE BENEFIT OF OTHER THINGS. THEREFORE, OUR GUARDIANS MUST KNOW THE GOOD IF OUR CITY IS TO BE PERFECTLY ESTABLISHED.

A.   Socrates is made to say in 506c2–3 that he does not know what the Good is, and there is no reason to suppose that Plato thought that he himself had a fully worked-out answer either. But one of the things that he does seem fairly certain of is that it is because of their relationship to the Good that other things are useful or beneficial or good. This view is of a piece with his general view that when an object can be said to be *F*, it is by virtue of a relation between it and the Form of *F* (see 475e–476d, n. B). This relation, "participation," usually seems to hold between sensible objects and Forms, but it can perhaps also hold between Forms too, e.g., between a Form and the Form of the Good (whether it can raises problems too involved to be treated here).

Another claim that he feels free to make here is that if we do not have knowledge of the Good, we can get no benefit from our knowledge of other things (505a–b). His point appears to be that without knowing what the Good is no benefit can be *guaranteed* or *secure*, and what he is interested in about the guardians' education is that they be capable of reaching and carrying out *stable* and *reliable* policies for the good of the city. His point, then, is the straightforward one that if you do not know what the good is, then you will be unable to plan effectively for the attainment of the good (cf. 603b–605c, n. B).

B.   Plato also maintains that every soul pursues the Good, and that whereas people are often satisfied with what merely seems beautiful or just (as Glaucon and Adeimantus in Book II, esp. 362d–368c, suggested that we should be satisfied with the mere appearance of justice), no one wishes what merely *seems* to be good but insists on trying to gain what really *is* good.

The idea behind this contention involves fundamental difficulties, but clearly Plato's view is that there is a distinction, which he claims we all recognize, between something's *seeming* to be good and its actually *being* good. What this means, at the least, is that what is good is not to be identified with what a person happens to want at a particular time, for it is certainly doubtful that we would all recognize a distinction between what we really want at a particular time and what we seem to want at that time. This is not to explain fully what the distinction between the actually good and the seeming good amounts to. But somewhat fuller explanation comes when Plato says that people often mistakenly hold that the good is pleasure or that it is knowledge. Evidently it is possible, in his view, for someone to have the resolute policy of pursuing pleasure, or pursuing knowledge, even though it is mistaken, on his part or anyone else's, to say that either of these things is *the* good. Plato is therefore clearly not a "relativist" about the good, in the sense that one might be a relativist about the good if one said that if a person steadfastly adopts the pursuit of pleasure or knowledge as his aim in life, then *for him* pleasure or knowledge must be the good. Plato accordingly believes that there is a fairly strong sort of *objectivity*, so to speak, about what is good, and that it is the task of the rulers to know what the objective facts about the good are (see further 519d–521b, n. E, Introd., sec. 3).

The identification of the good with either pleasure or knowledge is opposed in 505b–d by arguments that are only incompletely spelled out but which plainly anticipate, at least in certain respects, arguments on this matter later aired in the *Philebus*. Because the *Philebus* is quite clearly a later work than the *Republic*, it is reasonable to view it as, at least in part, carrying further the thoughts that Plato has here (whether or not there has been a change of view in Plato's mind between the two works). A certain kind of objectivity of goodness is also advanced by Plato in the *Theaetetus*, in 171–179 and 184–186.

C. It can hardly escape the notice of the student of modern ethics that Plato carries out this discussion of the good, like all of the rest of his discussions of the good in the *Republic*, without any recognition of certain differences among senses of the word "good" which modern philosophers have taken as paramount. For example, he draws no distinction comparable to the modern one between what is good and what is *morally* good, or between (some would say that this is much the same distinction) what is good or beneficial *to* or *for* a given person and what is good absolutely, i.e., not relatively to any given person, or (plainly a different distinction) between what is good in the sense of being *perfect* and what is good either in the sense of being beneficial to some person, or in some other sense. Moreover, we notice that Plato is capable of what appears to us a deliberate blurring of some of these distinctions, as in 505a when the notions of "good" and "benefit" appear without distinction and without a hint that only one sense of "good" corresponds to that of "benefit."

A natural reaction at this point is to say that Plato simply has not noticed these distinctions, and to proceed, rather uncomfortably, to try to extricate him from the apparent mistakes that this inadvertence seems to cause. On this showing, his ethical theory will seem rather primitive and clumsy.

There is a wiser reaction, which is both truer to the texts and more revelatory of philosophical views alternative to modern views. It is to take Plato's failure to make distinctions here, not perhaps as thoroughly considered and deliberate (it *is* true that the distinctions had not yet been drawn by philosophers, though *some* of them were drawn not long afterward by Aristotle), but as nevertheless part of a well-worked-out doctrine, which simply *did not allow* room for such differences among notions of goodness, and which strongly tended to say that the word "good" *ought* to be viewed as having a single meaning. This is the line of interpretation that seems to me wisest, and it will be pursued below (see 519d–521b, n. E, with Introd., secs. 3–4).

506b–507a: BUT WHAT IS THE GOOD? SOCRATES DISCLAIMS THE ABILITY TO ANSWER THIS QUESTION AND INSISTS ON AVOIDING THE STATING OF OPINIONS WITHOUT HAVING KNOWLEDGE. INSTEAD OF DISCUSSING THE GOOD HE OFFERS TO DISCUSS AN "OFFSPRING" OF THE GOOD WHICH IS LIKE IT, NAMELY, THE SUN.

A.   Plato does not suggest that there is no answer to the question what the good is, or that the good is somehow ineffable (although this idea has been adopted by some as an interpretation of 509b), but only that he is not certain what the good is. Cf. 531d–534d, n. C.

B.   The foregoing and following pages exhibit a certain vacillation between lower-case "good" and upper-case "Good". The latter is used when the connection with the Form of the Good, in the sense of Plato's theory of Forms, is strong; the former is used where ideas arising out of Plato's theory of Forms are far in the background or irrelevant.

507a–509c: *THE SIMILE OF THE SUN.* WE MUST RECALL (cf. 476d–480a) THE DISTINCTION BETWEEN GOOD THINGS AND

THE GOOD, AND BETWEEN BEAUTIFUL THINGS AND THE BEAUTIFUL, AND SO FORTH. THE FORMER ARE OBJECTS OF SIGHT AND THE LATTER ARE THE OBJECTS OF THOUGHT. LIGHT IS ESSENTIAL TO THE OPERATION OF SIGHT, AND IS PROVIDED BY THE SUN, WHICH IS THE OFFSPRING OF THE GOOD AND IS ALSO ANALOGOUS TO IT. JUST AS THE SUN IS NECESSARY FOR VISIBLE OBJECTS TO HAVE COLOR AND FOR EYES TO SEE, SO THE FORM OF THE GOOD IS REQUIRED FOR INTELLIGIBLE REALITIES TO HAVE TRUTH AND FOR THE KNOWER TO HAVE KNOWLEDGE. FURTHERMORE, JUST AS THE SUN IS THE CAUSE OF THE GENERATION OF THE THINGS THAT IT MAKES VISIBLE, SO TOO THE GOOD IS THE CAUSE OF THE BEING OF THE THINGS THAT IT MAKES KNOWABLE; AND JUST AS THE SUN IS NOT SUBJECT TO GENERATION, SO TOO THE GOOD, THOUGH IT IS THE CAUSE OF BEING TO OTHER THINGS, IS ITSELF BEYOND BEING. AND JUST AS THE SUN IS VISIBLE, THE GOOD IS KNOWABLE.

A. This suggestive passage, as Plato acknowledges in 509c, leaves out a great deal that might help to make its meaning clearer. It is a sketch rather than a complete picture of the role and importance of the Good. It is supplemented by the Simile of the Divided Line in 509d–511e and the Simile of the Cave in 514a–517c.

The purpose of the simile is to help us understand Plato's notion of the Form of the Good by means of the analogy between it and the sun. The main points of the analogy are four. First, the Good is said to be responsible for the possession of "truth" by things that are known, i.e., Forms (507b and 476d–480a, nn. A–B), and for our knowledge of them, just as the sun (Plato believes) is responsible for the colors possessed by sensible objects and our ability to see them (508d–e). Second, the Good is said to be the cause of the being of intelligible objects, just as the sun is the cause of the generation and growth of visible objects (509b). Third, the Good is said to be "beyond being in dignity and power," as the sun is not a process of generation (509b—see n. D). Fourth, just as the sun is visible, so too the Good can be known (508b–c). Let us take each of these points in turn. [Cross and Woozley, Chs. 9–10; Robinson, *PED*, Ch. X.]

B. Why is the Good the cause of knowledge and of "truth as known" (so I understand 508e3–4, with Shorey)? The usual and correct response is to say that to have knowledge of a thing, as Plato thinks, is to know that it bears a certain relation to the Good. The question is what this relation might be, and why the knowledge of it should be thought necessary for knowledge of the things that it relates. For the purposes of his overall argument in the *Republic*, Plato has no need to answer this question in any detail (nor does he spell out a clear answer elsewhere), so our own response must perforce be somewhat conjectural. I present an interpretation that seems to me the most plausible, without, however, attempting to explore or argue for it. Some further discussion can be found in sec. 3 of the Introduction.

The first part of the interpretation is this: the knowledge of every other Form involves the knowledge of the Good, because in general the Form of *F* is unqualifiedly *F* (see 476d–480a, n. C), and in that sense is *F* fully and without defect. From this Plato concludes that the Form of *F* is in a certain sense a *good F* (see Hare, pp. 35–6). We might say that the word "good" here is being used for the notion of something's being perfect, or, in a certain sense, good of its kind; but as we have seen, Plato does not wish to draw distinctions among various different senses of "good" (504d–506a, n. C, with 519d–521b, n. E, and Introd., secs. 3–4). In any case, to understand what each Form is, one would have to understand the notion of Goodness, because one would have to understand what it is for the Form to be a good *F* in this sense.

I call the foregoing the first part of the interpretation because it can be combined with another idea, which is that Plato is also here exploiting a kind of teleological conception of the Good. If we restrict ourselves to the *Republic*, then we find this view arising out of 601b–602c, where Plato maintains that the only person to have knowledge of a thing is the person who uses it, on the ground that the virtue or excellence (*aretē*) of a tool or an animal or an action aims at its use (*chreia*), which is explained as the use for which it is made or arises by nature (601d). This idea, of course, recalls the emphasis that Plato has placed on the notion of the task for which a thing is naturally suited (369e–370c) and the notion of the function or *ergon* of a thing (352d–354a, n. A, 369e–370c, n. F, 374e–376c, n. A, 422e–423d, n. A). According to this idea, an *F* would be a good *F* insofar as it serves the use or function of an *F*. To combine this idea with the foregoing would be to say that fully to serve the function of an *F* is to be an *F* non-defectively, i.e., unqualifiedly in the sense already explained (476d–480a, n. C). The connection of a thing with its use might apply, of course, only to the "tools, animals, and actions" to which 601d restricts Plato's point. Within this class of things, there is no reason why the two ideas should not be combined to yield a single interpretation of Plato's view of the Good, which would show why he thinks that knowledge of that Form is required for knowledge of all others. Elsewhere, the first part of the interpretations would apply alone. [Hare, pp. 35–36; Owen, *PPI*; Vlastos, *DRP*; Nehamas; Cooper, p. 154; Nettleship, pp. 222ff.; Shorey, *IG*, esp. pp. 199, 229; Guthrie, *HGP*, p. 507; Taylor, *PMW*, p. 294; Thayer. For accounts that also make the Good variously include, involve, or consist simply in, the ordering of the other Forms, see e.g., Taylor, *PMW*, p. 286; Krämer, pp. 128ff.; Irwin, *PMT*, p. 225; and Gosling, pp. 57–71.]

C.   That the Good should be regarded by Plato as the cause also of the being of intelligible objects, as well as of our knowledge of them, can be understood in parallel fashion. If to be the Form of F is to be unqualifiedly F and in that sense a good F, then the being of the Form (its *einai* and *ousia*, 509b7–8) can reasonably enough be thought of as involving, and in a sense made possible by, the Good.

The difficulty that arises from this statement, however, concerns what we might call "bad Forms," such as the Form of the Unjust or the Form of the Ugly (475e–476a). Is Plato saying that the Good is somehow the cause of the being of these things too? For some discussion of this difficult matter, see Introd., sec. 3, with the sixth point in 476d–480a, n. C.

D.   Another very difficult point in Plato's analogy between the Good and the sun is the statement that the Good is "beyond being in dignity and power" (509b9–10). Some have taken these words to mean that one cannot correctly apply the word "be" to the Good, or that it is somehow beyond or outside of the class of Forms. But it is difficult, especially in the light of 534b–c, to see why Plato should wish to make this claim, and the words that he uses here are not naturally used to make it. It is true that the Good has a special status among Forms, but this special status does not put it so far apart from them that it cannot be said to "be."

The line of interpretation suggested in nn. B–C offers another possibility. In the first place, Plato wishes to deny that the Good is the same thing as Being, just as in 509b4 he wishes to deny that the sun is the same thing as generation (see below). In addition, however, he wishes to indicate that for a thing to be a Form of F, and so for it in that way to "be" fully and without qualification (see 476d–480a, n. C, second point), is not yet for it to be the Form of the Good. That is, although the Form of the Good causes the other Forms to *be* (see n. C), this does not mean that the Form of the Good *is* Being. The reason why Plato bothers to make this point is that it constitutes an exception to his gen-

eral view about causation, which is that what causes something to be
F is the Form of *F* (see the citations in n. B on 379b–380c). Contrary to
the general rule, he is saying, from the fact that the Form of Good is
the cause of the being of other Forms it does not follow that the Form
of the Good *is* the Form of Being.

He does the same with respect to the sun in 509b4, which denies, as noted, that the
sun is the same thing as generation (*genesis*). Given this, the parallelism with the Good
implies that the Good is not the same thing as Being. If his point about the Good were
that we cannot say that it "is," then he would in parallel fashion have to be saying
about the sun that it is not *in* a process of *genesis*. But he is not saying this. Quite
apart from the question whether or not he believed that the physical universe was created or always existed, it is clear that the sun is a sensible object and as such is in at
least some varieties of *genesis*. It is not one of the intelligible objects which Plato urges
us to study in theoretical astronomy (528e–530e, esp. 529d). What he means here
is simply that although the sun gives *genesis* to sensibles, it is not itself *genesis*. That is,
although the sun causes sensibles to come-to-be, it is not the same thing as coming-to-
be. Hence the parallel with the claim that the Good is not the same as Being. As in the
case of the Good, his reason for making this claim about the sun is that he normally
adopts a different view of causation and so must cancel the suggestion that that view
would imply.

E.   The final part of the analogy is the idea that just as the sun can be
seen, so too the Good can be known. In 534b–c Plato makes it quite
clear that the Good can be known just as every other Form can be, in a
way that involves discovering a definition (see 531d–534d, n. C).

509d–511e: THE SIMILE OF THE DIVIDED LINE. WE HAVE
DIVIDED THINGS INTO THE REALM OF THE VISIBLE AND THE
REALM OF THE INTELLIGIBLE ON A LINE ASCENDING FROM (*A*)
to (*D*). THE VISIBLE REALM IS DIVIDED INTO (*A*) IMAGES AND
(*B*) THE THINGS THAT ARE PATTERNS OR MODELS AFTER
WHICH THOSE IMAGES ARE FORMED. IN THE INTELLIGIBLE
REALM WE HAVE A DISTINCTION BETWEEN (*C*) THE USE AS
IMAGES OF THE THINGS THAT WERE PREVIOUSLY MODELS
FOR IMAGES—WITH THE CONCOMITANT USE OF HYPOTHESES
OR ASSUMPTIONS—AND (*D*) THE USE OF FORMS ALONE, WITH-
OUT EITHER IMAGES OR HYPOTHESES. STUDENTS OF GEOM-
ETRY, ARITHMETIC, AND OTHER SCIENCES, USE HYPOTHESES
AND VISIBLE IMAGES. THE STUDENT OF THE SCIENCE OF DIA-
LECTIC, ON THE OTHER HAND, DOES WITHOUT EITHER OF
THESE, BUT ARRIVES AT A FIRST PRINCIPLE THAT IS NOT HYPO-
THETICAL, FROM WHICH HE DESCENDS TO CONCLUSIONS

HAVING ONLY TO DO WITH FORMS. THE CRUCIAL THING IS
TO DISTINGUISH BETWEEN THE SCIENCE OF DIALECTIC AND
OTHER PROCEDURES.

A.   Even more than the previous simile of the sun, this one glances at
ideas that Plato does not think he needs to take the time to explore fully.
His main aim here is to emphasize the distinction between sensible and
intelligible objects, to claim that there is a science of "dialectic" dealing with the latter and to insist that this science uses procedures different
from those of other sciences, in that the latter make use of sensible
images and rest on unproved hypotheses (526c–527c), whereas dialectic
dispenses with sensible images and, somehow, manages to reach a first
principle that is not hypothetical but can be accepted as more than a
mere assumption. It emerges later that this first principle (or, as it may
be, set of first principles) has something to do with the Form of the
Good (see 531d–534d, n. D) and may perhaps be a definition of the
Good, or a proposition or set of propositions about it.

As will emerge in Book VII, the rulers' education is to proceed through
a variety of sciences until it reaches dialectic, and culminates in the
acquisition by the rulers of a knowledge of the Good (531d–534d). But
Plato's explanation of that education does not appeal to the details of
philosophical reasoning that may be thought to lie behind this simile,
and so like the previous simile (see n. E on it), the present one may
be thought to convey, in its allusive and incomplete way, only that general outline of Plato's views which he thought necessary for the understanding of his main argument in this work. [On hypotheses, etc., see
Nettleship, p. 252; Robinson, *PED*, pp. 172–6; and White, pp. 95–99.]

Summary of the *REPUBLIC*

Book VII

- simile of the cave
- education of rulers - philosophy, math, etc

514a–517c: THE SIMILE OF THE CAVE. ORDINARY PEOPLE ARE COMPARED TO PEOPLE CHAINED IN A CAVE SO THAT THEIR EYES MUST BE DIRECTED TOWARD A WALL ON WHICH SHADOWS PLAY, WHICH ARE CAST BY ARTIFACTS CARRIED IN FRONT OF A LARGE FIRE. IT WOULD BE DIFFICULT AND PAINFUL FOR SOMEONE RELEASED FROM HIS CHAINS TO SEE WHEN TURNED TOWARD THE FIRE. IT WOULD BE MORE DIFFICULT STILL FOR SOMEONE LED OUT OF THE CAVE TO SEE IN THE SUNLIGHT. AT FIRST HE WOULD HAVE TO LOOK AT SHADOWS AND REFLECTIONS OF THINGS IN WATER; THEN HE WOULD BE ABLE TO LOOK AT THE THINGS THEMSELVES; AND FINALLY HE WOULD BE ABLE TO LOOK AT THE SUN. HE WOULD MUCH PREFER THIS STATE TO BEING IN THE CAVE; AND IF HE WENT BACK DOWN AGAIN HIS SIGHT WOULD AT FIRST BE POOR IN THE DARKNESS, AND HE WOULD BE DESPISED FOR THIS. THE SIMILE OF THE CAVE IS TO BE FITTED TO WHAT HAS GONE BEFORE: THE SUN HERE REPRESENTS THE FORM OF THE GOOD, WHICH IS THE CAUSE OF ALL THINGS THAT ARE RIGHT AND BEAUTIFUL, AND MUST BE SEEN BY ANYONE WHO IS TO BE ABLE TO ACT INTELLIGENTLY.

A. With this simile we are now in a position to understand the full significance for Plato's argument of the series of three similes which he has been setting forth since 507a, a significance that lies in their application to the philosopher-rulers' education. Plato's aim is to describe that education in such a way that it will be seen to suit the function that the rulers are to fulfill in the city, in particular, the function of guarding and preserving the city (412a–c, n. A). The special feature of that function to be stressed in Book VII is that for a good ruler, in the proper sense, the main requirement is, with seeming paradox, that he not wish to rule but that he prefer to do something else. This feature is crucial to the operation of Plato's city (see 519d–521b, nn. B, E).

That something else is philosophy, construed as intellectual activity concerning the Forms. The simile of the cave has the primary effect of dramatizing this idea by setting forth the relation between the sensible and the intelligible so as to highlight what Plato regards as the far greater attractiveness of the latter. (At the same time, the simile also dramatizes, in 516e–517a, the reasons already treated in 487b–489c for the reputation of true philosophers for being useless.)

B. Plato says that the Simile of the Cave must be fitted to what was said before in the other two similes just preceding. The fitting, however, is not without difficulty. Some, for example, have thought that Plato here indicates belief in the existence of an intermediate class of entities between Forms and sensibles, namely, "mathematical" objects (see, e.g., Wedberg), which are thought to figure in the second-highest segment of the Divided Line of 509d–511e; but if this is so, then these mathematical objects would seem to have disappeared from the Simile of the Cave. There are also difficulties surrounding the identification of the various objects in the Simile of the Cave itself. Are the shadows sensible objects? If so, then as the genuine objects in the outer world appear to be the Forms, we may wonder what the artifacts are that cast the shadows in the cave, and what the reflections are outside. Are the latter perhaps intermediate, mathematical objects? But there seems nothing especially mathematical about them. We may also ask whether the artifacts in the cave and the reflections outside of it represent the same type of objects in reality or not. These and other questions easily arise. Fortunately, although Plato says that we must fit the similes together, he leaves this as an exercise for us to pursue ourselves, rather than suggesting that it must be carried out in detail so that his main line of argument can be understood.

Let us, however, pursue the matter a little further, with a suggestion for an overall interpretation of the Simile of the Cave in conjunction with the other two similes. Start with three facts which are as plain as anything about the three similes. First of all, the real objects outside of the cave and the objects corresponding to the uppermost of the four segments of the line (i.e., segment D) both represent Forms. Secondly, as Plato makes equally explicit (509e–510a), the lowermost segment of the line, segment A, represents images of sensible objects, such as reflections and mirror-images (of, e.g., tables and chairs). Thirdly, the middle two segments, B and C, of the line *both*—notwithstanding the views of those who wish to see intermediate mathematical objects in the upper of these segments—are clearly said to represent the *same* objects, taken in segment B as the things of which the images are images, and taken in segment C as themselves images of the things above them, namely, of the Forms (510a–b). So far so good: segment A would contain, e.g., an image of a table, which table is in B considered as the model for that image, but is also in C considered as itself a copy or image of the Form of Table, which is in D. If we are to match the Line with the Cave, the next step is to say that the artifacts in the cave, which cast their reflections on the wall, and the images outside of the cave (the shadows and reflections of the real objects outside the cave, 516a) also represent the same objects, and thus correspond exactly to the two middle segments, B and C, of the line. In both cases, the objects in the middle serve as models for images on the one hand, and images of models on the other hand. (For the purposes of his simile, therefore, Plato groups together the various statues and reproductions that cast their shadows on the wall of the cave (514b–c), and the reflections and shadows outside of the cave which the viewer must look at before his eyes become accustomed to the light (516a). Both are images of the real objects outside of the cave, seen outside as such, and seen inside as models for yet further images.) What are these objects in this double-aspect middle group? Clearly enough—pending some further explanation—they are sensible objects, which are, in Plato's theory (cf. 596a–597e), both imitations of Forms and models from which further imitations can be made. But notice one further fact: the objects of the middle group are said to represent sensible objects of the sort that can be used by geometers, producing sensible diagrams in the sand, as images of the things that geometers really must talk about, namely, Forms of Square, Diameter, and the like. which are mentioned in 510d–e (again notwithstanding the mistaken idea that mathematical objects are "intermediates" rather than Forms). We shall see the importance of this fact shortly.

So far everything falls into a reasonable place, except one thing: the shadows on the wall of the cave. What are they? If they correspond to the lowest segment of the line, as we should insist that they do, they must be images of sensible objects. But this idea seems not to sit well with Plato's claim (515a–c) that most men sit fixed in such a way that they see nothing else throughout life. For surely Plato wishes to say that what men are forced to apprehend for the most part are not images but sensible objects themselves. So it would seem that we must unravel what we have put together and start all over again.

But no: Plato *does* think that what *most* men apprehend are merely images of sensible objects. *What* he means by this, and *that* he does mean this, can be seen from his discussion of poetry, painting, and images in Book X. For there he makes clear that the brute appearance that the painter represents is not *the object* that we might think of him as representing, but an *aspect* or *appearance* of an object, the one that it has when viewed from a particular angle (597e–598d with n. B, and 601b–602c, B–C, F–G).

What the painter gives us, we might say, is the object as it seems rather than the object as it is (though, of course, as it is only with qualification—cf. 476d–480a, n. C). But such appearances of objects are all that most people are aware of or consider. To be aware of anything more, Plato thinks, one must resort to something more than the mere use of the senses: one must resort to *measurement* and like techniques (Book X, 602c–603b). By doing this, one avoids errors caused by perspective, e.g., by discovering what the actual dimensions of a thing are, and what its real angles and shapes are, rather than those that are presented to bare and naïve perception (for example, when a round coin looks ovoid when seen from an oblique angle, or a square looks trapezoidal). But Plato clearly does not think that these techniques are available to the ignorant multitude in any very significant degree, inasmuch as they are associated with the reasoning part of the soul (602d–e). This is not to say that the ordinary man thinks that pennies are ovoid when they are not straight in front of him; it is to say that he does not have a complete grasp of the spatial interrelationships which are studied by geometry and kindred sciences. The ordinary man is in this sense constrained to apprehend the appearances that sensible objects present to him, and it is this fact that is portrayed in the Simile of the Cave.

As noted two paragraphs back, the objects dealt with by the geometer, and corresponding to the two middle segments of the line, are sensible objects as subjected to measurement. The geometer is thus a man who has turned around fully to see the fire in the cave and the artifacts carried in front of it; and he might in his capacity as geometer succeed in leaving the cave and seeing the images that are outside; but he does not reach the level of the philosopher, who is able to apprehend the real objects themselves and, ultimately, the sun—i.e., the Good—itself.

So, finally, the lowest segment of the line represents the appearances rendered by artists, reflected in mirrors, and presented to brute sensation. The next two segments represent sensible objects as subjected to measurement, regarded first as the things of which the appearances are appearances and imitations, and then—in the third segment—as imitations of the objects represented by the fourth segment, namely the Forms. It is the first group of objects that most men are forced by their chains to watch; the second group are apprehended by some, who realize that these are imitations of intelligible objects (see 509d–511e, n. A, 526c–527c); and the last group, the Forms, are apprehended only by those philosophers who are fully accustomed to activity of the intellect outside of the cave.

C. Let it not be thought that according to Plato there is no possibility of bringing reason to bear on what we apprehend by the senses. There is, if we understand what we are apprehending and what lies behind it. That this is so is clear from 518d–519b (see note A there), and also from the fact that Plato thinks that his rulers will be better rulers of their sensible city because of their study of the Forms (see esp. 534d–536b).

It is easy to think that 516c–d is meant to convey the contrary idea, as it seems at first sight to deny the possibility of predicting the future in the sensible world. But in fact this possibility is not what it denies, but rather the possibility of predicting the future on the basis *merely* of sensation—i.e., shadows on the wall of the cave—and *without knowledge of the Good*, by which one's actions should be guided. The kind of activity on which Plato is casting aspersions is the kind mentioned in 491b–494a, namely, the effort to predict the behavior of the "great beast," the multitude of men, and so to please it, thinking good only those things that have that effect. The multitude, Plato seems to think, is unpredictable (*Phaedrus* 269ff. perhaps suggests a different view). But an understanding of what the Good is, which enables one to aim at it directly rather than through the whims of the multitude, is the basis of reliable and prudent policy (cf. 520c, 475e–476d, n. B, 518d–519b, n. A).

(The idea that Plato expresses here is intended to be substantially the same as what he says in Book X about the way in which tragic poetry portrays and affects human beings. Tragedy presents situations in the light of people's emotional reactions to them, rather than in the light of a clear conception of what is good and bad about the situations [603b–605c, n. B].)

517c–518d: THERE ARE TWO WAYS, THEN, IN WHICH OUR ABILITIES TO APPREHEND THINGS MAY BE CONFUSED, ONE BY COMING FROM LIGHT INTO DARKNESS, AND THE OTHER BY COMING FROM DARKNESS INTO LIGHT. EDUCATION, AS OUR ACCOUNT INDICATES, IS NOT LIKE A PROCESS OF PUTTING EYES INTO PEOPLE WHO DO NOT HAVE THEM; IT IS A PROCESS OF TURNING EYES IN THE RIGHT DIRECTION. THE CAPACITY TO LEARN AND THE ORGAN WITH WHICH TO DO IT ARE ALREADY PRESENT IN EVERY PERSON'S SOUL.

A. In 502c–504d Plato began his explanation of the philosophical education of the rulers. In 504d–506a he stressed the role of the Good in this education, and the passages since then have in their various ways elaborated that theme. Now, against the background of the Simile of the Cave, he starts to indicate in more detail how the education will proceed.

In so doing, he begins to explain how wisdom is to be inculcated. Recall that in 485a–d the capacity for being wise was described in outline, but the nature of wisdom itself, as manifested in the philosopher, was left untreated until after Plato had introduced his views about Forms and especially the Form of the Good (485a–d, n. A).

B. Plato insists that this education is like turning eyes in the right direction rather than putting eyes into a person who did not have them, but he does not make explicit his reasons for so insisting. Some readers will see here an allusion to the theory of recollection in the *Meno* and *Phaedo*, according to which what seems to us to be learning is really recollection of what was known before birth. The business at hand, however, does not require Plato to explore the issue.

518d–519b: OTHER VIRTUES OF THE SOUL ARE UNLIKE THE VIRTUE OF INTELLIGENCE, IN THAT THEY ARE NOT PRESENT AT FIRST BUT ARE ADDED BY HABIT AND PRACTICE. MEN WHO ARE BAD BUT INTELLIGENT EMPLOY THEIR INTELLIGENCE FOR BAD PURPOSES. IF THEY HAD BEEN WELL EDUCATED FROM CHILDHOOD, THE SAME CAPACITY THAT IS EXERCISED ON SENSIBLE OBJECTS WOULD BE DIRECTED INSTEAD TOWARD THE TRUE REALITIES.

A.   We have noted that Plato allows for the possibility of bringing reason to bear on sensibles (514a–517d, n. C). Here he indicates that the same capacity (*dynamis*, 518e3) should be thought of as employed both for sensibles and for intelligibles, depending on, so to speak, the direction in which it is turned. In similar fashion he says in 553d that the reasoning part of the soul (*to logistikon*), ordinarily concerned with Forms, is the part used by the oligarchic man to calculate how he may gain financially.

B.   By contrast to intelligence, which Plato views not as acquired but as developed, other virtues or excellences of soul are not developed but acquired, by habit and practice. But Plato does not explore this matter further here. (Had he done so, he, rather than Aristotle, might have been commonly regarded as the first to stress the importance of practice and habit in moral education.)

519b–d: WE MUST ALLOW TO BE RULERS NEITHER THOSE WHO ARE UNEDUCATED NOR THOSE WHO ALLOW THEMSELVES TO SPEND THEIR WHOLE LIVES BEING EDUCATED. WE MUST EXCLUDE THE FORMER BECAUSE THEY DO NOT HAVE A SINGLE END AT WHICH THEY AIM IN ALL OF THEIR ACTIONS, AND THE LATTER BECAUSE THEY WOULD REFUSE TO ACT. THE BEST NATURES MUST STUDY, SO THAT THEY MAY SEE THE GOOD, AND THEN THEY MUST RETURN TO THE CAVE TO RULE.

A. One must not underestimate the importance to Plato of the idea presented here, which will be elaborated in the rest of Book VII, namely, that those who rule must be those who are educated to the point of apprehending the good but nevertheless leave the study of it and of the other realities in order to return to practical matters and govern the city. A ruler who is fit for his task must combine both of these activities.

The reasons for this are not superficial but arise out of basic features of Plato's line of reasoning, as he will make clear in the following section, when he explains that the city must be ruled by those who do not wish to rule, but must be "forced" (*anagkasai*, 519c9) to do so.

B. In 519c Plato maintains that those who are not educated in philosophical matters will not have a single goal by which to regulate all of their actions. He does not expand on this idea much here (Aristotle, as is well known, pursued it later), but it is evidently connected with the principle that each person should pursue one and only one task (see 369e–370c, n. B), and the idea that if a person is not governed by reason, then he will not have a unified plan of life (see 559d–562a, nn. A–B, 573c–576b, n. B). As we shall see (519d–521b, nn. B–E), the unity of the philosopher-ruler's goal must arise from the fact that he is able to apprehend the good and devote himself to trying to see it exemplified as much as possible in the sensible world. By adopting this aim, and by being so trained and educated that his other desires allow him to pursue it, he avoids the kind of psychological conflict with which all others are afflicted (573c–576b, n. B). [Nettleship, pp. 220–21; Shorey, *UPT*, p. 18.]

519d–521b: GLAUCON OBJECTS THAT WE ARE DOING THE RULERS AN INJUSTICE BY GIVING THEM A WORSE LIFE WHEN THEY MIGHT HAVE A BETTER. AS BEFORE (420b), SOCRATES AGAIN REMINDS GLAUCON THAT THE EFFORT WAS NOT TO GIVE ANY ONE GROUP WITHIN THE CITY A GOOD LIFE, BUT TO GAIN ADVANTAGE FOR THE WHOLE CITY BY BRINGING ITS CITIZENS INTO HARMONY AND BINDING THE CITY TOGETHER. IN COMPELLING THE RULERS TO SERVE AS RULERS AND GUARDIANS, WE ARE LAYING ON THEM A JUST INJUNCTION, AS THEY WILL SEE WHEN WE POINT OUT TO THEM THAT BECAUSE THEY HAVE BEEN RAISED AND EDUCATED BETTER THAN OTHERS, THEY ARE ABLE TO HAVE BOTH KINDS OF LIFE, THAT OF RULING AND THAT OF PHILOSOPHY. ONLY IF THE CITY IS RULED BY THOSE WHO DO NOT WISH TO RULE

BUT HAVE OTHER THINGS THAT THEY WOULD PREFER TO DO, CAN THE CITY BE WELL RULED.

A.   Here we have one of the most important passages in the *Republic* concerning the role of the rulers and their motivation to adopt it. Plato has already warned us of the importance of this matter. He brought it up at the beginning of Book IV, when he made Glaucon ask whether Socrates' scheme was granting sufficient happiness to the guardians. But Plato postponed the issue until the present, that is, after he had expounded enough of the situation to deal with it (see 419a–421c, nn. B–C).

B.   We must begin our examination of the passage by considering Plato's contention, already adumbrated in 519b–d (n. A there), that the only way in which the city can be well ruled is for it to be ruled by people who do not wish to rule but have something else that would be better for them to do (520e–521a).

He has been preparing for this idea since 473b–474c, where he first introduced the notion that his city should be ruled by philosophers. It there became part of his project to show that the tasks of ruling and philosophizing are not really two tasks but one, for which people have to be trained by a single program of education (474b–d, n. B, 484a–d, nn. A–B, 485a–d, n. A, 485d–487a, n. A). He has argued in one way for this view by showing how the knowledge gained by philosophy is essential for a ruler. But he is now making a further point: philosophizing is essential to ruling because it is the activity that is preferable to ruling, and so the activity that the ruler *must* have *available* to him if he is to wish *not* to rule, where wishing not to rule is, paradoxically, what makes it possible for him to rule well. Thus the total task of ruling, properly construed, must *include* the activity of philosophy, both as a lure from the practical side of actually managing the affairs of the city, and as a source of that knowledge by which the managing is guided. The upshot is that philosophizing is not thought of by Plato as a task somehow additional to that of ruling, but as an essential part of effective ruling.

What makes this point so important, aside from the fact that it enables us to see the cohesive plan in Plato's argument, is its bearing on the primary point of this section, that ruling is an unattractive pursuit by contrast to philosophy. For it is vitally important that when the philosopher-rulers face this unattractiveness and rule in spite of it, they are not, according to Plato, forced to do something entirely unconnected with philosophical activity. See further nn. D–E.

C.   Glaucon's challenge here echoes his challenge in 419a–421c, but this time it has two distinct parts. The first is that by compelling philosophers to rule, we shall be making them *less well off* than they would otherwise be. The second is that we shall thereby be treating them *unjustly.* Plato responds to both parts together, but it will be helpful for us to keep his responses to them separate.

D.   His response to the charge of injustice is to deny it. As in 420–421, he says in 519e–520a that our aim is not to make any one group in the city as well off as it could possibly be, but to make the whole city as well off as it can be by binding it together and making it harmonious (see n. G below, and 422e–423d, n. B). However, the point of doing this, as we have seen, is in part to make the city as just as possible (432b–434c), so he can take it as shown that the treatment of the rulers under scrutiny here is not unjust. This is especially so because this treatment was designed precisely to make the rulers perform their task, which is part of what the justice of the city consists in (see *ibid.*).
   Moreover, the justice of making the rulers rule even though they do not wish to becomes even clearer, by Plato's standard, when we realize that, as we have seen (n. B), the full task of ruling actually is *ruling even though it is not what they most wish to do.* For, he says, if one has rulers in a city who want to rule, then they will *compete* for the opportunity to do so, with the result that the city will be afflicted with strife (520d). Thus, for the city to be just, the rulers must perform their task; and in order that strife be avoided, this task must be not simply ruling, as we normally think of it, but ruling even while having something else that is preferable to do. So, he holds, the ruler's position *is just* because an essential part of his task is that very discontent with ruling that might superficially appear to show that his position is *not just.* This is the burden of the explanation that is given to the rulers in 520b–d, where it is pointed out that the rulers' education suits them for *both* philosophizing and ruling, and that a city cannot be well governed unless its rulers do not wish to rule. A further consideration offered to defend the justice of the treatment of the rulers appears in 520b. It is the suggestion that the education given the rulers lays on them a debt to repay by consenting to rule. This consideration links Plato's argument with a more ordinary notion of justice (cf. 442d–443b, n. B), according to which justice involves the repayment of debts (cf. 331c–d).

E.   It is more difficult for Plato to reply to the other part of Glaucon's challenge, which is that his treatment of the rulers makes them less well off than they could be. For this part of the challenge casts doubt on the idea that the rulers will actually be motivated to rule as Plato says that they should, and thus on the idea that by putting philosophers in charge of the city, he really is showing that the establishment of the city is in some sense possible, as he claims in his response to the third wave (see 449a–450c, n. A, 472e–473b, n. A, 419a–421c, n. C). For if philosophers could in some way avoid ruling and merely philosophize instead, and if they would be moved strongly enough to take that way, the city would be without its necessary rulers and would collapse.

Nevertheless, Plato wishes to maintain that the philosopher-rulers in his city will be moved to rule even though they are aware of another, better activity that they could engage in. He speaks of their being "forced" to rule, but he also speaks of them as regarding the justice that requires them to rule as something essential or necessary (cf. 540d–e), and (in 540b) as ruling "for the sake of the city." Therefore, when he says that they are forced, he does not mean that they do not in any sense choose to do so but are compelled against their wills. Rather, he means that they consent to rule in spite of the realization that they could otherwise be better off. Moreover, their training has prepared the way for their consent, because it has been designed to harmonize their spirited and philosophical tendencies, not allowing the latter to grow completely unchecked (see 410a–412a, n. A).

Plato clearly believes that there is a manner of life that makes one better off than the life of both philosophizing and ruling. In addition to saying what he says here, he has described such a life in 496a–497a, led by a man of philosophic temperament in retirement from the political activities of actual cities, and in 591a–592b he also urges such a life on philosophically-minded people in the world as it actually is (cf. 520b). Such a life does not fully develop the capacities of the philosophic person, for, as we have seen (474b–c, n. B, 496a–497a, n. A), such a person has as much of a natural tendency to be a ruler as he does to be a philosopher. But in spite of this fact, we saw that Plato does not maintain that philosophers in actual cities wish to rule because that would make them happier or better off (496a–497a, n. A). Nor does he say, what one might have expected him to say, that a refusal by philosophers to rule will deprive them of the opportunity to philosophize. He never suggests that the philosopher-ruler's motive for managing the city is, or ought to be, to safeguard his own philosophical activity. Such a supposition, moreover, would completely undercut his contention that his rulers are to rule even though they wish to do something better instead. For according to this supposition, there really is no better life than that which the rulers have, because if they chose to stop ruling the city then the only alternative would be, e.g., the dissolution of the city and the destruction of their opportunities to engage in philosophy. Plato must clearly mean, therefore, that the rulers do, as he says, eschew the chance of a better life which is actually available to them.

What does he think their motivation to do such a thing will be? In Book I, at 346b–347e, he has suggested one reason that good men have for ruling, that it is extremely distasteful, "the greatest punishment," to be ruled by someone worse than oneself. This, however, although it may be why he thinks good men consent to rule in actual cities, is not what he says to explain why the philosopher-rulers will rule in the city which he has constructed. From 520b–d it is obvious that in his view they will be moved to rule because they apprehend that it is *just* for them to do so, and that the justice of the city, and its benefit, will be advanced. This claim is reiterated at the end of Book VII, in 540d–e, where he says that the rulers will regard justice as "the greatest and most essential (or necessary) thing" (*megiston kai anagkaiotaton*), having said just before (540b) that they will rule *"for the sake of the city,"* not as something fine or splendid (*kalon*) but as something essential or necessary (*anagkaion*). So the rulers are motivated by the thought that ruling is just and by the idea of doing so for the sake of the city. It accordingly appears that he is attributing to them an attachment to justice for its own sake, and to the city for its own sake, too.

This, however, is not a complete account of the matter, because it leaves out the most important element of Plato's views about motivation, which is the role of the notion of goodness. For when we ask what he actually says that human beings aim at, we must recall that he has answered quite explicitly in 504d–506a that *the Good* is what all souls pursue, even if they often are ignorant or confused about what it is.

Although it is easy to think that this passage says that all souls pursue what is genuinely *good for themselves*, i.e., what is to their own benefit, and although it is especially easy to think this if one is subject to a misapprehension to be combated shortly, nevertheless, it is quite clear that the passage does not say this. The passage does say that the Good is what makes just things and other things useful and beneficial (505a, e); and it says that knowledge of other things is of no benefit to us if we do not have knowledge of the Good (505a); and it also says that all men wish to *possess* what is really good and not merely what seems to be good (505d). But none of these things is tantamount to asserting that when one pursues *the Good*, as Plato holds in 505d–e that we all do, one is thereby pursuing *one's own benefit* or *what is good for one-*

self. Moreover, that all men pursue nothing but their own benefit is something that Plato cannot intend to maintain. We have just seen that the rulers in certain respects do not do this. And in 540a–b, one of the passages in which, as we just saw, Plato maintains that the rulers will pursue justice and act for the sake of the city against what would be better for themselves, he says that they would act in this way precisely as a result of using *the Good* as a paradigm or model (a8–9; cf. 500b–e). So treating the Good as a paradigm does not always lead to an effort to increase *one's own* wellbeing.

A little reflection shows that it would be very unlikely for Plato to think that an effort to pursue the Good is simply an effort to gain what is good for oneself. For (quite apart from the particular interpretation of the theory of Forms expounded in n. C on 476d–480a) it is generally agreed to be certain that for Plato the Good is in some sense unqualifiedly or absolutely good, rather than a relative notion that each person must scrutinize, so to speak, only with reference to himself. And if this is so, then it cannot be that in seeking the Good each person is simply pursuing his own benefit (cf. 531d–534d, n. E).

The point is even clearer, and Plato's whole line of thought is given greater coherence, if we do exploit the theory of Forms as explained in 476d–480a, n. C. For just as in general the Form of *F* is unqualifiedly *F*, or *F* without reference to surrounding conditions or in particular respects, so too the Form of the Good must be good in the same totally unqualified way. Therefore, the Form of the Good is not, in and of itself, good *for you* or good *for me*, and the ability to apprehend or understand the Good is not the ability to apprehend or understand what is good *for oneself*, but, precisely, the ability to understand the notion of what is good *without reference to* any particular person (or circumstance).

Given these facts, we can comprehend more firmly the importance of the observation at 504d–506a, n. C that Plato does not have any use for one of the distinctions between notions of goodness that many contemporary philosophers take as paramount, namely, that between what is good or beneficial *for* a particular person and what is *morally* good. For Plato, the notion of what is unqualifiedly good includes much of what we think of as moral goodness, viewed (as, e.g., Kant viewed it) as something not relative to particular circumstances or particular interests. But the notion of something's being good *for* a particular person is not regarded by Plato as another notion of goodness on a par with this one. Rather, a thing that is good for one person, but possibly not for some other person, is viewed as possessing *qualifiedly* the attribute (so to speak) that the Form of the Good possesses *un*qualifiedly or absolutely. When a thing must be thought of as a benefit and we must ask *whom* it is a benefit *for*, then, in Plato's view, it is being thought of as a manifestation or exemplification of the Form of the Good, which is something that must be thought of as good *without* reference to whom it might be good for. Cf. Introd., sec. 3.

A ruler, then, is someone who not only has a firm grasp of the notion of the Good, but who is also moved to pursue it and the exemplification of it in the world, rather than to follow any particular interest of his own which may conflict with it. The workings of this motivation are not explained by Plato in any detail. As is recognized, however, he evidently attributes to human reason a kind of motive force of its own (this view is obviously contrary to that of Hume), and in particular he attributes to human reason the tendency to try to see exemplified in the sensible world those Forms (or at least many of them) that it apprehends (see, e.g., Demos, and Introd., sec. 4). The sacrifice that the ruler makes in this connection is not overwhelming, because Plato certainly thinks that he is very happy indeed (521a4, 465c–466c), and, what is more, far happier than anyone who is positively unjust (this is the conclusion reached by the end of Book IX; see 358a–362c, n. D, and 576b–578b, n. A). What makes him rule is not a desire for his own wellbeing or happiness, but an understanding of and attraction to the kind of goodness that—as Plato will try to show (see esp. 531d–534d)—his philosophical education equips him to comprehend and be influenced by.

It is very common not to appreciate these facts about Plato's view, and to think that even the rulers of Plato's city must be wholly moved by the desire to gain their own benefit, happiness, or welfare. One reason for this misapprehension is that in Book III (412d–e) the guardians are said at an earlier stage of their education to need to be taught a coincidence of their interest with that of the city. That stage, however, is a stage of their education far earlier than the one at which the elect among them, now philosopher-rulers, reach an understanding of what the Good is. The other chief reason for the misapprehension is a mistaken inference from the fact that the whole *Republic* is, after all, an argument for the proposition that the just man is happier and better off than the unjust man (358a–362c, esp. n. D), which is Plato's way of "praising justice." In fact, however, it is perfectly consistent for Plato to hold that the rulers sacrifice their own interests in choosing to rule as well as to philosophize, and at the same time to argue, as he indeed does, that if one is just one will be happy and, in particular, that the completely just man is far better off than the completely unjust man. On this matter see further Introd., sec. 3 with secs. 1 and 4.

[Interpreters of the *Republic* have been caused untold discomfort by failing to realize that there is no incompatibility between Plato's praise of justice and his claim that the rulers, although they are extremely happy, do sacrifice some measure of happiness by not simply being philosophers. The sacrifice is, however, too patent not to have been widely noted. It is remarked on by, e.g., Prichard, p. 108; Adkins, pp. 290–1; Shorey, *WPS*, p. 235; Kraut, *ELP*, pp. 330–1; Cooper, p. 156. Prichard and Adkins suppose that it is inconsistent with the main burden of Plato's view. Kraut does not make this mistake. See also Zeller, pp. 870–6; Ritter, *EPP*, pp. 82–3; Sidgwick, *OHE*, pp. 40, 48; Shorey, *Rep.*, I, pp. 50, 314–5; Demos, p. 55. Failure to see the importance of the sacrifice results in serious difficulties of interpretation: see, e.g., Gosling, pp. 39–40, 68ff. (though pp. 70–1 are nearer the mark); Irwin, *PMT*, pp. 240, 243–8. Of recent accounts, Cooper's is the closest to the truth, because he sees clearly both that the rulers' interests are sacrificed (p. 156) and much of why this is so (pp. 153–6); but he then partially reverses himself and seems to be struggling for a way of saying that this is not so after all (pp. 156–7). (For articulations of a quite different view of Plato's ideas about the Good, see esp. Shorey, *IG*, pp. 231–4, and Irwin, *RPT*.]

F. The reader will have noticed that the questions of motivation dealt with in the foregoing note pertain only to the rulers in Plato's city, and neither to other inhabitants of that city nor to those living outside of it. For further remarks on the motivation of these people, see Introd., sec. 4, and 590c–591a, nn. C–D.

G. In this passage Plato continues to give prominence to the theme of the desirability of the cohesiveness of the city. The reason why rulers must accept the task of ruling even while wishing not to do so (cf. nn. B, D) is that if they do not, there will be competition for rule among those who do wish it, with the consequent development of dissension or strife (*stasis*—see 520d3) and the destruction of the city. Cf. 422e–423d, n. B, 461e–462e, n. B, and 545c–547c, n. A.

521c–d: BUT HOW ARE WE TO TRAIN SUCH PHILOSOPHER-RULERS AND TURN THEIR SOULS UPWARD TOWARD THE FORMS?

A. This passage now begins the full-scale discussion, promised in 502c–504d, of how the education of the rulers (that is, that part that they do not share with the auxiliaries) is to be organized and what it is to deal with. The leading question is always how they are to be brought to have knowledge of the Forms, and particularly the Form of the Good.

521d–522e: OUR GUARDIANS WERE TO BE SKILLED IN MILITARY MATTERS. IT WOULD BE GOOD IF THE STUDIES THAT COME NEXT WERE USEFUL IN SUCH MATTERS, THOUGH CLEARLY NEITHER PHYSICAL TRAINING NOR TRAINING IN

THE ARTS IS WHAT WE NOW NEED. BUT THERE IS SOMETHING THAT IS NEEDED IN ALL TYPES OF THOUGHT, AND WHICH EVERYONE MUST LEARN AT THE START, NAMELY, THE SCIENCE OF NUMBER AND CALCULATION, WHICH IS PLAINLY ALSO NECESSARY FOR MILITARY PURSUITS AS WELL.

A.   Plato begins by showing a link between the function of the rulers as philosophers and knowers of Forms, and their function as the military guardians of the city, by indicating that their philosophical education must begin as an extension of a study that they already need in their military capacity, namely, the study of numbers.

523a–524d: THERE ARE TWO KINDS OF STUDIES, THOSE THAT LEAD TO THE USE OF INTELLIGENCE AND THOSE THAT DO NOT. THE LATTER INVOLVE THOSE IMPRESSIONS ABOUT WHICH SENSATION CAN JUDGE SUFFICIENTLY; THE FORMER INVOLVE MATTERS IN WHICH SENSATION DELIVERS SIMULTANEOUS CONTRARY JUDGMENTS ABOUT THE SAME THING. FOR EXAMPLE, A THING JUDGED BY SENSATION TO BE A FINGER IS SO JUDGED REGARDLESS OF ITS POSITION AND DOES NOT SEEM AT THE SAME TIME TO BE THE CONTRARY OF A FINGER. BUT A THING THAT IS JUDGED BY SENSATION TO BE LARGE WILL ALSO AT THE SAME TIME APPEAR SMALL. ONE IS THEREFORE FORCED TO RELY ON INTELLIGENCE TO DISCOVER WHAT THE LARGE IS, BECAUSE SENSATION DOES NOT TELL ONE WHAT IT IS AS IT DECLARES THE SAME THINGS TO BE BOTH LARGE AND SMALL. IN THE CASE OF VISIBLE THINGS LARGE AND SMALL ARE MINGLED IN THE SAME THING; BUT THIS IS NOT SO IN THE CASE OF WHAT IS INTELLIGIBLE.

A.   Plato's aim here is not to give an exposition of his theory of Forms, but simply to show how certain studies tend to turn our minds toward the Forms.

B.   The distinction that Plato uses here is between predicate expressions that appear to sensation to apply to sensible objects simultaneously with their contraries, and predicate expressions that do not do so. His point is that consideration of the former, unlike consideration of the latter, will induce us to ask something of the form "What, then, *is F*, if the same objects appear to be both *F* and non-*F*?" and to conclude that it must be a non-sensible object. He expects us, that is, to follow the same line of argument that he has given in 479a–b for the distinctness of "what is" from sensible objects (476d–480a, n. C).

C.   Notice that Plato does not say here that "finger" applies to sensible objects without qualification. What he says is that it does not give *simultaneous* appearances of applying and not applying. But it will still apply to a sensible object only with temporal qualification (485a–d, n. B). (Notice, too, that Plato does not make a distinction—except perhaps in much later works—between a predicate's not being true of a thing and its contrary's being true of the thing.)

524d–525c: NOTIONS HAVING TO DO WITH *NUMBER* AND *UNIT* ARE OF THE KIND THAT LEAD TO THE USE OF INTELLIGENCE AND TO CONSIDERATION OF INTELLIGIBLE OBJECTS, BECAUSE THE SAME OBJECT THAT APPEARS TO BE ONE, OR A UNIT, ALSO APPEARS TO BE MANY. SO BOTH THE WARRIOR AND THE PHILOSOPHER MUST STUDY NUMBERS, AND LIKEWISE RULERS MUST DO SO.

A.   So, Plato argues, the study of numbers is suited to both the military and the philosophical aspects of the rulers' task (521d–522e, n. A).

B.   Plato makes clear that he sometimes thinks of number-words as predicates, so as to say that something "is one," in the sense of being unitary or a unit, or that something "is three," in the sense of being composed of three units.

525d–526c: THIS FACT ABOUT THE STUDY OF NUMBERS IS IL-LUSTRATED BY THE VIEWS OF ARITHMETICIANS, WHO REFUSE TO ALLOW THE UNIT TO BE VIEWED AS A PLURALITY; THEY WOULD ACKNOWLEDGE THAT THEY ARE NOT THEREIN SPEAKING OF SENSIBLE OBJECTS. MOREOVER, THOSE WHO ARE GOOD AT THE STUDY OF NUMBERS ARE CLEVER AT OTHER STUDIES AS WELL, AND THE STUDY OF NUMBERS IT-SELF MAKES THEIR WITS SHARPER.

A.   Plato maintains that his view of the salutary features of numerical concepts is corroborated by the practice of arithmeticians, in that they refuse to allow something to be treated simultaneously as both a unit and a plurality of units. But he does not seem to attribute to them a clear awareness that they are therefore committed to regarding numbers as intelligible rather than sensible objects.

526c–527c: *GEOMETRY* MUST ALSO BE STUDIED, BOTH BE-

CAUSE OF ITS USEFULNESS IN WARFARE AND BECAUSE IT TOO TENDS TO MAKE ONE THINK OF INTELLIGIBLE OBJECTS AND THE FORM OF THE GOOD. FOR CONTRARY TO THE WAY IN WHICH GEOMETERS TALK, STRICT GEOMETRY IS NOT CONCERNED WITH SENSIBLE FIGURES BUT WITH INTELLIGIBLE ONES.

A. Once again Plato takes note of the dual usefulness of the rulers' course of study (521d–522e, n. A).

B. This passage echoes Plato's earlier claim that geometers of his day mistakenly cling to a reliance on sensible figures (509d–511e, n. A), and indicates that their mistake is reflected in their manner of speaking. [Robinson, *PED*, Ch. X; Hare; White, pp. 95–99.]

527d–528e: AS THE NEXT PART OF THE RULERS' EDUCATION WE SHOULD MENTION, NOT ASTRONOMY, BUT *SOLID GEOMETRY*, WHICH IS IMPROPERLY NEGLECTED. ITS USEFULNESS WOULD BE EVIDENT IF IT WERE PURSUED.

A. Plato believes that solid geometry is as worthy of study as plane geometry, though it does not receive it. But beyond this there seems to be no special reason for the special attention he gives solid geometry here.

528e–531d: AS *ASTRONOMY* IS PRACTICED, IT LEADS THE SOUL DOWNWARD TOWARD CONSIDERATION OF SENSIBLE OBJECTS, THROUGH THOUGHTS OF VARIABLE SENSIBLE THINGS, SUCH AS RELATIONS OF NIGHT TO DAY AND DAY TO MONTH. BUT AN ASTRONOMY THAT DEALT WITH INVARIABLE RELATIONS WOULD LEAD THE MIND UPWARD. ANALOGOUSLY, THE STUDY OF *HARMONY* THROUGH AUDIBLE SOUNDS PLAYED ON SENSIBLE MUSICAL INSTRUMENTS SHOULD BE REPLACED BY THE RELATIONS OF HARMONY AMONG NUMBERS. SUCH STUDIES WILL BE APPROPRIATE FOR THE RULERS AND WILL HELP THEM TOWARD THE APPREHENSION OF THE BEAUTIFUL AND THE GOOD.

A. Plato's idea here is somewhat difficult to understand, and he does not stop to explain it. In the case of the study of harmony he seems to have in mind the replacement of the study of relations among audible notes by a discipline involving certain relations among numbers (*not*, it should be noted, among inaudible *sounds*; cf. 603b–605c, n. C). But his suggestions concerning astronomy are less clear. Does he have in mind a study of—somehow—non-sensible, non-physical *motions?* Or something else? He leaves the matter unexplored.

531d–534d: THE FINAL STUDY IS *DIALECTIC*, WHEREBY THE RULERS CAN GIVE AND RECEIVE AN ACCOUNT OF THE THINGS THAT CAN BE KNOWN. THEY MUST NOT STOP UNTIL THEY KNOW WHAT THE GOOD ITSELF IS. A PERSON CANNOT BE SAID TO HAVE A KNOWLEDGE OF THE GOOD UNLESS HE CAN GIVE AN ACCOUNT OF IT THAT DISTINGUISHES IT FROM OTHER THINGS. THOSE WHO CANNOT DO SO NEVER HAVE ANYTHING MORE THAN MERE OPINIONS ABOUT IMAGES OF THE GOOD.

A.   The rulers' course of study ends with their acquisition of knowledge of the Good. This is what was being aimed at from 504d–506a, when it was first said that the most important knowledge for them to have was of the Good, and that it was this knowledge that would enable them to govern reliably and well (n. A there).

B.   As we have seen (519d–521b, n. E), it is the pursuit of the Good that motivates all that the rulers do. Like everyone else, they aim for what is good, but unlike others they have a firm grasp of what it is at which they are aiming (505d–e).

In saying that the rulers pursue the Good and that they are thereby able to govern well, Plato has in mind that the rulers will see to it that the Good is as much exemplified in the sensible world as it can be (cf. 519d–521b, n. E, 540a–b, and Introd., sec. 4). The clarity of their understanding of what the Good is will be what enables them to do this effectively. See further 536b–540c, n. A.

C.   Plato's remarks in 534b–c show his belief that a full knowledge of the Good must include the ability to give, and to recognize as correct, some sort of definition of it that will distinguish it from other things, and thus help to avoid such mistakes as the identification of the Good with pleasure or knowledge (504d–506a). [*Contra*, e.g., Taylor, *PMW*, pp. 287–9.]

D.   Although he does not explicitly say so, he certainly gives the impression in 533b–d and 534b–c that the knowledge of the Good will provide the unhypothetical first principle of the dialectician, from which other knowledge will apparently be derived by some kind of deductive procedure (see 509d–511e, n. A).

Plato does not seem concerned to present here an account of exactly how all of this might work. What does interest him is simply *that* some such knowledge must be possessed by the rulers. His failure to pursue the matter further, however, has left him open to criticism, on the ground that he presents no criterion for determining goodness, or way of telling whether one actually has successfully apprehended the Good if one thinks that one has. I have already mentioned that his criterion of the goodness of something is not simply its being chosen by reason (Introd., sec. 4, and 441c–442d, n. F). Perhaps he thinks that there is some other criterion. Perhaps, on the other hand, he does not think that there is or needs to be any such criterion. Some interpreters have held that his remarks about the Good suggest the idea of a kind of blinding illumination that the apprehension of the Good causes, which is somehow thought to eliminate the need for a criterion of correctness (see e.g., 527d–e, 532c). This interpretation may be correct. If it is, then Plato is saying that when someone asks how one can tell whether one has apprehended the Good, the response is *simply* that one *can* tell, and that there is no need or possibility of a *way* of telling. If it is not correct, then one must say that in the *Republic* Plato does not provide us with a way of telling. [Shorey, *IG*, pp. 231–9; Shorey, *Rep.*, II, p. xl; Robinson, *PED*, pp. 172–7; White, pp. 102–103.]

E. It seems again fully evident, as remarked (519d–521b, n. E), that when we are told that the rulers must gain knowledge of the Good, we are not being told simply that they must gain knowledge of what is really to their benefit (see also 536b–540c, n. A).

534d–536b: THIS, THEN, IS THE COURSE OF STUDY THAT OUR RULERS MUST FOLLOW, ENDING WITH DIALECTIC. THOSE WHO ARE TO FOLLOW THIS COURSE OF STUDY MUST HAVE THE RIGHT NATURAL DISPOSITION. THEY MUST BE QUICK TO LEARN, WITH A GOOD MEMORY, BUT THEY MUST HAVE A GENUINELY PHILOSOPHICAL DISPOSITION AND ALSO BE GENUINELY DISPOSED TO HAVE ALL OF THE OTHER VIRTUES. IF WE SELECT SUCH PEOPLE, WE SHALL BE ABLE TO PRESERVE THE CITY AND ITS CONSTITUTION.

A.   Plato ends his discussion of the rulers' philosophical education with a reiteration of the idea that the selection of those with naturally philosophical tendencies, and the training of those who will develop those tendencies, will produce rulers who are able to perform the task of guarding and preserving the city (536b; cf. 369e–370c, n. B, 412a–c, n. A, 484a–d, nn. A, C). He also attempts briefly to make clear that a philosophical disposition is just the sort of disposition that is needed by those following the course of study laid down since 521d.

536b–540c: AS CHILDREN, FUTURE RULERS WILL LEARN CALCULATION AND GEOMETRY THROUGH PLAY, NOT COMPULSION. DURING THEIR LATE TEENS THEY WILL GIVE UP SUCH STUDIES AND PURSUE PHYSICAL TRAINING EXCLUSIVELY. AT TWENTY, THOSE SUITED TO BE RULERS WILL BE SELECTED AND GIVEN EDUCATION IN THOSE SCIENCES THAT WILL SHOW THEM HOW THEY ARE AKIN TO EACH OTHER AND TO THE NATURE OF REALITY, AN EDUCATION ALSO DESIGNED TO TEST THEIR STEADFASTNESS. AT THIRTY, THE BEST WILL BE SELECTED AGAIN AND WILL BE TAUGHT DIALECTIC AND TESTED IN IT, TO SEE THAT THEY ARE INTERESTED IN TRUTH AND ARE BY NATURE ORDERLY AND STEADY. (FOR WHEN IT IS TAUGHT UNDER THE WRONG CIRCUMSTANCES, AND TO THE WRONG SORT OF PEOPLE, DIALECTIC HAS A WAY OF REMOVING ONE'S EARLIER BELIEFS AND LEAVING ONE WITH THE TENDENCY TO DISPUTE SIMPLY FOR THE SAKE OF PRODUCING CONTRADICTIONS, AND NOT FOR THE SAKE OF TRUTH.) AT THIRTY-FIVE, THEY WILL BE COMPELLED TO TAKE ON THE TASK OF RULING IN MATTERS CONCERNING WAR AND THE YOUNG, AND IN THIS THEY WILL BE TESTED AGAIN FOR FIFTEEN YEARS. AT FIFTY, THEY WILL BE LED TO A KNOWLEDGE OF THE GOOD ITSELF, AND THEY WILL SPEND A GREAT DEAL OF TIME IN PHILOSOPHICAL ACTIVITY. BUT THEY WILL BE COMPELLED TO TAKE THEIR TURNS RULING, FOR THE SAKE OF THE CITY, USING THE GOOD AS A PARADIGM, AND REGARDING THE ACTIVITY OF RULING NOT AS SOMETHING FINE AND SPLENDID BUT AS SOMETHING NECESSARY, UNTIL THEY DEPART LIFE FOR THE ISLES OF THE BLESSED.

A.   This section sums up the results since 521c–d and surveys the rulers' education.

The final result, as we have seen (531d–534d, n. B), is that the rulers, having acquired a knowledge of the Good, employ the Good as a paradigm in some way, so as to guide their activity of ruling, the aim being to further the exemplification of the Good to the extent that they can. It is again made clear that the Good in question is not their own good, or what is beneficial to them (*ibid.*, n. E), and that their ruling of the city involves a kind of sacrifice of their wellbeing, because it impinges on their philosophical activity (519d–521b, nn. C–E). The efforts of the rulers to see the Good instantiated are quite general, at least to the boundaries of their city (cf. 469b-471c, n.A).

540d–541b: OUR CITY IS POSSIBLE, PROVIDED THAT, PHILOSOPHERS BECOME RULERS. THEY WILL DESPISE WHAT ARE GENERALLY NOW THOUGHT OF AS HONORS, WILL VALUE WHAT IS RIGHT AND THE HONORS ARISING THEREFROM, AND WILL CONSIDER JUSTICE THE GREATEST AND MOST NECESSARY THING. THEY MIGHT ESTABLISH THE CITY BY SENDING AWAY ALL THOSE OVER THE AGE OF TEN AND BY EDUCATING THE CHILDREN WHO REMAIN IN THE MANNER THAT WE HAVE DESCRIBED. THIS WOULD BE THE QUICKEST WAY TO ESTABLISH OUR CITY, SO THAT IT WILL BE HAPPY AND WILL PROVIDE THE MOST BENEFIT FOR THOSE AMONG WHOM IT IS ESTABLISHED. WE HAVE THUS COMPLETED THE ACCOUNT OF THIS CITY AND THE MAN WHO IS LIKE IT.

A.   This section marks a break in the *Republic*. Plato ends his description of the city and the man who resembles it, and likewise ends his response to the difficulties raised by his interlocutors at the start of Book V. Thus he brings himself back to the point where he was at the end of Book IV, about to describe the cities and people who are less good than his city and the rulers of it (445c–e).

  So far he has described the city, discovered that it is just and what the justice in it is. He has also described the corresponding sort of man, and shown that he is just and what the justice in his soul is. He has established, he believes, that both the city and the man are good (though in a sense only provisionally, because he has not supported his argument with a final account of what the Good is). Further, he has argued, or at least maintained (521a, 465c–466c), that the lives of the rulers will be very good and very happy. But he has *not* yet—and it is very important to remember this fact—established that justice is *better* for one who possesses it than injustice is for its possessor, or that justice makes one happi*er* than injustice does. And he has therefore *not* yet met the challenge that was laid down by Glaucon and Adeimantus in Book II. It is to the fulfillment of this obligation, then, that the rest of the work, especially Books VIII–IX (see 576b–578b, n. A), is devoted.

B.   Plato suggests that his city might be established if philosophers could be found to rule who would send away all people over the age of ten years and start organizing the city by educating those who were left. Although much the same idea has already been set forth in 500e–502c, it seems odd enough for people to have wondered whether Plato means it to be taken entirely seriously.

Nevertheless, there is clearly a serious point lying behind it, which is essential to an understanding of the *Republic*. That point is that the *Republic* is not a description of a process of reform which any city or person may freely adopt to achieve some improvement of character. Plato's main vehicle for improving the character of individuals is education, beginning at an early age. For many adults, he clearly thinks, time has run out. Of course, many of these people who are in a city such as he has described may be able to be controlled by the rulers (590c–591a, nn. C–D). But he does not think that a philosopher-ruler will be able to take an established group of adults and necessarily be capable of bringing it, as it is, into a tractable condition (see *ibid.*).

Book VIII

- types of cities - gov't
- ~~education of guardians~~
- ~~division of guardian class~~

543a–c: SO IF THE CITY IS TO BE WELL GOVERNED, THEN
WIVES, CHILDREN, EDUCATIONS, AND OCCUPATIONS MUST BE
IN COMMON; THE RULERS WILL HAVE NO PRIVATE PROPERTY,
AND THEIR WAGES MUST BE ONLY THOSE OF GUARDIANS AND
SOLDIERS, I.E., JUST ENOUGH TO SUPPORT THEM, THEIR DUTY
BEING TO CARE FOR THEMSELVES AND THE CITY.

A. Plato sums up the main features of the rulers' and guardians' lives,
with which he will now contrast the lives of people of other types. Once
again the leading ideas are that the task of being a guardian must be
strictly kept to, and that the lives of the guardians must be bound together by a community of possessions and activities, so that the city as a
whole may be held together (465b, 545c–d).

543c–544d: WE MUST RETURN TO THE POINT (I.E., THE BE-
GINNING OF BOOK V) AT WHICH, HAVING DESCRIBED A GOOD
CITY AND A GOOD MAN, WE WERE GOING TO EXAMINE FOUR
OTHER TYPES OF CITY, SO AS TO SEE WHICH WAS THE BEST
AND WHICH WAS THE WORST, AND WHETHER THE BEST MAN
WAS THE HAPPIEST AND THE WORST THE LEAST HAPPY. THE
FOUR TYPES ARE (NOT INCLUDING OUR CITY, WHICH IS *KING-
SHIP OR ARISTOCRACY*, DEPENDING ON HOW MANY RULERS
THERE ARE: (1) THE CRETAN OR LACONIAN TYPE, I.E., *TIMO-
CRACY*, (2) *OLIGARCHY*, (3) *DEMOCRACY*, AND (4) *DICTATORSHIP*

OR *TYRANNY*. OTHER TYPES OF CONSTITUTION FALL BE-
TWEEN THESE.

A. Plato here returns to the point at the beginning of Book V, 449a,
where he had said that there were four types of defective city and was
about to describe them, when Adeimantus broke in with the demand
that Socrates explain the sense in which wives and children were to be
held in common.

B. In 543d1–544a1 it is cryptically suggested that Plato has yet a
better city and a better man to tell of than the ones described so far.
Plato has said nothing explicit in this vein, and indeed Glaucon indicates
(by "it seems", *hōs eoikas*) that he realizes this. It seems doubtful, however, that Plato would not make this suggestion without some purpose.
If we are to guess what it is, then we should probably say that it concerns the idea that a disembodied soul might be in a better state than
an embodied person, and that there might even be a city of disembodied
souls (see 611a–612a, n. B). But if this is Plato's idea, it plays no central
role in his argument here. [Shorey, *WPS*, p. 238.]

544d–545c: THERE MUST BE FIVE TYPES OF MEN CORRESPOND-
ING TO THE FIVE TYPES OF CITY, BECAUSE THE CITIES MUST
GET THEIR CHARACTERS FROM SOME OF THE MEN IN THEM.
THE MAN CORRESPONDING TO THE GOOD CITY (ARISTOCRACY
OR KINGSHIP) IS THE GOOD AND JUST MAN; AND LIKEWISE
THERE ARE FOUR LESS GOOD TYPES OF MEN. AFTER WE EX-
AMINE THESE WE MUST COMPARE THE MOST JUST, WHOM WE
HAVE ALREADY DESCRIBED, AND THE LEAST JUST, WITH
RESPECT TO HOW HAPPY THEY ARE.

A. As we observed earlier (358a–362c, n. B), Plato explicitly presented
his task in Book II as one of showing that the purely or completely just
man is happier and better off than the purely or completely unjust man
(545a5–7), rather than one of showing that one's amount of happiness
is always directly proportional to one's degree of justice. He does the
same here, and subsequently in 587d–e. Nevertheless, the following discussion gives us the distinct impression that although he does not argue
the point at all, he thinks that those whom he is about to describe are,
as a rough generalization, less happy insofar as they are less just (see
580a–c, n. A, and Introd., sec. 3). (Remember, however, that he is not
aiming to show that an increase in justice will *always* bring an increase

in happiness, or vice versa—see 519d–521b, n. E., and notice that although he does seem to think that a rough proportionality of justice and happiness holds among those whom he is about to describe, he never states it, much less emphasizes it.

B.   There is an echo here of the previously enunciated idea (435c–436b) that characteristics of cities arise from characteristics of its inhabitants. As before, however, the idea plays no crucial role in Plato's argument, beyond that of helping us to know what to expect. For he takes it to be clear from observation, and independently of this idea, that the five types of cities and men that he has enumerated exist, along with various intermediate types as well.

On the other hand, Plato does believe that there is a correspondence between the cities and the men, which consists partly in the fact that a city takes on characteristics from the men who are most actively involved in governing it. The other part of the correspondence is that the structure exhibited by the classes in the city is supposed to be analogous to the structure exhibited by the parts of the corresponding man's soul, as was the case with the good city and the good man in Book IV.

545c–547c: *THE DEVELOPMENT OF THE TIMOCRATIC CITY.* THE CITY THAT WE HAVE DESCRIBED, LIKE EVERYTHING THAT COMES INTO EXISTENCE, MUST EVENTUALLY PERISH. AS IN THE CASE OF ALL POLITICAL CHANGE, THIS HAPPENS BY THE BREAKING OUT OF DISSENSION AMONG THE RULERS, WHICH CANNOT OCCUR WHEN THE RULERS ARE OF ONE MIND. IN THE PRESENT CASE CHANGE OCCURS WHEN THE RULERS FAIL TO FOLLOW THE CORRECT PROCEDURES FOR PRODUCING FUTURE GUARDIANS AND RULERS. AS A RESULT, SUBSEQUENT GENERATIONS NEGLECT TRAINING IN THE ARTS FIRST OF ALL, AND THEN PHYSICAL TRAINING ALSO. THE ABILITY TO JUDGE THE NATURES OF MEN DETERIORATES, AND THE CLASS OF RULERS BECOMES NO LONGER HOMOGENEOUS, SO THAT DISSENSION AMONG THEM RESULTS. BY A COMPROMISE BETWEEN THE BETTER AND THE WORSE AMONG THEM, LAND AND HOUSES ARE DISTRIBUTED AS PRIVATE PROPERTY; AND THE RULERS NOW REGARD AS THEIR SLAVES THOSE WHOM THEY PREVIOUSLY GUARDED AND VIEWED AS THEIR FRIENDS AND PROVIDERS.

A.   The deterioration of his city is traced by Plato to violations of the principles on which he has based his construction of it. One is the Principle of the Natural Division of Labor, and the need for each person to perform the task for which he is naturally suited. The other is the need for concord and unity within the city and within the class of rulers. (See 369e–370c and 422e–423d, n. B.) The former comes into play because when future rulers are not properly bred, they turn out not to be suited to the task of ruling (the metaphor of the metals as representing natural dispositions echoes 414b–415d). Failures of guardianship ensue. One failure is that the educational system is allowed to deteriorate (cf. 401d–403c, n. B, where Plato made the overseeing of education a part of the guardianly function). Another is marked in 547c, where it is said that in the timocratic city the rulers do not see themselves as fulfilling the role of guardians of those whom they rule (cf. 341c–342e, n. A).

The latter principle, concerning the need for unity, appears in 545c–d, where the cause of change of constitution is said always to be dissension in the ruling group leading to dissension within the city as a whole. (In 465b Plato has said that unity among the guardians of his city guarantees the unity of the city.) The same theme is repeated in 547a.

B. The purpose of Plato's sketch of various political changes is intimately connected with his overall argument. It shows the mechanisms by which he thinks a city operates, those whose disruption leads to a change of constitution. The leading idea, as he says in 545c–d, is that dissension in the ruling group leads to dissolution. The explanation of these mechanisms leads in turn to an explanation of the dynamics of the individual soul that produce deviations from the best type, i.e., the philosopher-ruler in Plato's city. It is important to be aware that what Plato is ultimately aiming at here is an understanding of the individual soul. For his final goal is to put us in a position to understand the state of soul of the completely unjust man, so that we may compare his soul with the soul of the philosopher-ruler (i.e., the perfectly just man) and see which of the two is happier. For this determination was the original task laid down in Book II (358a–368c). From this standpoint, the account of the intermediate souls and cities has the chief purpose of giving us a better grasp of the workings of the soul and of how it may go awry, finally to reach the ultimate extreme of the completely unjust dictatorial man (573c–576b).

C. That said, it still remains true that there is some interest in viewing Book VIII as a kind of hypothesis about historical development, whether or not Plato really intended it to be taken so. Cf. 371e–373c, n. C.

[Nettleship, pp. 295–6, 299; Adam, II, pp. 195–6; Diès, pp. lxxxix–ciii.]

D. In 547c we have a brief glimpse of how the rulers in Plato's city, by contrast to timocratic rulers, are supposed to regard those whom they rule. In the first place, the ruled are *guarded* (*phylattomenous*) by the rulers, i.e., they are those in relation to whom the rulers perform their task of guardianship. They are also providers (*tropheas*), people who fulfill a certain function within the city which is essential to the existence and well-being of both the city and the rulers themselves. (This idea recalls Plato's earlier point that human beings are not self-sufficient; see 369b–d.) In addition, the ruled are also "free" (*eleutherous*) and "friends" or "dear" (*philous*) to the rulers (see 588b–590a, n. B). They are free because, as Plato sees the matter, they are not subject to the arbitrary desires and whims of the rulers and therefore fit into a scheme in which both their tasks and those of the rulers are equally prescribed. They are friends to the rulers because the rulers view their activity in fulfillment of their tasks as important to their own task. (Notice that this is in certain important ways different from our present-day notion of friendship and involves no real notion of sympathy or altruism.)

E. It is unclear how seriously Plato takes the discussion of numbers in 546b–d, though people have remarked that it at least shows his belief in the importance of numerically expressible patterns in the sensible world (see also 587b–588a).

547d–548d: THE CHARACTERISTICS OF THE TIMOCRATIC CITY. THIS CITY IS MANAGED BY RULERS WITH MORE OF A TASTE FOR WAR THAN FOR PEACE. THEY VALUE HONOR BUT ARE ALSO SECRETLY GREEDY FOR MONEY. THEIR EDUCATION HAS OVERESTIMATED PHYSICAL TRAINING AT THE EXPENSE OF TRAINING IN THE ARTS, LEAVING THE CITY A MIXTURE OF GOOD AND BAD, BUT FOSTERING AN EXCESSIVE DESIRE FOR MILITARY VICTORY AND HONORS.

A. The timocratic city is dominated by those members of the class of guardians who were primarily suited for fighting, namely, the auxiliaries (412e–414b). Plato has stressed the idea that the guardians' education must aim at a blending of aggressive and peaceful tendencies (374e–376c, 410a–412a). The rulers of the timocratic city are those in whom such a blending has not been successfully accomplished, and who, though they presumably could be fighters in Plato's city, are not now subject to the moderating influence of true rulers.

B.   Plato says that timocratic men will harbor a secret fondness for wealth (548a). This is because they will be anxious to have private resources rather than having everything in common (547b, 416e–417a). It would appear that Plato thinks of money as having the major characteristic of being easily disposable by the individual for his own private purposes.

548d–549b: *THE CHARACTERISTICS OF THE TIMOCRATIC MAN.* THE MAN CORRESPONDING TO THIS TYPE OF CITY HAS AN INCOMPLETE EDUCATION, WHICH HAS EMPHASIZED PHYSICAL TRAINING AT THE EXPENSE OF TRAINING IN THE ARTS. HE IS HARSH TO THOSE WHO ARE SUBORDINATE TO HIM. HE WELCOMES MONEY MORE AS HE GROWS OLDER. AND HE IS NOT PURE WITH RESPECT TO EXCELLENCE OR VIRTUE, BECAUSE HE HAS LACKED THE BEST SORT OF GUARDIAN, NAMELY, THE EXERCISE OF REASON COMBINED WITH THE ARTS.

A.   The ideas expressed here are much the same as those expressed in the previous sections. In general, Plato of course cannot completely separate his treatment of a city from that of the corresponding man, nor his treatment of development from his description of the product thereof.

549c–550c: *THE DEVELOPMENT OF THE TIMOCRATIC MAN.* THE TIMOCRATIC MAN IS THE SON OF A GOOD MAN WHO LIVES IN A BADLY RULED CITY. THE FATHER IS NOT ESTEEMED BUT LIVES A PRIVATE LIFE CONCENTRATED ON HIS THOUGHTS. THE SON IS PULLED IN TWO DIRECTIONS, TOWARD THE USE OF REASON BY HIS FATHER, AND IN THE DIRECTION OF APPETITES BY OTHERS, WHO URGE HIM TO SEEK MORE ACTIVELY AFTER HONOR.

A.   In 550a–b Plato attributes the development of the timocratic man directly to a conflict within his character arising from two contrary influences. This explanation is to be compared with the earlier explanation of the way in which dissension among rulers leads to political change (545c–547c).

B.   Plato also shows here how he thinks that the development of the timocratic city is linked to the decline of justice in the city. For it emerges that in such a city there is little esteem for restricting oneself to one's own affairs in the city (the phrase for minding one's own affairs or business, *ta hautōn prattein* at 550a2–3, is one that Plato has frequently used as a rough expression of the notion of justice, as at 443c–e). The major manifestation of this feature of the timocratic city is the fact that the performance of the task of guardianship has broken down (545c–547c, n. A).

550c–551b: THE DEVELOPMENT OF THE OLIGARCHIC CITY. OLIGARCHY DEVELOPS FROM TIMOCRACY WHEN MEN BECOME PREOCCUPIED WITH MONEY, AND A PROPERTY QUALIFICATION FOR PUBLIC OFFICE IS ESTABLISHED.

A.   The development of the oligarchic city from the timocratic city is the development from a city characterized by a love of honor to a city characterized by the desire for money, which Plato associates with the appetitive part of the soul (see 580e–581a, and 553a–e, n. A). In 550e Plato says that the desire to be excellent or virtuous gives way as the desire for money increases. The former desire had already been weakened in the timocratic city (549b), and this process continues in subsequent cities (556c). This is a manifestation of the kind of mistaken view of the Good which Plato had said must be avoided by the rulers of his city (504d–506a).

551b–552e: THE CHARACTERISTICS OF THE OLIGARCHIC CITY. THE OLIGARCHIC CITY IS NOT ONE CITY BUT TWO, THE CITY OF THE RICH AND THE CITY OF THE POOR. MOREOVER, THE RULERS WILL BE AFRAID TO ARM MANY SOLDIERS, AND SO EITHER WILL HAVE NO EFFECTIVE DEFENSE FOR THE CITY, OR WILL THEMSELVES HAVE TO FIGHT, THUS PERFORMING MORE THAN ONE TASK. IN ADDITION, A MAN WILL BE ABLE TO LOSE ALL OF HIS PROPERTY AND THUS NOT BE A GENUINE PART OF THE CITY EVEN THOUGH HE LIVES IN IT. AND EVEN THE MAN WHO IS STILL RICH WILL BE MERELY A SPENDER RATHER THAN A MAN WITH A TASK THAT IS GENUINELY PART OF THE OPERATION OF THE CITY. THE CITY WILL BE FULL OF DRONES, INHABITANTS WITHOUT ROLES, THE STINGLESS ONES BEING BEGGARS AND THOSE WITH STINGS BEING CRIMINALS WHO MUST BE KEPT UNDER CONTROL BY FORCE.

A.   Plato regards the oligarchic city as markedly worse than the timocratic city in both of the same respects in which the timocratic city was worse than his aristocratic city (see n. A on 545c–547c). In the first place, the oligarchic city is clearly no longer one city but two cities (cf. 422e–423a). In the second place, the assignment to each person of his natural task has been seriously disrupted. For one thing, there are none who perform solely the task of guardianship (cf. 547c). Moreover, the many poor people in the city have no function in it at all, being merely drones. But not only do the poor have this characteristic of tasklessness; the rich do too, because their main activity is money-making and Plato considers this, like the spending of money, not to be a task genuinely contributing to the maintenance of the city (cf. 421c–422a). In sum, the city both lacks unity and fails to conform to the Principle of the Natural Division of Labor. [Bosanquet, p. 322.]

B.   In 552b–e Plato tries to explain the occurrence in an oligarchy of the kinds of actions that, the reader will notice, were mentioned in 442d–443b as those deemed to be unjust or criminal by ordinary standards. In so doing he is trying to show a connection between injustice as it is ordinarily conceived and injustice as he explains it in his discussion of cities and individual souls. For what is responsible for these crimes, he thinks, is the lack of what he has called justice in both city and individual (cf. 590a–c, n. B).

553a–e: THE DEVELOPMENT OF THE OLIGARCHIC MAN. THE OLIGARCHIC MAN ARISES WHEN HIS TIMOCRATIC FATHER IS RUINED BY SOME MISFORTUNE AND LOSES ALL OF HIS PROPERTY. IN FEAR, THE SON SUBORDINATES ALL OF HIS DESIRES AND ENERGIES TO THE DESIRE FOR MONEY, FORCING REASON TO SERVE THIS END AND SUPPRESSING OTHER APPETITES TO THE EXTENT THAT THEY INTERFERE WITH IT AND CAN THEMSELVES GO UNSATISFIED.

A.   Expressed in terms of Plato's theory of the soul, the difference between the timocratic and oligarchic man is that the former is dominated by a desire of the spirited part of the soul, whereas the latter is governed by one of his appetites of the lowest part of his soul, the desire for money (see 553d with 580e–581a, 550a–b). The idea appears to be that this greed for money arises because of fear brought on by his father's financial ruin, which in turn was brought on by unsuccessful efforts to live life in the pursuit of honor. As Plato stresses both here and in the next section (see n. B there), this leads to a suppression of other desires, including those of the appetitive part of the soul.

554a–555a: THE CHARACTERISTICS OF THE OLIGARCHIC MAN. THE OLIGARCHIC MAN SUBORDINATES ALL OF HIS OTHER DESIRES TO MAKING MONEY, SATISFYING ONLY HIS NECESSARY DESIRES. HE HAS OTHER APPETITES, AND THEY ARE STRONG BECAUSE OF HIS HAVING BEEN POORLY EDUCATED, BUT HE HOLDS THEM IN CHECK. BECAUSE OF HIS CONFLICT WITHIN HIMSELF, HE IS NOT ONE MAN BUT TWO. THE OLIGARCHIC MAN THUS CORRESPONDS TO THE OLIGARCHIC CITY, ESPECIALLY IN THAT HE IS AFRAID TO SPEND MONEY TO SATISFY HIS APPETITES, JUST AS THE CITY IS AFRAID TO ARM ITS CITIZENS (551d–e).

A.   Like the oligarchic city, the oligarchic man is torn by conflict, his desire for money holding other desires in check. (The normal situation would appear to be that the desire for money serves other desires, accumulating the wherewithal for them to be satisfied; see 580e–581a.)

B.   It should be noticed that being dominated by a single appetite is not enough, in Plato's view, to give one a soul that is harmonious and unified (see 573c–576b, n. B). For what the desire for money lacks, and the motivation arising from reason has, is the impulse to oversee all of the desires and motivations, and the arrangement thereof. As a result, domination by greed requires the *suppression* of other desires (which remain strong in spite of being suppressed), rather than the moderate satisfaction of the necessary ones and the training of them (note 554b) so that they will not get out of hand or threaten the harmony of the whole soul (see *ibid.*).

C.   The fact that the oligarchic man is dominated by only one element of the appetitive part of his soul should remind us that, as noted in n. A to 435c–436b, the appetitive part is not really a unitary part of the soul but rather a collection of heterogeneous and often conflicting desires.

555b–557a: THE DEVELOPMENT OF THE DEMOCRATIC CITY. THE DEMOCRATIC CITY ARISES WHEN THE OLIGARCHIC CITY IS RUINED BY EXCESSIVE GREED. MONEY-MAKERS, CARING ONLY ABOUT GREATER GAINS, ALLOW PEOPLE TO BORROW FOOLISHLY TO SATISFY THEIR APPETITES, AND THEN TO BE

FINANCIALLY RUINED SO THAT THEY ARE DRONES WITHIN THE CITY. EVENTUALLY, THE CITY FALLS INTO STRIFE, AND WHEN THE POOR ARE VICTORIOUS, DEMOCRACY EMERGES.

A. In keeping with Plato's general view, the fall of oligarchy is caused by disunity and dissension (556e, *stasiazei*). No mention is made of dissension within the ruling group, as one would have expected from 545c–d, but the omission is not surprising, because there has not been any indication that the ruling group in the oligarchic city has ever been substantially unified.

B. At 555c it is said that the esteem of money is incompatible with the acquisition by the citizens of a sufficient degree of moderation. This statement illustrates a point made earlier about Plato's view of appetites, that they are cravings without any natural limit (see n. E on 358a–362c, 422e–423d, n. C, 437b–439b, n. B). There is no such thing, for example, as a desire that is simply a desire for a modest amount of money; rather, there is only the possibility of the desire for money to be limited by some other factor. [Kraut, *RJR*, pp. 223–4.]

557b–558c: THE CHARACTERISTICS OF THE DEMOCRATIC CITY. IT IS A CITY IN WHICH ONE CAN DO ANYTHING THAT ONE PLEASES, AND SO IT IS FULL OF ALL KINDS OF PEOPLE AND, AS IT WERE, CONTAINS ALL KINDS OF CONSTITUTIONS. THERE IS NO COMPULSION TO RULE OR TO BE RULED, AND PEOPLE DO WHAT THEY LIKE IN DISREGARD OF THE LAW. A KIND OF EQUALITY IS ACCORDED TO BOTH EQUALS AND UNEQUALS.

A. Democracy, too, deviates from the pattern and principles of Plato's city. As oligarchy was not one city but two (551d), so democracy contains all sorts of constitutions and is a sort of emporium of constitutions (557d). Presumably, Plato means that it contains many organizations exhibiting all different sorts of structure (e.g., clubs with property qualifications for membership, analogous to oligarchy, and even aristocratic philosophical societies like Plato's Academy). In any case, the emphasis is on the variety and lack of cohesiveness in a democratic city. This lack of cohesiveness is attributed by Plato to the fact that in a democracy one is free, not to act in performance of a task to which one is naturally suited, as in Plato's city, but to do whatever one wants (*boulesthai*, 557b7; *epithymein*, e5). In this way the democratic city is analogous to the appetitive part of the soul, which is a jumble of desires rather than a single one (435c–436b, n. A).

B.   A closely related feature of the democratic city, harking back to the parable of the ship of state and the metaphor of the beast (487b–489c, 491b–494a), is that it honors only what happens to please the multitude at the moment (558b–c). It therefore has no coherent policy or plan of government (cf. 519c), and what laws it does have possess no force (557e–558a).

558c–559d: BEFORE WE DESCRIBE THE DEVELOPMENT OF THE DEMOCRATIC MAN, WE MUST EXPLAIN THE DISTINCTION BE-TWEEN TWO KINDS OF APPETITES, THE NECESSARY OR PRO-FITABLE ONES, AND THE UNNECESSARY OR SPENDTHRIFT ONES. THE FORMER ARE THOSE THAT WE ARE UNABLE TO DIVERT OR SUPPRESS, AND THAT BENEFIT US WHEN THEY ARE SATISFIED; FOR WE NECESSARILY PURSUE THE SATISFAC-TION OF SUCH APPETITES BY NATURE. THE LATTER SORT ARE THOSE THAT WE CAN GET RID OF BY PRACTICE FROM A YOUNG AGE, AND THAT EITHER DO NO GOOD OR DO HARM.

A.   This distinction among appetites (*epithymiai*) is based on two cri-teria. (At 559c9 it is implied that there is an analogous distinction among pleasures, *hēdonai*; cf. 561a.) One is whether or not the appetite can be gotten rid of by practice and education. The other is whether or not the satisfaction of the appetite produces benefit. But Plato evidently thinks that these two criteria coincide, and he makes no provision for the possi-bility that a desire might be ineradicable but yet produce harm or be eradicable but yet produce benefit. And he speaks of those that are both ineradicable and beneficial as natural (558e2).

B.   The distinction is meant to classify appetites belonging to the third, appetitive part of the soul. Plato is therefore saying that some of these are necessary and natural—a position that fits with his earlier points, that men have needs that they cannot satisfy by themselves, such as the needs for food and shelter (369b–d). We see once again that Plato is concerned with how human life is to be lived in the physical world as it is, with all of the difficulties engendered by "physical" needs and desires (369b–d, n. B). Whether he thinks that the afterlife offers some-thing else is another question (611a–612a, n. B).

559d–562a: *THE DEVELOPMENT AND CHARACTERISTICS OF THE DEMOCRATIC MAN.* THE DEMOCRATIC MAN APPEARS WHEN THE SON OF AN OLIGARCHIC MAN IS ENCOURAGED BY OTHERS TO DEVELOP HIS SPENDTHRIFT APPETITES. HE IS

FULL OF CONFLICT BETWEEN THESE AND HIS NECESSARY AP-
PETITES; AND HIS FATHER, BECAUSE OF HIS IGNORANCE OF
PROPER EDUCATION, IS UNABLE TO MAKE HIM CLEAVE TO
THE LATTER. EVENTUALLY, THE BAD COMPANY THAT HE
KEEPS LEADS HIM TO GIVE IN AND HE INDULGES IN UNNECES-
SARY PLEASURES. LATER IN LIFE HE REGAINS SOME OF THE
MODERATE APPETITES AND THEN PUTS ALL PLEASURES ON
AN EQUAL FOOTING, YIELDING DAY BY DAY TO WHICHEVER
IS AT HAND, LEADING A LIFE OF NO ORDER OR DISCIPLINE.

A. Like the democratic city, the democratic man is characterized by a
lack of plan and organization in his life. He has no rationale for particular activities and indulgences, but simply follows whim, i.e., whatever
desire happens to be strongest at the time (as 561c–d shows, this is sometimes a desire of one of the upper two parts of the soul).

B. It is worthy of note that Plato does not treat of the democratic man
in two distinct sections, one on his development and another on his characteristics, as he has done for the other types of men in Book VIII. The
reason is perhaps that unlike the other men, the democratic man does
not reach a clearly defined point at which he remains stable and fully
developed for the rest of his life (though a kind of mellowing sets in,
Plato says). Rather, as 561a–b indicates, his development extends late
into life, and he never has any fully fixed pattern of activity.

C. As elsewhere, Plato emphasizes at 559e the great effect on one's
character exerted by the company that one keeps (see *e.g.*, 549e–550b
on the timocratic man). (The other major influence that he especially
attends to is, of course, education; see 560a–b.) The metaphor that he
uses to describe the situation is that of the city with one type of constitution coming to the aid of a sympathetic faction within another city. The
general idea is that of a part of a soul or of a city receiving help from
outside when it is unable by itself to overcome opposing parts. This
same idea is exploited later, in 590c–591a, in Plato's account of how the
reason of the rulers ought to serve those in the city whose own reasoning
is too weak to prevail within them alone.

562a–564b: LIKE OLIGARCHY, DEMOCRACY IS DESTROYED BY
EXCESSIVE INDULGENCE IN WHAT IT DEFINES AS THE GOOD,
NAMELY, LIBERTY OR FREEDOM. IN A DEMOCRACY, LIBERTY
IS CARRIED TO THE POINT OF ANARCHY, SO THAT ALL ARE
TREATED AS, AND TRY TO ACT AS, EQUALS, BECAUSE THEY

WANT TO AVOID ANY APPEARANCE OF CONTROL. THIS EX-CESS OF LIBERTY LEADS, IN DICTATORSHIP, TO AN EXCESS OF SLAVERY (AS, IN GENERAL, AN EXCESS OF ONE SORT USUALLY PRODUCES A CHANGE IN THE OPPOSITE DIRECTION).

A.   Before giving his account of the fall of democracy and the rise of dictatorship, Plato makes the general observation that both democracy and oligarchy are destroyed by excessive indulgence in what they call good. It is of course crucial that their view of the good be a mistaken one, not the correct one that governs the actions of the rulers in Plato's own city. The defective types of city all err in their conceptions of the Good, each mistaking it for something else. Thus, the timocratic city treats honor as the Good; the oligarchic city treats money as the Good, and democracy defines the Good (562b9) as liberty. (But Plato does not say that timocracy is destroyed by excessive indulgence in honor.) It is the avoidance of such misidentifications that enables Plato's city to maintain itself in a good condition (504d–506a, 534b–c).

564b–566d: *THE DEVELOPMENT OF DICTATORSHIP.* IN A DE-MOCRACY THREE PARTS MAY BE DISTINGUISHED. ONE CONSISTS OF THE DRONES, WHO ARE FAR MORE POWERFUL THAN THEY ARE IN AN OLIGARCHY, AND INDEED, THEY MANAGE MOST OF THE BUSINESS OF THE CITY; ANOTHER CONSISTS OF THE WEALTHIEST, ON WHOM THE DRONES HOPE TO PREY; AND THE THIRD CONSISTS OF THE PEOPLE, WHO ARE THE MOST POWERFUL ELEMENT WHENEVER THEY ARE ASSEMBLED. STRIFE BREAKS OUT WHEN THE LEADERS OF THE PEOPLE AT-TEMPT TO GAIN WEALTH FOR THEMSELVES AND THE PEOPLE, AND ACCUSE THE WEALTHIEST OF PLOTTING AGAINST THE PEOPLE; IN RESPONSE THE WEALTHIEST ATTEMPT TO ACT AS OLIGARCHS, AND A STRUGGLE RESULTS. THE PEOPLE ELEVATE ONE MAN AS THEIR CHAMPION, AND OUT OF THIS SITUATION THERE GROWS DICTATORSHIP. SUCH A MAN DOMINATES THE PEOPLE, AND TURNS TO ALL SORTS OF CRIMES TO GAIN POWER, AT THE SAME TIME ENTICING THE PEOPLE WITH PROMISES OF GAIN FOR THEM. TO PROTECT HIMSELF AGAINST THE OPPOSITION OF THE WOULD-BE OLIGARCHS, HE ASKS FOR A BODYGUARD, WHICH THE PEOPLE GRANT HIM, AND HE NOW BECOMES A DICTATOR.

A.   Once again the cause of political change is said to be division within the city (545c–547c, n. A). The rivalry and strife among the three politically active parts of a democracy are what allow dictatorship to emerge. [On the translation "dictator" (instead of "tyrant") for *tyrannos* see Grube, *Rep.*, p. 195, n. 3.]

566d–569c: THE CHARACTERISTICS OF DICTATORSHIP. THE DICTATOR GENERALLY TRIES TO STIR UP WAR, SO THAT THE PEOPLE WILL NEED A LEADER, SO THAT THEY WILL BE DISTRACTED FROM PLOTTING AGAINST HIM, AND SO THAT HE WILL HAVE EXCUSES TO SUPPRESS THOSE WHOM HE SUSPECTS OF OPPOSING HIM. HE MUST ELIMINATE ALL PEOPLE OF ABILITY, WHETHER FRIENDS OR ENEMIES, LEST THEY RIVAL HIM. HE WILL ENLIST IN HIS BODYGUARD FOREIGN DRONES, SLAVES THAT HE HAS TAKEN FROM OTHERS. HE WILL SUPPORT HIS EFFORTS BY SPENDING THE SACRED TREASURES OF THE CITY AND THE PROPERTY OF HIS VICTIMS, AND HIS OWN FATHER'S ESTATE. WHEN THE PEOPLE TRY TO GET RID OF HIM, HE WILL NOT HESITATE TO BE HARSH TOWARD THEM, AND EVEN TOWARD HIS OWN FATHER, AND PEOPLE WILL DISCOVER FINALLY THAT THEY HAVE BEEN ENSLAVED.

A.   The sketch of dictatorship is a prelude to the description of the dictator, and for obvious reasons concentrates on his actions. In particular, Plato stresses the crimes and injustices committed by the dictator (esp. 568d–569c). As in the section on oligarchy (551b–552e, n. B), Plato here tries to show a connection between the injustice of a city in his own sense (the failure of parts to perform their natural tasks, 432b–434c) and the occurrence in it of what would ordinarily be called unjust actions (see 590a–c, n. B).

B.   Plato's claim at the beginning of this section, that he is going to discuss the "happiness" of the dictator, is of course ironic. His sarcastic treatment in 568a–d of poets who eulogize dictators is a foreshadowing of his discussion of tragic poetry in Book X (595a–608b).

C.   In 567c–e (see also 575d) Plato reacts in a particularly scandalized way to the idea that the dictator will appropriate slaves and foreigners to serve as his bodyguard. The idea of making use of outsiders in the management of the city has significance within Plato's scheme. For it illustrates the lack of cohesiveness of the city under dictatorship, insofar as the city is ruled with the help of people who do not even belong to it (cf. 552a–c, on the presence in an oligarchy of those who are not truly a part of it).

Book IX

571a–572b: BEFORE WE CONSIDER THE DICTATORIAL MAN, WE MUST MAKE ANOTHER CLASSIFICATION OF APPETITES (CF. 558c–559d), OF THOSE THAT WE HAVE CALLED UNNECESSARY, SOME ARE LAWLESS AND ARE LIABLE TO BREAK FORTH IN ANYONE'S SLEEP IN THE FORM OF DREAMS, THOUGH IN A FEW THEY ARE PERHAPS ELIMINATED OR WEAKENED. BUT A MODERATE MAN, HAVING STIMULATED THE REASONING PART OF HIS SOUL, AND HAVING NEITHER STARVED NOR OVER-INDULGED HIS APPETITES, AND HAVING CALMED HIS SPIRITED PART AND NOT GONE TO SLEEP ANGRY, WILL BE ABLE TO EXERCISE HIS RATIONAL PART WHILE ASLEEP.

A.   This passage starts from the classification in 558c–559d, and treats a subclass of the appetites there marked off as unnecessary, namely, the subclass labeled "lawless" appetites. It may seem from Plato's manner of speaking here that these appetites ought to be called necessary rather than unnecessary, on the ground that people seem unable to get rid of them (572b). But in fact Plato wishes to say that they are unnecessary, in the sense that life can be lived without any actual *satisfaction* of them, even if the desires themselves cannot be completely eliminated.

B.   It is very important to realize that Plato's view of the optimum human condition in the physical world does not present us with a thoroughgoing ascetic ideal. The reasonable man is pictured in 571e–572a as neither overindulging *nor starving* his necessary appetites (see 573c–576b, n. B, 588b–590a, n. B). But this does not mean that just anyone could put himself in a contented or ideal condition by cutting down the satisfaction of his unnecessary appetites, because in many people, as they actually are, some of these appetites are so strong that the people would be miserable if the appetites were not overindulged. Moreover, some people of this kind have obsessions that are, in the actual state of affairs, incurable, though perhaps in the past they might have been forestalled from arriving at such a state. But more than this, Plato clearly believes that some people have by nature such weak reasons and strong appetites that even from birth their condition is irredeemable. Such people, when they are in Plato's city, are to be selected for placement in the lowest class (414b–415d, 590c–591a). Although their condition can be ameliorated by education, they would be unable on their own to moderate their desires (590c–591a).

572b–573c: *THE DEVELOPMENT OF THE DICTATORIAL MAN.* THE MAN OF THIS TYPE IS THE SON OF A DEMOCRATIC MAN. THE SON IS PULLED IN THE DIRECTION OF LAWLESS DESIRES BY OTHER PEOPLE WHO CORRUPT HIM, AND WHO END UP BY ENCOURAGING LUST IN HIM AS THE LEADER OF THOSE APPETITES THAT APPROPRIATE WHATEVER IS AT HAND. THIS LEADING APPETITE BECOMES STRONGER AND DRIVES OUT ALL SHAME AND MODERATION.

A. Among the various appetites of the lowest part of the soul, "lust" (*erōs*) is depicted by Plato as having a special nature that makes it capable of holding the position of, first, leader (*prostatēs*, 572e6) of the other appetites, and later as dictator or tyrant (573d4) among them. The idea as it appears in 572e–573a is evidently that whereas other unnecessary appetites are insistently active whenever their objects are at hand, lust is the sort of nagging appetite that, once it arises, is just as insistent whether its object is present or not. The distinction is one between a strong but evanescent desire and an unremitting obsession.

B. It is because of this unremitting character of lust that Plato thinks it has the particular tyrannical or dictatorial nature which he will go on to explain more fully below (see 573c–576b, n. B), a nature that makes it thwart the satisfaction of other desires.

C. As Plato views it here, *erōs* is simply sexual *craving* (cf. 437b–439b, n. B), rather than any other form of love or attraction. (But at 559c6 he distinguishes sexual desire that is useful from sexual desire that is "spendthrift," and in the *Symposium* and the *Phaedrus* he gives much more elaborate discussions of the nature of *erōs*.)

573c–576b: THE CHARACTERISTICS OF THE DICTATORIAL MAN.
IN THIS MAN LUST DIRECTS ALL ACTIONS, LEADING HIM TO
ALL SORTS OF CRIMES AND SHAMELESS BEHAVIOR. HE BE-
COMES IN FACT AS HE WAS IN THE DREAMS IN WHICH THE
LAWLESS APPETITES MANIFESTED THEMSELVES. HIS CRIMES
ARE FAR GREATER THAN THOSE OF PETTY CRIMINALS. HIS
ASSOCIATES ARE ALWAYS FLATTERERS; HE IS ALWAYS EI-
THER THE MASTER OR THE SLAVE OF THOSE HE IS WITH,
AND HE NEVER KNOWS TRUE FRIENDSHIP. HE IS AS UN-
JUST AS A PERSON CAN BE, BY OUR PREVIOUS STANDARD OF
JUSTICE.

A.   Just as the philosopher-ruler or kingly man was the most just man,
so the dictatorial man is the most unjust. In accordance with Plato's
explanation of justice and injustice in the soul (441c–442d, 444a–e), this
means that the dictatorial man's soul is that in which there is the most
disorder, and whose parts are farthest from performing their own
natural tasks.

B.   Why is the soul that is by this standard the least just the one in
which lust rules? Because, according to Plato, when lust is dominant,
that part of the soul rules that is least suited to do so, rather than reason, which is best suited by nature for the task of ruling. For, as will become clear in the following sections (esp. 576b–578b, 587a–b), the rule
of lust, unlike the rule of reason, involves a lack of any guidance or
directing force in the soul, to see to the orderly satisfaction of all necessary desires, and to the orderly pursuit of the task that the person is
naturally suited to perform. Lust is obsessed with pursuing its own satisfaction, and the person governed by it will do no genuine planning for
the sake of any other end. The satisfaction of other desires will therefore
be thwarted, or at best be a matter of catch-as-catch-can. By contrast,
Plato pictures reason as endowed with a desire for the orderly planning
of the satisfaction of *all* necessary desires, both its own and those of the
other parts of the soul, so that the pursuit of its own ends does not involve the thwarting of other desires in the way that the pursuit of the
ends of lust does (see 571a–572b, n. B, 588b–590a, n. B).
   That lust should be pictured as working toward the thwarting of other
desires fits with Plato's representation of it, in the previous section, as a
kind of obsession which is always insistently at work once it gets out
of hand (572b–573c, n. B). [Irwin, *PMT*, p. 236.]

C.   Because a person dominated by lust is in this manner obsessed, it follows that he cannot concentrate his attention and activity on any single task within a city. Given that the task of ruling a city is as Plato has described it in Books II–VII, it is clear that a dictatorial man who is ruling in his city cannot, because of the predominance of lust in him, genuinely perform the task of ruling the city, any more than lust can perform the task of ruling in the soul.

D.   At 576a Plato says that the dictatorial man never stands to anyone in the relation of true friendship. In this he is to be compared with the timocratic people portrayed in 547c, who were said to have ceased to regard those whom they ruled as friends, as the genuine guardians in Plato's city had done.

576b–578b: LET US NOW SEE WHETHER THE DICTATORIAL MAN IS THE WORST, AND ALSO THE LEAST HAPPY. WE MUST KEEP IN MIND THE RESEMBLANCE BETWEEN THE DICTATORIAL MAN AND THE CITY GOVERNED BY DICTATORSHIP. BOTH THE CITY AND THE MAN ARE THE WORST OF THEIR KIND. BUT HOW IS IT WITH RESPECT TO HAPPINESS AND MISERY? IT IS OBVIOUS THAT A DICTATORSHIP IS THE MOST MISERABLE OF CITIES, FOR THE CITY AS A WHOLE AND THE BEST CITIZENS IN IT ARE SLAVES AND CAN LEAST DO WHAT THEY WANT. LET US NOT, THEN, BE DECEIVED BY THE SUPERFICIAL SHOW OF HAPPINESS THAT THE DICTATOR PRESENTS. FOR WHEN WE LOOK INSIDE HIS SOUL WE CAN SEE THAT, IF THE INDIVIDUAL IS INDEED LIKE THE CITY, THEN THE SAME ARRANGEMENT MUST PREVAIL THERE, SO THAT THE SOUL AS A WHOLE AND THE BEST PARTS IN IT ARE ENSLAVED, AND IT IS RULED BY A SMALL PART WHICH IS THE WORST. SO JUST AS THE DICTATORSHIP IS LEAST ABLE TO DO WHAT IT WANTS, SO TOO THE DICTATOR IS IN FACT THE LEAST ABLE TO DO WHAT HE WANTS. IT THEREFORE DOES APPEAR THAT AS THE DICTATORSHIP IS THE MOST MISERABLE OF CITIES, THE DICTATOR IS LIKEWISE THE MOST MISERABLE OF MEN.

A.   We are now finally nearing the completion of Plato's long comparison, begun in Book II, of the lives of the just man and the unjust man, and his effort to demonstrate his claim that the former is better off than the latter. As he announces explicitly in 580a–c, he is now giving his first argument for the claim. It is readily seen that this argument began as far back as 368c, with the considerations that he now advances having been in the process of development since then.

This *first argument* runs to 580a, its conclusion being stated at length in 580a–c. Then Plato presents two more arguments for much the same thesis. His *second argument* extends from 580c through 583a, and the *third argument* is given in 583b–586d. Further rounding off of the arguments and of their conclusion occupies the remainder of Book IX, to 592b.

B.   The special feature of the first argument, repeatedly stressed by Plato (576c, 577c1–2, d1–2, 579e), is that it depends heavily on the analogy between city and soul, not only on the claim that they possess similar structures, but also on the claim that because of this similarity of structure, an individual of dictatorial character must be unhappy in the same way and to the same degree as the corresponding city (577c–d). It is because of this heavy reliance on this analogy (which Plato earlier asserted to rest on what he acknowledged as a hypothesis, 436b–437a) that he supplements this argument by the two others.

The first argument asks us to suppose that because we can observe the widespread suppression of desires and damage to the wellbeing of people in the dictatorially governed city, we may safely infer that the analogous thing is happening in the corresponding sort of man. Some have regarded 576e–577b as an indication that in judging the happiness of the dictatorial man, Plato was relying on his own personal acquaintance with the dictator Dionysius I of Syracuse, and the passage probably does allude to that acquaintance. But we are plainly not asked to believe Plato's conclusion simply on the basis of his claims about his own experience. Rather, the ability to enter into a character and discern it, spoken of in 577a, is supposed to come from the awareness one must have of the analogy in structure between city and soul on which Plato's argument is based. [Diès, pp. cii–ciii.]

C.   Plato's analogy between city and soul, and his use of it here to show the just man happier than the dictatorial man, raise in a new form a question that we have already discussed in connection with the claim that his city is happy (see 419e–421c, n. D). We earlier asked whether he construes the happiness of the city as a whole as simply the sum of the net quantities of happiness of the individual citizens, or instead construes it as something like an orderly arrangement or distribution of happiness among them. Although it appeared that he did not ever pose this issue explicitly, we saw that his line of thought tended in the latter rather than the former direction. But we have since seen that he sometimes talks as though the parts of the soul are rather like people, with interests of their own that sometimes do and sometimes do not conflict with each other (441c–442d, n. E). So we may ask now whether the happiness of the whole soul (577e) is regarded by him as simply the sum of the quantities of happiness (or possibly satisfaction) of the parts of the soul, or is instead a kind of appropriate or harmonious arrangement of such component happinesses. (Notice that, of course, there might be a conflict between maximizing total happiness of the parts and achieving a harmonious arrangement, so that it can make a difference which of these Plato wishes us to aim for—unless we could somehow be assured that the appearance of conflict is illusory.) Once again our answer to this question has to begin with the observation that he does not pose the issue explicitly and so does not answer it explicitly either. It is true that 587b–588a is strongly suggestive of the idea of maximization of a total quantity of pleasure of the parts of the soul, but the rest of his examination of the whole matter is free of this idea. My own belief is that the later dialogue, the *Philebus*, was primarily intended by him as a discussion of the question whether a man's good or welfare ought to be thought of in such—so to speak—quantitative terms, but that in the *Republic* he does not make a clear statement on the matter. [Bosanquet, pp. 126, 366; Taylor, *PMW*, p. 410; Hackforth, p. 6.]

578b–580a: BUT EVEN MORE MISERABLE IS THE MAN OF THIS TYPE WHO ACTUALLY IS A DICTATOR IN A CITY. HE IS WRACKED BY NEEDS AND FEARS, PARTICULARLY BECAUSE HE IS CONSTANTLY THREATENED WITH UPRISINGS AND ATTACKS BY THOSE WHOM HE HAS ENSLAVED. HE IS HIMSELF ENSLAVED AND IN THE GREATEST NEED TO FLATTER THOSE MEN WHO ARE BAD ENOUGH TO HELP HIM MAINTAIN HIS POSITION.

A. Plato's main interest has all along been to show the unhappiness of a man of a certain sort of character, namely, the unjust man, because his aim has been to show that a lack of justice brings unhappiness. Here, however, he turns explicitly to external circumstances and maintains that an unjust man who actually is a dictator is even worse off than an unjust man who is not a dictator. In addition to the ills that he suffers as an unjust man, the unjust dictator has also to contend with fears that arise from the insecurity of his position.

B. Notice that Plato does not consider the dictator who is not of unjust character. Why not? Partly because he is responding to people like

Thrasymachus, who believe that the chief motivation for being a dictator is to be able to satisfy whatever appetites one wishes, and who would therefore not urge this possibility on Plato as one that urgently required to be treated. And partly, and more importantly, because Plato too does not think that any other sort of person has the desire to occupy the position of a dictator in a city. The only advantage of being in such a position is that one has the ability to minister to obsessions which a man in a better condition of soul will lack. No use, then, wishing that you were a person with a philosopher-ruler's temperament and the external opportunities of a dictator.

580a–c: THE FOREGOING HAS BEEN THE *FIRST ARGUMENT* FOR THE PROPOSITION THAT THE BEST, THE HAPPIEST, AND THE MOST JUST PERSON IS THE MOST KINGLY PERSON, WHO RULES LIKE A KING OVER HIMSELF; WHEREAS THE WORST, MOST UNJUST, AND MOST MISERABLE PERSON IS THE MOST DICTATORIAL PERSON, WHO HOLDS BOTH HIMSELF AND HIS CITY UNDER DICTATORSHIP.

A. As noted (358a–362c, nn. B, D, and 544d–545c, n. A), Plato concentrates in the *Republic* on comparing the degrees of welfare of the completely just and the completely unjust man, paying relatively little heed to the question how well off those people are who possess intermediate amounts of justice. Here, however, although he is mainly concerned to state the results of this comparison, he shows in 580b that, in his view, the order of presentation of diminishing degrees of justice in Book VIII to some degree reflects the order of diminishing degrees of happiness. But he does not pause to argue the point.

B. The present passage makes explicit once again what we saw before in Book IV (444a–e with n. B; cf. 427e–428a), that the man who is completely just is also the man who is, quite generally, best (*aristos*). By the same token, the completely unjust man is also the worst man (*kakistos*). And what Plato has just argued, of course, is that of those surveyed in Books VIII–IX the former is the happiest (*eudaimonestatos*) and the latter is the most miserable (*athliōtatos*). [Grote, pp. 120–1.]

580c–581e: THE SECOND ARGUMENT FOR THE SUPERIORITY OF THE LIFE OF THE JUST MAN: BEGINNING. THE SOUL OF EACH PERSON IS DIVIDED INTO THREE PARTS, TO EACH OF WHICH THERE CORRESPONDS A KIND OF PLEASURE, AND A

KIND OF APPETITE, AND A KIND OF RULE OR GOVERNANCE.
DEPENDING ON WHICH PART RULES, WE HAVE THREE KINDS
OF MEN: THE PHILOSOPHIC, THE VICTORY- AND HONOR-
LOVING, AND THE MONEY-LOVING (SO CALLED BECAUSE HE
DESIRES TO HAVE MONEY TO SATISFY OTHER APPETITES IN
THE APPETITIVE PART OF THE SOUL). WHEN EACH OF THESE
IS ASKED WHICH LIFE IS THE MOST PLEASANT (APART, THAT
IS, FROM THE QUESTION WHICH IS THE MOST BEAUTIFUL OR
THE BEST), HE WILL ANSWER THAT HIS OWN IS.

A.   This second argument for the superiority of the life of the just man
is devoted to arguing that such a life is the *most pleasant*. At 581e Plato
explicitly distinguishes this sort of superiority from considerations about
which life is the most beautiful or finest (*kalon*) and that of which is
the best (see *ameinon*, "better," e8). What the interrelationships among
these issues are he does not say, and in particular he does not say how
the question which life is the most pleasant bears on the question which
life is best or finest. (Here, however, we have another issue that is pursued further in the *Philebus*; cf. 576b–578b, n. C, and 587b–588a, n. B.)
[Guthrie, *HGP*, pp. 541–2; Crombie, *EPD*, p. 136; Sidgwick, *OHE*,
p. 50.]

B.   Plato's distinction among the three types of men, corresponding to
the three parts of the soul that may dominate, shows that he does not
regard the "appetitive" part of the soul as the only part that may be
said to have "appetites" or "desires" (*epithymai*, 580d8). Both the reasoning part and the spirited part have them too. Thus we see once again
that he does not adopt the view, often associated with Hume, that the
word "reason" designates something without motivating force or desires
of its own. (Cf. 437b–439b, n. C.) [Cross and Woozley, pp. 117–9;
Grube, *PT*, p. 136; Kraut, *RJR*, pp. 21ff.]

C.   Plato's remark at 580d–e shows clearly (see 435c–436b, n. A) that
the appetitive part of the soul is not regarded by him as a genuinely
unitary part, but as a hetereogeneous collection of various desires and
impulses. The only title that he can find to denote it is "money-making,"
on the ground that its other desires are often satisfied by means of
money.

D.   In his statement of this argument, Plato has changed the terms in
which he characterizes the types of men being compared. Instead of

labeling them according to their roles in a city, as he did in the previous argument (580b), he now designates them according to what they predominately seek (581a–b; though his usage varies, as in 587b). One reason for the change is that in the present argument Plato concentrates on this latter point. Another reason is that the present argument does not, as the previous argument did (576b–578b, n. B), depend on the analogy in structure between city and soul. Notice in particular that Plato is comparing the man with a philosophic temperament and the man with a dictatorial temperament and is not now concerned with issues arising from their ruling of their respective cities. Thus, he is not saddling the philosophic man with the sacrifice that he must make in order to rule (519d–521b, n. E) and likewise is not burdening the dictatorial man with actually being a dictator (578b–580a).

581e–583a: THE SECOND ARGUMENT FOR THE SUPERIORITY OF THE LIFE OF THE JUST MAN: CONCLUSION. HOW ARE WE TO DECIDE AMONG THESE THREE CLAIMS? THERE ARE THREE THINGS THAT SHOULD ENABLE US TO DO SO: EXPERIENCE, KNOWLEDGE, AND REASONING. FIRST, ONLY THE PHILOSOPHIC MAN HAS EXPERIENCE OF ALL THREE TYPES OF PLEASURE, SO ONLY HE CAN JUDGE THEM ON THAT BASIS. SECOND, ONLY HE HAS EXPERIENCE WITH KNOWLEDGE. THIRD, WE MUST MAKE THE JUDGMENT THROUGH REASONING, WHICH IS THE TOOL OF THE PHILOSOPHER. THEREFORE, THE VERDICT OF THE PHILOSOPHIC MAN AS TO THE GREATER PLEASANTNESS OF HIS LIFE IS TO BE ACCEPTED.

A. There are three parts of Plato's argument for accepting the philosophic man's judgment about which life is the most pleasant.

The first part rests on the contention that only the philosophic man has adequate experience of the three types of pleasure being assessed. For whereas all men have some acquaintance with the pleasures of the appetitive part of the soul, philosophers also know those of the spirited part; and only philosophers know the pleasures of the reason. It is sometimes responded that the philosophic man, although he has a taste of the lower two types of pleasure, does not know what a whole life devoted to them would be like, and so cannot really make the comparison required of him by Plato's argument. Evidently, however, Plato thinks it possible to extrapolate from the taste.

The second part of the argument, indicated only fleetingly at 582d4–5, is that only the philosopher has "experience with or accompanied by knowledge" (*meta phrōneseōs*). The exact idea here is unclear, but Plato seems to mean that only the philosopher is able to use his experience to arrive at knowledge (*phronēsis*). Just what sort of knowledge he means is not explained. (*Phronēsis* is not his standard word for distinguishing between knowledge and opinion in his epistemological theory, e.g., at 476d–480a, 511d–e, 523a–524d; so it does not appear that he is thinking of the sort of knowledge that is concerned with Forms.)

The third part of the argument (d7–14) turns on the claim that reasoned argument (or reasoned calculation, or perhaps simply argument—*logos*), which is what only the philosopher truly engages in, is the only other means whereby we can decide which life is the most pleasant.

B. The present argument certainly raises deep issues that cannot be dealt with adequately here. Some will disagree with his conclusion about which life is the most pleasant. Others will disagree with his arguments for accepting the judgment of the philosophic man, and even with his claim about what the judgment of the philosophic man would be. But still others will disagree with his view that there is a matter of fact here to be argued over at all. For they will say that pleasantness, at least in this context, is a relative matter, depending on the likes and dislikes of the individual involved; so that, given that there are three different types of tastes in lives, there is no way of adjudicating which of them is, somehow objectively, most pleasant. Now we have seen that Plato adopts that view that goodness in general is not simply a matter of individual tastes or even interests, and that there is a coherent notion of what is good "objectively," and not relatively to any person (519d–521b, n. E, and Introd., secs 3–4). But in the same way, as is clear both from this argument and the next one (583b–587b), he believes in a notion of the objectively pleasant, which is not merely pleasantness (relative) to a particular person. [Sidgwick, *ME*, pp. 141, 148; Nettleship, p. 316; Guthrie, *HGP*, p. 537; Irwin, *PMT*, p. 285.]

C. Notice that Plato continues without comment his identification of the perfectly just man with the philosophic man, i.e., the type of man suited to be a philosopher-ruler in his city (cf. 580c–581e, n. D). As Plato has argued in Books III–VII, the perfectly just man is the man whose soul is ordered by a governing reason whose understanding of how to order the soul rests on its philosophical knowledge. So the present argument, purporting to show that the philosophic man is right to judge his life the most pleasant, is by its very nature an argument purporting to show that the completely just man is right to judge his life the most pleasant.

583b–585a: *THE THIRD ARGUMENT FOR THE SUPERIORITY OF THE LIFE OF THE JUST MAN: BEGINNING.* THERE IS PLEASURE AND THERE IS PAIN, AND THERE IS THE INTERMEDIATE STATE BETWEEN THE TWO. PEOPLE ACCORDINGLY BECOME CONFUSED, BY MISTAKING FOR PLEASURE THE PASSAGE FROM PAIN TO THE INTERMEDIATE STATE, AND IN OTHER SIMILAR WAYS, AND THEY START TO THINK, WRONGLY, THAT PLEASURE IS NOTHING BUT THE ABSENCE OF PAIN. THE CONFUSION ARISES PARTICULARLY BECAUSE MOST BODILY PLEASURES AND ALSO PLEASURES OF ANTICIPATION REALLY ARE OF THIS KIND, SO THAT PEOPLE TEND NOT TO RECOGNIZE THE EXISTENCE OF GENUINE PLEASURE, WHICH IS NOT MERELY A RELEASE FROM OR AN ABSENCE OF PAIN.

A.   This passage is a preliminary stage of the third argument, designed primarily to convince us that we can be mistaken about the nature of pleasure and therefore about what is really pleasant. By convincing us of this, he hopes to be able to convince us next that there are pleasures much greater than those we ordinarily experience, which are pleasures of the body and pleasures of anticipation (584c). The greater pleasures are those gained through the exercise of reason, as the next sections show.

B.   Plato's view of what is pleasant is of a piece with the views that go to make up his theory of Forms, and particularly with the view that the appearance or non-appearance of many attributes in the sensible world is dependent on the circumstances in which sensible objects and the observers of them happen to be placed. Thus, for example, a given object or state of affairs will seem to have a given attribute or not, depending on surrounding circumstances or the proximity of other states of affairs. In particular, Plato thinks that most pleasures of the body are of the type that depend for their seeming pleasantness or proximity to and contrast with pains, notably pains associated with deprivation of and desire for something to be supplied to the body.

By contrast to things that are, or seem, pleasant only in certain circumstances, Plato believes that there are pleasures that are independent of circumstances. These are the things, he holds, that are genuinely pleasant, and not merely qualifiedly so. The situation is analogous to the one described in 523c–e, in which he says that a finger may appear large or small depending on whether it is viewed next to a smaller or a larger finger. The Form of the Large, on the other hand, is not large in this qualified and relative way (476d–480a, n. C, and Introd., sec. 3).

Plato wishes to say that the most genuinely pleasant things are those whose appearance of being pleasant is least dependent on contingent circumstances. And what he will go on to argue is that by this test, the so-called bodily pleasures are not genuinely pleasant (though he explains why we think they are—cf. n. A), and that the things that are genuinely pleasant are things connected with the exercise of reason. See further 603b–605c, n. B.

585a–e: THE THIRD ARGUMENT FOR THE SUPERIORITY OF THE LIFE OF THE JUST MAN: SECOND STAGE. JUST AS HUNGER AND THIRST ARE A KIND OF EMPTINESS OF THE BODY, SO IGNORANCE IS A KIND OF EMPTINESS OF THE SOUL. THE KINDS OF THINGS THAT FILL THE LATTER EMPTINESS HAVE MORE BEING OR REALITY, AND TRUTH, THAN THOSE THAT FILL THE FORMER. THE SOUL, WHICH IS FILLED BY THINGS HAVING MORE BEING AND TRUTH, IS ACCORDINGLY MORE REALLY AND TRULY FILLED THAN THE BODY, WHICH IS FILLED BY THINGS HAVING LESS BEING AND TRUTH, AND SO THE SOUL THEREFORE MORE TRULY HAS TRUE AND LASTING PLEASURE.

A.   This is the central part of the third argument for the claim that the pleasure gained by the activity of reason is in a certain sense greater than any other.

B.   For Plato's intentions here to be properly understood, one must read the present passage with an eye on certain parts of his theory of Forms, some of which were just mentioned in 583b–585a, n. B. The first point to remember is that according to Plato, one of the ways in which objects may bear attributes only qualifiedly is by bearing attributes only with temporal qualification, i.e., only at certain times but not at others (485a–d, n. B). Because he thinks of the sensible world as in some way constantly changing, he tends to think of sensible objects as in this way having predicates true of them only qualifiedly. The second point is that he thinks that sensible objects may bear attributes more or less qualifiedly, that is, that qualified bearing of attributes can be a matter of degree. This is the basis of his view that one sensible object can approximate a Form (the unqualified bearer of the attribute) more or less closely than another, or than itself at a different time. The third point is that in his view, an object that more closely approximates the Form of *F* than another can be said to be both "more *truly F*" than the latter object, and also, apparently, simply "more *F*" than it is. Thus the Form of

Beauty is pictured, because it is unqualifiedly beautiful, as being more beautiful than any sensible object (see *Symposium* 209–212).

This line of thought involves an idea that requires special attention in the present context. It is the idea that because a thing is less qualifiedly *F*, it therefore is more *F*, no matter what the qualification involved. For when *we* ordinarily say that a thing is more *F*, we frequently have in mind something other than the general lack of qualifiedness of its being *F*. In particular, it seems odd to say, simply on the ground that one thing is more permanently *F* than another, that it is by virtue of that fact "more *F*." For we ordinarily use the phrase "more *F*" to indicate something different, such as something's being, e.g., more *intensely* *F* than another thing. We shall see the relevance of this point shortly (see n. D).

C. Plato's application of these ideas to the case of pleasure is fairly straightforward. His basic point, as 585b–c makes clear, has to do with the stability and instability of different sorts of pleasant experiences, and of the objects or events in which pleasure is taken. Up until 585d10 he is going on the assumption that pleasure is associated with the filling of an emptiness or lack (585a–b). And he is saying that the more stable the thing with which something is filled, the more stably the latter thing is filled, and that the more stably the latter thing is filled, the more truly and really it can be said to be filled. In the case of bodily pleasures, he believes, the instability of the things with which the body is filled makes the body less stably, and so less really and truly, filled. But because Forms, which are what knowledge is concerned with, do not change, they do not provide reason to worry that one's knowledge of them might be unstable (485a–d, n. B). One may of course forget, and Plato realizes that one's cognitive states are not immune to change (see *Symposium* 207e–208a). He does not, however, here maintain that the pleasures a man gets from knowledge are totally stable, but only that they are much more so than bodily pleasures, because the latter are involved with much more unstable objects than the former.

D. The difficulty that arises for Plato's argument is the one broached just above in n. B. Even if we accept the idea that pleasures are rendered less stable by the instability of the objects in which pleasure is taken, there is real difficulty in passing from the claim that a certain pleasure is less stable than another, to the claim that the former is less truly and genuinely a pleasure, and thence to the claim that it is in any significant sense *less pleasant*. If by saying that it is less truly and genuinely a pleasure, all we mean is that it is a pleasure only with more (temporal) qualification, then we may accept the first of these two steps. But in this case the second step seems all the more difficult, because in our ordinary manner of looking at the matter, something's being only temporarily a pleasure or pleasant thing does not *necessarily* make it less pleasant. And we may say this even while granting that the measurement of degrees of pleasantness, and even the understanding of the concept of degree of pleasantness, presents very severe philosophical difficulties.

There are various replies that Plato could make to this line of objection, but he does not make them here. Like other issues in Book IX, however (cf. 576b–578b, n. C, 580c–581e, n. A), this matter of degrees of pleasantness is further treated in the *Philebus*, which attempts to distinguish between being more pleasant and having a greater quantity of pleasure (esp. 53b–c).

586a–e: THE THIRD ARGUMENT FOR THE SUPERIORITY OF THE LIFE OF THE JUST MAN: THIRD STAGE.

A. The chief importance of this passage is that it provides us with a clearer account than Plato has thus far given of the proper governance of reason within the soul, and in its stress on the fact, already emphasized (571a–572b, n. B), that reason is to provide a moderate amount of satisfaction for all three parts of the soul. The basis of this idea at this point must be in the foregoing argument, and so it must be that the moderate satisfaction of necessary desires leads to a relatively stable condition of soul, free from rapidly alternating cycles of emptiness and repletion, and possessing instead more lasting periods of satisfaction (see 571e–572a).

587a–b: THE THIRD ARGUMENT FOR THE SUPERIORITY OF THE LIFE OF THE JUST MAN: CONCLUSION. BUT WHEN ONE OF THE LOWER PARTS OF THE SOUL RULES TO ANY EXTENT, IT CANNOT FIND ITS OWN PLEASURE, AND IT FORCES THE OTHERS TO PURSUE PLEASURE THAT IS ALIEN TO THEM. THE ELEMENTS OF THE SOUL THAT ARE FARTHEST FROM PHILOSOPHY AND REASON ARE MOST LIKELY TO DO THIS, NAMELY, THE LUSTFUL AND DICTATORIAL APPETITES. ACCORDINGLY, THE DICTATOR WILL BE THE FARTHEST FROM ENJOYING TRUE PLEASURE, AND THE KINGLY OR PHILOSOPHIC MAN WILL BE THE CLOSEST. THEREFORE, THE LATTER WILL LEAD

THE MOST PLEASANT LIFE, AND THE FORMER THE LEAST PLEASANT.

A. Plato's conclusion is that the kingly man, i.e., the completely just man (581e–583a, n. C), will be the happiest man because he will have more true pleasure than anyone else, precisely because his reason will order the satisfaction of his desires so as to avoid the condition described in the previous section.

B. According to Plato's view, when some part of the soul other than reason rules, neither that part nor any other is able to gain its own pleasure. Just why this is so is not explained. One part of the idea might be that, e.g., when lust rules it somehow turns other desires away from their natural purposes. For example, perhaps Plato is thinking of people who, instead of drinking beverages that will satisfy thirst, drink alcoholic beverages to show a kind of prowess in the eyes of potential sexual partners, with the result that they drink too much and consequently suffer pain.

587b–588a: IN FACT, A CALCULATION SHOWS THAT THE KING LIVES 729 TIMES AS PLEASANTLY AS THE DICTATOR. AND IF THE GOOD AND JUST MAN HAS A LIFE SO MUCH MORE PLEASANT THAN THE BAD AND UNJUST MAN, THEN PLAINLY THE FORMER'S LIFE WILL HAVE MORE GRACE, BEAUTY, AND EXCELLENCE OR VIRTUE THAN THE LATTER'S.

A. How seriously Plato takes the mathematical calculation recorded here is an open question. Clearly, however, he does not insist that his readers accept it or even understand its basis, since he treats it only briefly and tangentially without trying to justify its use. As in an earlier passage, however (see n. E on 545c–547c), he shows his view that the sensible world exhibits certain mathematically expressible patterns.

B. From the claim that the just man's life is so much more pleasant than the unjust man's life, Plato infers that the former must also have much more grace, beauty, and excellence (588a). These are features that he explicitly put aside from consideration in 580c–581e, when he first broached the question which life was the most pleasant. Although he does not develop the issue, it is clear that in his eyes there is more to the question what life is best than simply the question what life is pleasantest. Cf. *ibid.*, n. A. But because he is arguing mainly against people like

Thrasymachus, he contents himself, in the latter two of his three arguments for the superiority of the just life, with arguing for superiority in respect of pleasantness. That the just life is superior in these other ways he must think fairly obvious, at least to those who are interested in them.

588b–590a: REMINDING OURSELVES OF THE BEGINNING OF OUR EFFORT TO PRAISE JUSTICE, LET US FASHION AN IMAGE OF THE SOUL, COMPARING IT TO A GROUP CONSISTING OF A MANY-HEADED BEAST, A LION, AND A MAN, CORRESPONDING RESPECTIVELY TO THE THREE PARTS OF THE SOUL. A MAN WHO PRAISES INJUSTICE IS THEREBY FAVORING THE ENSLAVEMENT OF THE BEST PART, THE MAN, TO THE WORST PART, THE BEAST. TO FAVOR JUSTICE, ON THE OTHER HAND, IS TO MAKE THE MAN THE STRONGEST, SO THAT HE WILL TEND THE BEAST, FOSTERING THE TAME DESIRES AND PREVENTING THE SAVAGE ONES FROM GROWING, MAKING THE LION HIS ALLY, AND CARING FOR ALL IN COMMON AND MAKING THEM FRIENDLY TO EACH OTHER AND TO HIMSELF. ONE CAN SEE THAT JUSTICE IS SUPERIOR, FROM THE POINT OF VIEW OF PLEASURE, OF REPUTATION, AND OF BENEFIT.

A.   Plato sums up the results of his arguments for the superiority of the just life and presents an image of the soul to illustrate those results. The image neither is nor provides what Plato intends as an *argument* for the superiority of the just life. Rather, arguments for this claim are provided in the foregoing passages. (Nevertheless, Plato's image here does suggest something that *other* philosophers, from Aristotle onward, have used as an argument for something like the same claim. It is based on the idea that being just, or morally good, is somehow a peculiarly human trait or capacity. Along with the premise that it is desirable to develop one's peculiarly human traits or capacities, this yields an argument of sorts for being just or morally good.)

B.   The true and fundamental grounds of the superiority of justice, as Plato has shown them to us, have to do (not with being characteristically human, but) with having a kind of order established in one's soul or character. The point is made plain in 589a–b (cf. 573c–576b, n. B, 571a–572b, n. B). It is that reason tends all of the elements of the soul in common (*koinēi* in 589b4 is the same word that was used frequently in Book V to express the idea that the guardians of the city must have all aspects of their lives in common; see on 449a–550c, n. A). It prevents the growth of unnecessary and lawless appetites (571a–572b) but it provides the others with what they need. In this way it ensures the harmony of the whole soul, by making all of its parts friendly to each other and to itself (*phila*—cf. 547c2 and 545c–547c, n. D). By contrast, under the rule of the beast they are not friendly (*philon*, a3) but fight among themselves. (We have seen, of course, that there is a question whether this harmony is desirable for its own sake or rather because it makes possible a maximization of total satisfaction of some kind; cf. 576b–578b, n. C.)

Also made clear in this passage is that the rule of the soul by reason is not something that Plato values simply for its own sake or without the possibility of its being justified by further considerations. The rule of reason is desirable because under reason the soul is in a particular condition of orderliness and unity which yields the balance of satisfactions just described. (Cf. 441c–442d, n. F, 531d–534d, n. D, and Introd., sec. 4.) [Bosanquet, pp. 369–70.]

C.   The image given here continues Plato's tendency to picture the parts of a human character as comparable to actual independent persons, each with interests of its own (cf. 441c–442d, nn. D–E, 590c–591a, n. E).

The near-personification of the parts of the soul makes one ask how, for example, Plato might try without metaphor to express the idea that reason can make all of the parts of the soul "friendly" to each other. The idea evidently is that by training and education, certain desires are simply weakened to the point where one can assuage them without depriving other desires of the time and resources for their satisfaction. We do not, that is, always have to think of the spirited and appetitive parts of the soul as actually *agreeing*, in some quasi-rational way, to taking less than they·really want, like a small child who is argued into grumblingly accepting less than a full portion of cake. Rather, Plato believes, desires can be trained (largely by not being overindulged) so that they simply become less insistent. It is in this way that we should perhaps construe Plato's identification in 441c–442d of moderation in the soul with a kind of agreement by all parts about who should rule. The idea would then simply be that non-rational desires are weak enough that they do not nag when required by a rational plan of action or life to adjust themselves to the overall demands of the whole person. (But this does not mean that all of Plato's remarks about the soul can be construed without personification of them: see 590c–591a, n. E.) [Penner, *passim*.]

D. In 589c Plato says that justice is superior to injustice from the point of view of reputation, or good repute (*eudoxia*). This statement appears to be an anticipation of what he will be arguing in Book X (612a–e) and is not strictly germane to what he has been arguing in Books II–IX (see 362d–368c, nn. A–B). On the other hand, he may not mean here that justice brings the benefits of good reputation, as he will argue in Book X, but that praise, or good reputation, of justice is justified.

590a–c: THE REASON WHY LICENTIOUSNESS HAS LONG BEEN CONDEMNED IS THAT IT INVOLVES LETTING THE BEAST LOOSE MORE THAN IT SHOULD BE LET LOOSE. OBSTINACY AND THE LIKE ARE CONDEMNED WHEN THE LION-LIKE PART OF THE SOUL IS LARGER THAN IT SHOULD BE, WHEREAS SOFTNESS OF CHARACTER IS CONDEMNED BECAUSE IT INVOLVES EXCESSIVE WEAKENING OF THIS SAME PART. FLATTERY AND SLAVISH-NESS OCCUR WHEN THE SPIRITED PART IS UNDER THE RULE OF THE BEAST. AND BASER OCCUPATIONS ARE PROPERLY CONDEMNED ONLY WHEN THE BEST PART OF ONE'S SOUL— REASON—IS WEAK AND CANNOT GOVERN ONE'S APPETITES, SO THAT ONE WORKS ONLY TO SATISFY THEM.

A. This unobtrusive passage is more important than it appears. In the first place, it attempts to show that the bad reputation of certain activi-ties and traits is not simply arbitrary but is the result of their connection with certain conditions of soul which Plato has already argued to be undesirable. His reason for making this point is to rebut the views of those who think that the ordinary disapproval of such things is merely the result of fortuitous convention, exactly as they think that the dis-approval of injustice is merely conventional (358a–362c). Plato, on the other hand, wishes to show that these ordinary standards have their basis in objective facts about certain conditions of the human soul which are not established by convention.

B. In the second place, however, this attempt has an important bearing on Plato's need, already remarked on (442d–443b, nn. B–C), to show that his notion of justice in the individual is closely enough linked to the ordinary notion of justice for the purposes of his argument. In gen-eral, he wishes to maintain that with certain exceptions, ordinary standards of justice in behavior coincide with those endorsed by his account of the soul, at least to a certain extent. That is, he wishes to maintain that behavior condemned by those standards is caused by states of the soul that can be seen to be undesirable in the light of his account of the soul. This means, according to 442d–443b, that what ordinary standards count as injustices are, in general, those actions detrimental to the establishment and maintenance of a just condition of soul. The burden of the present passage is to suggest something along this line. What the passage says, however, is something different. It says that behavior violating ordinary standards is *caused by* an unjust condition of soul, rather than that it tends to the establishment and maintenance of such a condition. But because Plato's view is that overindulgence of desires is what makes them become excessive, he probably holds that the actions caused by injustice in the soul are generally those that promote it. See 443b–444a, n. F.

The present passage is supplemented in this regard, by much of the description of deficient characters in Books VIII–IX. For in those books, and especially in the descriptions of the oligarchic and dictatorial men, Plato has done much to try to show how criminal behavior in the ordinary sense is caused by deficiencies in the state of people's souls. Moreover, Plato no doubt tends to believe that when criminal behavior occurs, it is generally caused, except in unusual circumstances, by such deficiencies, as they are expounded in his theory of the soul.

But Plato seems to stop short of any attempt to show that *every* action that would be condemned by ordinary standards as unjust is in fact caused by or productive of injustice in a person's soul, or that *every* action that is so caused or so productive is a violation of ordinary standards of justice. He clearly allows for actions that are just under conventional views but that are performed, so to speak, for the wrong reasons, and out of the wrong condition of soul (see e.g., 619c–d and *Phaedo* 68e–69c); and he quite probably counts the historical Socrates as someone who violated conventional strictures but was just nevertheless. Moreover, some of Plato's own judgments about justice, and his views about how his city should be organized, run violently against the views current in Athens, or anywhere in Greece, in his time. An obvious example is his system of eugenics (see esp. 449a–550c); another is his whole system of education (451c–452e, n. A). Clearly, therefore, there is less than a perfect fit between his conception of justice and the ordinary one, with regard to particular cases. That there is a considerable fit, however, is something that he takes himself to establish here and in the rest of Books VIII–IX. Moreover, he plainly thinks that there is a close enough fit for the argument of the whole *Republic*, dealing as it does with his own conception of justice, to be relevant to the thesis ad-

vanced by Thrasymachus in Book I (442d–443b, n. B), which involved a
different and more ordinary conception of justice. For he hopes that,
especially in the light of Books VIII–IX, his readers will be convinced
that his conception of justice is really a clearer version of what we are
struggling to articulate when we employ the ordinary conception. [Cf.
the bibliographical references at the end of 442d–443b, n. B, esp. Grote,
pp. 102–118; Sachs; Vlastos, pp. 90–92; see also Crombie, *PMA*, pp.
135–6, 142–3, 158–9; Sidgwick, *OHE*, pp. 41–3; Sidgwick, *ME*, p. 171;
White, pp. 93–4 with nn. 20, 21.]

C. The somewhat obscure remarks in this passage about the baser occupations and the use of one's hands is meant to indicate that, as Plato
thinks, those who work with their hands usually do so mainly in order
to earn money, the purpose of which is to enable them to satisfy their
appetites (whence the appetitive part of the soul is called the money-
loving part, 580e–581a). This is why he assigns artisans to the lowest
class in his city. His point here is that there is nothing intrinsically
wrong with such occupations; the basis of his condemnation of them is
simply that they usually indicate, he holds, the predominance of appetites in those who practice them.

590c–591a: BUT THERE IS A WAY IN WHICH A PERSON RULED
BY HIS APPETITES CAN BE RULED BY THE SAME ELEMENT
THAT RULES IN THE BEST MAN, NAMELY, BY BEING THE SLAVE
OF THE RATIONAL MAN WHO RULES HIM, NOT FOR HIS DETRI-
MENT, BUT BECAUSE IT IS BETTER FOR EVERYONE TO BE
RULED BY REASON. IT WOULD BE BETTER IF THE PERSON
RULED BY APPETITE HAD A RULING REASON WITHIN HIM, BUT
IF HE DOES NOT, THEN HE MUST BE RULED BY ONE FROM
THE OUTSIDE, SO THAT, TO THE EXTENT POSSIBLE, ALL PEO-
PLE WOULD BE ALIKE AND FRIENDLY TO EACH OTHER, BEING
RULED BY THE SAME THING. THIS WILL BE THE AIM OF LAW
AND EDUCATION.

A. Plato returns to consideration of the way in which his city will be
governed and the rule of reason can operate in all citizens.

B. His phraseology here seems to run counter to what he had said in
547c, in a passage that suggested that the relation of ruler to ruled in
his city was sharply different from the relation of master to slave. No
doubt Plato intends to be talking of different aspects of the relationship

in the two passages, but certainly many will object that it really *is* one of slavery, and in an objectionable sense. The present passage is of course meant to emphasize the necessity for control of appetites by reason. If one asks for the justification of this procedure within the city, particularly as it yields a relationship so comparable to slavery, then of course Plato's response must be to point back to the whole of his argument in Books II–IV for saying that a city such as he described is good (427e–428a).

C. But the argument in Books II–IV leaves what to modern eyes looks like a major gap concerning the motivation that the subjects in Plato's city could have to acquiesce in being ruled as Plato prescribes, and whether being so ruled could benefit them.

As is made clear in 590e–591a (cf. 499a–500b, n. B, 500b–e, n. B, and 430c–432a, n. B), Plato does not think that the rule of others by philosopher-rulers will be maintained, once established, entirely by brute force. (His descriptions of timocracy, oligarchy, and dictatorship make clear that he thinks that those forms of rule rely on force for their maintenance; democracy does not, because it has very little rule to maintain.) Rather, once the city is established, control is exercised primarily through education, though the mention of law suggests that punishment also plays a part. Yet this does not mean that Plato sees any such pacific way, or indeed any way at all, of inducing a group of people, trained and educated *as they are in actual societies,* to accept the governance of philosopher-rulers. Rather, as we saw in 540d–541b, n. B, to establish his city Plato considers it probably necessary to begin the education of its citizens from scratch, starting only with children educated by philosophers. So in reply to the question whether there could be motivation for the lower classes to accept the rule of philosopher-rulers, he admits that in actual cities such motivation has been eliminated or submerged, but maintains that it could be fostered by education of the young.

D. This response, however, still leaves us uninformed about what that motivation is and how it should be described. Would it, for example, take the form of a desire on the part of a member of a lower class for his own happiness, and a belief that this could best be gained by cooperating in the rulers' scheme? Or would it be some appreciation, however dim, of the fact that the way in which the city is ruled is in fact good? Or would it simply be a full and undivided desire to work at a particular task, e.g., carpentry, to which the rulers have perceived his affinity and so assigned him? In other words, is he simply trained in such a way that his other desires and appetites do not interfere with the performance of his task, which he pursues without any substantial reflections either on his own good or on goodness in general? This last suggestion might appear to fit with Plato's depiction of the members of the lower classes as dominated by non-rational parts of their souls, which do not even attempt to calculate the good but simply act on certain impulses (cf. 588b–590a, n. C, and 603b–605c, nn. B–C, and notice that the reason is often spoken of as the *logistikon*, the calculative part of the soul—cf. Shorey, *Rep.*, I, p. 397). Against this suggestion, however, it may be pointed out that both the timocratic and the oligarchic man, who are dominated by parts other than their reasons, are said to have their own views about what the *good* is, the former choosing honor and the latter, money. Moreover, the fact that a person is dominated by the desires of one part of his soul need not mean, on Plato's psychological theory, that he is entirely unable to formulate views about the good. In particular, it does not mean that his reason, even though it may not be "strong" enough to influence his actions decisively and is in that sense dominated by another part of his soul, cannot have a correct view, at least some of the time, about the good. Perhaps Plato thinks, then, that the reason of an appetite-dominated person can welcome, and understand the rationale of, the control of his appetites which is exercised, from outside of himself, by the reason-dominated rulers. But although this idea is perhaps compatible with some of Plato's psychological theory, he does not make it thoroughly clear that this is what he means to say.

We are left, then, in some uncertainty about the motives of people not dominated by reason, and in particular about whether they can be said to be governed by a conception of what the good is, or are instead to have their behavior explained by saying simply that they have certain impulses or cravings (cf. 437b–439b, n. B), without any clear conception of good to be gained by satisfying them. And because of this uncertainty, it is difficult for us to tell exactly what the motivation is of those people not dominated by reason. When they live in a city that is governed in accordance with reason, why do they abide by the arrangements prescribed by the rulers there? To the extent that Plato leaves this matter unclear, he must be said to have left it likewise unclear that his city really is the coherent possibility that he claims it to be (472e–473b, n. A). For if his city is to be a coherent possibility, then it must be possible to say what motivates the members of the lower classes to play the part in the city that he wishes them to play. Cf. 430c–432a, nn. A–B, 369b–d, n. C, 419a–421c, n. D, and 427e–428a, n. B.

Moreover—as goes without saying for many of us—if Plato does not give some more adequate explanation of the motivations of those who are ruled in his city, he leaves himself especially vulnerable to the charge that in spite of his protestations (427e–428a, 461e–462e), he has not in fact contrived a truly good city, nor one with institutions that are conducive to the benefit and happiness of itself as a whole (419a–421c, 519d–521b). For it will be denied by the tradition opposing Plato's conception of the good society that the cohesiveness and stability of a society are as important in this regard as he makes them out to be (422e–423d, n. B), and it will be urged that more attention must be paid to the satisfactions, and also the liberties, of those living in the society. This tradition will urge that Plato is mistaken to put so much weight on these structural features of his city, and on the capacity and motivation of the rulers to ensure them, and too little weight on the motivation of others to accept them, on the benefit or harm gained by those others in accepting them, and on the bearing of these issues on the question how well off Plato's city really is. [Bosanquet, pp. 174–5; Grote, pp. 186–7.]

E. We saw in the previous note that Plato leaves it unclear how the control by reason from outside (*exōthen*, 590d5) is exercised on those whose own reasons are weak, and what the psychological reaction is of those who are subjected to this control. A considerable part of this difficulty arises from a still more basic difficulty in Plato's whole theory of the soul and its division into parts. This more basic difficulty is caused by the existence of two distinct tendencies within his thought. On the one hand, he wishes to treat the *logistikon* as the only part of the soul that can engage in truly rational thought, particularly about the good, and wishes to treat the other two parts as, in a sense, non-rational vessels of inarticulate impulses and cravings (437b–439b, nn. A–B). On the other hand, he also has an inclination to treat the lower two parts of the soul as possessing a kind of rationality themselves, as though they were comparatively brutish human beings who, along with reason, dwell within a single person (see esp. 441c–442d, n. D). Plato never attempts to show how he would reconcile this apparent conflict.

Though this is a far-reaching topic, we can see at least a partial explanation of the coexistence within Plato of these two tendencies. If we start with the former tendency just described, it is clear how the latter can arise. It does so when one tries to describe the influence that the reason may have—as Plato believes—on the desires of the lower parts of the soul. Thinking as one does of reason as an articulate, rational agent, one moves easily to the idea that its influence must be exercised through its powers of articulation and rationality. Having made this move, however, one is already tending to think of the reason as *speaking*, as it were, to the other parts of the soul and endeavoring to persuade them to follow its lead. But once one has done this, one is almost irresistably drawn toward thinking of the other parts of the soul as capable of *understanding* what reason says and thus as, at least to that degree, rational. If, therefore, we think of Plato as beginning with a conception of the soul as containing only one rational, articulate element, the reason, we can see how he was easily able also to be subject to the other tendency. (The only way to resist this latter tendency, given the former, would seem to be to think of reason as exercising its influence over the other elements of the soul, not through their understanding of what it says, but rather through something like their susceptibility to its tone of voice, or some other thing that it does that requires no understanding or rationality. But this might be argued to require us to think of reason as having some other, as yet unexplained, power in addition to its rationality.) [Penner.]

F.   Plato's difficulties in this matter are intimately connected with the question of his reaction to the Socratic identification of virtue (or excellence, *aretē*) with knowledge. In the *Republic*, Plato does not say whether he agrees or disagrees with this identification, nor, if he disagrees, just how he disagrees. We may say roughly that Socrates arrived at this identification by asking, and being unable to answer, the question how one and the same person could both know what was good in a particular case and fail to pursue it. It is usually said that in the *Republic*, Plato went some way, at least, toward denying the identification by providing an answer to this question. His answer was, on this interpretation, to appeal to his theory of the tripartite soul, and to suggest that even though one's reason might know the good, one might be deflected by the influence of other parts of the soul. I think it evident that his response to Socrates was considerably more complicated than this. Indeed, I think that the reason why he did not in the *Republic* explicitly confront the question of the identification of virtue and knowledge was that he knew that the complexity of his psychological theory made a straightforward and simple response to it impossible.

G.   Plato's idea is that people in his city who are not ruled by their own reasons are ruled by reason from outside (n. E, *init.*). Are such people virtuous, and just, by Plato's standard? Not, it would seem, by the account of justice given in Book IV, 441c–442d, because that account clearly has reference to what occurs within a person's soul. Nor does it seem that Plato has been thinking of such people while arguing in Book IX that the just man is happier than the unjust man, for all three of his arguments compare the unjust man with the fully just or philosophical man (see 581e–583a, n. C), and thus do not argue anything about the happiness of the man who is a member of one of the two lower classes in his city. Plato's only word about these people has been his claim at 421c that nature will provide them with the appropriate amount of happiness. Clearly, they will be trained or educated so as to fulfill their functions within the city, and clearly Plato believes that even if they cannot themselves be called fully virtuous or just in their own right, they will have a kind of borrowed virtue and justice, and that they will not be as miserable as they would be if they were not subject to the rule of reason administered by the rulers in his city. Nevertheless, one must say that Plato has neglected to treat this matter will full explicitness. [Vlastos, *JHR*, pp. 92–94.]

591a–592b: SO IT IS MISTAKEN TO SAY THAT INJUSTICE AND SHAMEFUL ACTIONS ARE BENEFICIAL IF THEY ARE UNDISCOVERED. THE MAN OF SENSE WILL AVOID SUCH THINGS AND CULTIVATE THOSE ACTIVITIES THAT MAINTAIN ORDER, HARMONY, AND CONSONANCE IN HIS SOUL. HE WILL AVOID THE MULTITUDE'S VIEW OF HAPPINESS, AND ATTEMPT TO HAVE NEITHER TOO MUCH MONEY NOR TOO LITTLE, AND LIKEWISE TO AVOID HONORS THAT WOULD DISTURB THE CONDITION OF HIS SOUL. AND HE WILL AVOID POLITICAL ACTIVITY IN ANY ACTUAL CITY. FOR THE CITY THAT WE HAVE DESCRIBED DOES NOT APPEAR TO EXIST ANYWHERE ON EARTH BUT IS A PARADIGM LAID UP IN HEAVEN FOR A PERSON TO REGARD IN ESTABLISHING THE GOVERNANCE OF HIS OWN SOUL.

A.   Plato concludes his argument with a recapitulation of many of the themes that have run through it from its beginning in Book II. In particular, there is the emphasis on harmony (422e–423d, n. B), the connection between harmony and moderate behavior (442d–443b, 573c–576b), and the status of Plato's city as a kind of goal (472e–473b, n. A).

B.   Recall that the present argument, in Books II–IX, has been that justice is beneficial "for its own sake" to the person possessing it (357b–362c). The idea that justice is also good "for its consequences" will be taken up in Book X.

C.   The upshot of Plato's argument so far, as he views it, is that a man in a position to do so will cultivate justice in his soul, thereby gaining the benefit that results from so doing. But in order to cultivate justice in his soul, Plato believes, a man will have to refrain from political activity in any actual city and lead the kind of quiet, retired life to which philosophic men are forced by prevailing political conditions (496a–497a).

There are two ways in which this result will raise questions in our minds. In the first place, our ordinary conception of justice will make it seem odd that the pursuit of justice should be thought to involve not merely a retired and apolitical life, but also one that seems so thoroughly self-serving. For it appears that according to Plato, the just man or the man aspiring to greater justice will not engage in efforts—or at least large-scale efforts—to ameliorate the condition of his city or of his fellow man. How, we may well ask, can justice be so regarded? In the second place, this idea seems odd not only when judged by our ordinary standards, but also when taken in conjunction with Plato's own views about the conduct and motivation of the rulers in his city. For we saw Plato explicitly holding that a philosophic man in such a position will sacrifice his own interest for the sake of justice and the interests of the city as a whole (519d–521b, nn. D–E). But why should such self-sacrifice not be engaged in just as much by the philosophic man outside of Plato's city as it is by the philosophic man who happens to be a ruler in such a city?

This is an issue taken up at length in sec. 4 of the Introduction, and it cannot be developed in full detail here. But a couple of the major points can be briefly made. The first is that what Plato is saying is this: his city, unlike existing cities, is a place in which the effort to augment one's own justice and one's own goodness (444a–e, n. B), and the effort to augment the justice and the goodness of the surrounding society, both coincide. This may seem a cruel fact, but Plato nevertheless believes that it is a fact. Even so, the question remains why in a situation of conflict between the two efforts, such as he believes to obtain in actual societies, he holds that one should choose to further one's own goodness (and justice, and benefit), rather than that of society or other people. The answer lies in his firmly-held pessimism about actual societies and the fate of efforts to improve them. Plato does not believe that, in the absence of very unusual circumstances, the efforts of one philosophic man or a few philosophic men can produce much improvement in political conditions. Although in Book VIII he seems to present the deficient cities in order of decreasing degree of justice, he has no tendency to advocate that we try to bring about timocracy as against the other three; and indeed he has kind words about democracy, precisely because—it seems—such a city allows scope for a wide variety of activities, including the sort of philosophical activity in which he himself engaged. The only thing that might bring about significant political change is, he believes, luck, namely, the sort of luck that might bring a philosophic person to power in a city so that a genuinely good city might be established (592a; cf. 473b–474b). This is a kind of eventuality that, although possible, he has no suggestions about how to bring about. There seems little doubt that he would advocate seizing such a chance if it occurred (presumably, he viewed his own expeditions to Sicily in this way), and would say that justice dictated it. But short of such a piece of good fortune, he plainly does not see much scope for action by the individual philosopher. The condition of his own soul, however, is something that he thinks a person has the power to affect, at least if he has a certain basic modicum of native capacity, and perhaps also the condition of soul of those who are near to him (in the way in which some of Socrates'. disciples were near to him). For this reason, he concentrates his attention on the efforts that may be made to keep one's own soul just, and urges people to eschew larger aims. There is a kind of egoism involved in this attitude, but it is an egoism borne of a considered assessment of the possibilities. [Crombie, *PMA*, p. 187.]

D.   In 592a–b Plato speaks of his city as a model or paradigm (*paradeigma*) in heaven. The use of this word, along with the idea expressed, recalls to us the fact that his city in certain respects plays the role of a Form, in the sense given by his metaphysical theory, though we have also seen that it cannot actually be one (see 472b–d, n. B, 472e–473b, n. B, and 370c–371e, n. B).

For our efforts to order our souls, Plato presents us with the model of a city. Why did he not construct a soul as a paradigm, given that he views the desired order of a soul as analogous (442e–423d, n. B, 444a–e, n. B)? The reason is the same as the reason why he began with a description of the city instead of the soul in the first place, in Book II: the workings of the city are much easier for us to grasp, as is the role therein of justice, and its connection with our ordinary use of the term (368c–369b, n. B), and the soul is the subject of particular difficulties, which Plato is seemingly not certain how to solve (611a–612a).

Book X

595a–c: WE WERE RIGHT NOT TO ADMIT POETRY INVOLVING IMITATION INTO OUR CITY, AND THIS FACT IS PARTICULARLY CLEAR NOW THAT WE HAVE DISTINGUISHED THE THREE PARTS OF THE SOUL. ALL SUCH POETRY WILL DAMAGE THE THOUGHT OF ITS HEARERS, UNLESS THEY HAVE AS AN ANTIDOTE A KNOWLEDGE OF ITS NATURE. WE MUST SAY THIS IN SPITE OF OUR LONGSTANDING LOVE AND RESPECT FOR HOMER, WHO IS THE TEACHER OF ALL TRAGIC POETS.

A. The transition from the previous section to this one is abrupt. Although we have noticed that the division of the *Republic* into books does not always follow natural articulations (cf. introductory n. to Bk. III), we can easily see why a division came to be established here. On the other hand, it cannot be said that Book X itself is highly unified, and although it can be seen not unreasonably as an appendix to the whole work, it is not a fully cohesive one, and this fact has caused some commentators to wonder whether it was originally composed as a single whole. The main break comes between 608b and 608c, where Plato moves from a discussion of poetry to an account of the immortality of the soul and the respective consequences, particularly after death, of being just and unjust.

In fact, however, there is a reasonably substantial connection both between the parts of Book X, and between Book X itself and the rest of the *Republic*. Both parts of the book have to do with the exercise of rational prudence and foresight (see esp. 617d–621b, n. D). By this fact they are linked to each other, and to Books II–IX, which have promised an account of it (see 612a–e, n. A). [Nettleship, pp. 340-1, 355; Shorey, *Rep.*, II, p. lxi; Else.]

B. Plato has more than one reason for returning to the subject of poetry, already treated at some length (see 392c–398b). One is that because of their important position in Greek culture, the poets—and especially Homer—were Plato's main rivals. For they were thought to be authorities on all matters pertaining to government and the behavior of people. If Plato wishes successfully to promulgate his own views on how a city should be ruled and how its citizens should act, he must somehow combat the quite different views of poets. Another reason for his returning to poetry is that he is now in a position, he thinks, to place his critical remarks about it on a firmer philosophical footing. For he has now expounded a substantial portion of his doctrine of Forms, on the basis of which he can explain why he thinks that the imitative aspects of poetry—or rather, of imitative poetry—are undesirable. And he can also explain, on the same basis, the way in which a philosophical understanding of the nature of poetry can serve as an antidote to its unsalutary effects.

As Plato indicates here, he concentrates his attack on a particular kind of poetry, namely, tragic poetry, because he thinks that it exemplifies most clearly the aspects of imitative poetry of which he disapproves. For the reason why, see 603b–605c, n. C. [On 595a–608b, see esp. Bosanquet.]

595c–597e: WE NEED TO SEE QUITE GENERALLY WHAT IMITATION IS. WE HAVE A FORM WHEN THERE IS A PLURALITY OF THINGS WITH THE SAME NAME, E.G., THE FORM OF BED; IN ADDITION THERE ARE THE BEDS ON WHICH WE SLEEP, WHICH ARE MADE BY ARTISANS; AND THERE ARE APPEARANCES OF BEDS, WHICH CAN BE PRODUCED BY MIRRORS OR BY PAINTING. THE ARTISAN DOES NOT MAKE THE FORM OF BED, BUT ONLY A PARTICULAR BED; THE GOD MADE THE FORM, WHICH IS NECESSARILY UNIQUE. THE PRODUCT OF AN IMITATOR, SUCH AS A PAINTER, IS AT THE THIRD REMOVE FROM THE FORM. WE SHALL SEE THAT THE TRAGIC POET IS SUCH AN IMITATOR.

A. This initial characterization of imitation (*mimēsis*; see below, n. B) broaches two ideas which are to be explained further. One is that the tragic poet is like a painter. This Plato tries to establish in the ensuing discussion (esp. 603b–c, 605b). The other is that their products are, in both cases, at the third remove from Forms, being imitations of imitations of Forms (to say that they are at the "third" remove is to count the first member of the series, in the Greek manner; cf. 587c).

B.   It is often thought that Plato's treatment of imitation here is inconsistent with his treatment of it in Book III, or at least that his emphasis is very different. For in the earlier passage, the imitation of good men is apparently exempted from the prohibition of imitation (396c, 397d), whereas here the prohibition seems to be exceptionless.

We must remember, however, that the issue there was different from the one being treated here. There, the main question was concerned with the sort of poetic performances that prospective guardians would be allowed to *take part in* during the course of their education, and the question what sort of poetry would be permitted in the city was secondary. Plato's point about prospective guardians was that *they* should be allowed to imitate good men, because in this way they would be helped to become good themselves. There was no worry, of course, that *they* might be at the third remove from the Forms. (For this reason, it is tempting to translate the Greek word *mimēsis* by "impersonation" in Book III, though not in Book X; see Grube, *Rep.*, p. 63, n. 21.) Here, however, the issue is what sort of poetic *works* will be allowed in Plato's city. But even here Plato's proscription of imitation is not a blanket one but applies only to those literary and artistic products that have certain undesirably deceptive features which he tries to explain (597e–598d, 602c–605c). As we shall see (603b–605c, n. D), there does not emerge here, any more than in Book III, a prohibition of the impersonation of good men by the young being educated, nor even of literary and artistic products that accurately show what is good and encourage good practices.

597e–598d: THE PAINTER IS NOT MERELY AN IMITATOR; HE ALSO IMITATES THINGS NOT AS THEY ARE BUT AS THEY APPEAR. FOR EXAMPLE, A BED LOOKS DIFFERENT FROM DIFFERENT ANGLES EVEN THOUGH IT IS NOT DIFFERENT; BUT THE PAINTER WILL RENDER IT AS IT APPEARS, THAT IS, DIFFERENTLY FROM DIFFERENT ANGLES. THE REASON WHY IMITATORS CAN IMITATE EVERYTHING IS THAT THEY RENDER ONLY A SMALL PART OF EACH THING, I.E., SOMETHING OF

ITS MANNER OF APPEARING. SO IF WE HEAR SOMEONE SAY THAT HE HAS MET A MAN WHO KNOWS ALL ARTS AND EVERY-THING ELSE, WE CAN TELL THAT HE MUST UNKNOWINGLY HAVE ENCOUNTERED AN IMITATOR.

A. Plato believes that it is impossible to master all skills. This is a corollary of the Principle of the Natural Division of Labor, and the idea that each man is naturally able to perform only a single task (see 369e–370c). The claims made by some, that Homer had knowledge of all subjects and could be consulted on any of them (598e), therefore are said to be absurd. The impression that there are people who have mastered all skills, he thinks, is created by the fact that imitators render only appearances of things, which requires little or no knowledge of the things themselves (601b–602c).

B. It seems somewhat odd to say that painting is defective because a picture of a bed must necessarily be made from one perspective or another, but Plato is willing to draw the distinction between how sensible objects appear and how they are (598a5) and say that the painter only renders the former. The fundamental idea is that when we walk around an object such as a bed and thus see it from different points of view, nevertheless the bed does not change. See further 602c–603b, nn. B and F.

598d–601b: WE MUST THEREFORE NEXT EXAMINE TRAGEDY, TO SEE WHETHER IT IS INDEED THIS SORT OF COUNTER-FEIT, OR WHETHER POETS REALLY DO HAVE KNOWLEDGE OF THE THINGS OF WHICH THEY WRITE. TO LEAVE ASIDE LESS IMPORTANT SUBJECTS, WE MUST ASK WHETHER HOMER REALLY DOES HAVE KNOWLEDGE OF WHICH ACTIVITIES MAKE MEN BETTER IN BOTH PRIVATE AND PUBLIC LIFE, SO AS TO BE ABLE TO ESTABLISH GOOD GOVERNMENTS AND WAYS OF LIFE, AS WISE MEN ARE REPUTED TO HAVE DONE. SURELY IF THIS WERE SO, MEN WOULD HAVE USED THIS KNOWLEDGE OF HIS, WHICH THEY HAVE NOT DONE. SO WE MAY SUPPOSE THAT THE POET IS LIKE THE PAINTER, AND HAS NO KNOWLEDGE OF HIS SUBJECT-MATTER, BUT COPIES MERELY THE APPEAR-ANCE, ADDING TO HIS WORK THE COLORING OF RHYTHM AND THE LIKE.

A. Plato carries his comparison of the poet to the painter a step further here, resting on the shortly-to-be-improved-on ground that Homer has not engendered any usable expertise about the founding and management of cities, as one would have expected him to have done if he really did have knowledge of statecraft.

B. In 601a–b, Plato intensifies his comparison of poetry and painting, by suggesting that the poet and the painter both employ analogous devices to render the appearances of things: the painter uses shape and color, and the poet uses meter and melody (as before—see n. D on 398c–400c—we must remember that Greek poetry was sung poetry). Plato once again exhibits (cf. 386a–398b) his view that poetry can be straightforwardly analyzed into content on the one hand and poetic ornamentation on the other. On his view of the effects of the ornamentation, see 603b–605c, n. G.

601b–602c: THERE ARE THREE ACTIVITIES IN CONNECTION WITH A THING: THE USE OF IT, THE MAKING OF IT, AND THE IMITATION OF IT. THE ONLY PERSON WHO HAS KNOWLEDGE OF WHAT A THING IS LIKE IS THE MAN WHO USES IT, BECAUSE THE EXCELLENCE OF A THING HAS TO DO WITH ITS USE. THE MAKER OF A THING, RECEIVING HIS INSTRUCTIONS FROM THE USER, THEREBY HAS RIGHT OPINION, WHEREAS THE IMITATOR HAS NEITHER KNOWLEDGE NOR RIGHT OPINION. BECAUSE THE IMITATOR HAS NEITHER KNOWLEDGE NOR RIGHT OPINION OF WHAT A THING OF A GIVEN KIND IS REALLY LIKE, HE CAN ONLY IMITATE WHAT HE THINKS WILL APPEAR BEAUTIFUL TO THE IGNORANT MULTITUDE.

A. Plato here tries to show why the imitator of a thing does not have any expertise concerning it at all, not even to the extent of having true or right opinion or belief (*doxa* or *pistis*) about it. Plato's view rests on the idea that for the rendering of a thing to be fully satisfactory, it would have to be the outcome of the knowledge of the use (*chreia*) of the thing. The user of the thing knows its use, at first hand, and can therefore tell what distinguishes a good specimen from a bad one (601e4–5). The maker of an artifact receives this information from the user and so has it at second hand or by hearsay, and thus can be said to have only true opinion (given, that is, that his informant is reliable, which the maker cannot check for himself). If someone is merely imitating the appearance of an artifact, however, he does not need either to know at first hand, or even to consider, how it is used or what distinguishes a good specimen from a bad one. From this Plato concludes that the imitator's skill can consist in nothing beyond an ability to render images of things that will appear beautiful to those who are ignorant of the things themselves. For if the imitator were to produce imitations that appealed to the knowledgeable, the imitations would have to embody information about the things themselves, which would have to come from the use thereof. Therefore, if someone produced an artifact that really embodied such information, he would, after all, turn out to be a maker and not an imitator. Thus, if one were trying to render not merely the way in which a bridle *looks*, but to show with *full* accuracy all of the features that contribute to its use, one would by that very fact be trying to produce bridles rather than pictures of them. [White, pp. 3–4, 19.]

B. The present argument applies most naturally to artifacts, and Plato has been talking of such things as beds and bridles since the beginning of the treatment of poetry (see 506a). From the previous sections, however, it is clear that he intends an analogy between the triad, using/ making/imitating, and the triad, Form/sensible instance/imitation. We must exercise care, however, in determining just how far he intended this analogy to be carried. It seems incorrect to suppose that Forms can, strictly, have a use. On the other hand, we have earlier encountered signs of Plato's view that knowledge of the Form of *F* involves an understanding of what makes an *F* a good specimen of its kind (507a–509c, nn. B–C, and 352d–354a, n. A). And although Forms themselves cannot be used, he can still think of a kind of goodness as attaching to the Form of *F* in virtue of its representing what, generally speaking, an *F* must have in order to be unqualifiedly and non-defectively an *F* (see *ibid.*).

C. It is not difficult to see why Plato thought that the rendering of mere appearances must go along with a failure to render (and the lack of need to consider) all of the features necessary for the use of a thing. He thought of an appearance, as we have seen (597e–598d), as an appearance from a single perspective. But all of the things that we use, it seems, are three-dimensional objects, having features relevant to their use over and above the features that can be observed or depicted from one angle alone. (Perhaps he would have some reason to say that motion pictures are less defective in this respect.)

D. The notion that the virtue or excellence (*aretē*, 601d4) of a thing has to do with its use (*chreia*) was first introduced in Book I, at 352d–354a. (The terminology was slightly different: though *aretē* was used,

353b2 and e2, "function," *ergon*, was used instead of *chreia*.) The notion of a function appeared in the Principle of the Natural Division of Labor (369e–370c, n. F), and something close to it is involved in Plato's notion of goodness (507a–509c, n. B). Notice that Plato does not restrict the term "use" only to artifacts: things that are produced by nature (see *pephykos*, 601d6) also have a "use."

602c–603b: THE EFFECTS OF IMITATION ARE OPPOSED TO REASON. CONSIDER APPEARANCES PRESENTED BY SIGHT, SUCH AS THE FACT THAT THE SAME THING WILL APPEAR CROOKED IN WATER BUT STRAIGHT WHEN OUT OF WATER, AND WILL APPEAR TO BE OF DIFFERENT SIZES WHEN SEEN FROM DIFFERENT DISTANCES. PAINTING USES JUST SUCH DIFFICULTIES ABOUT APPEARANCES TO PRODUCE ITS EFFECTS. COUNTERACTING SUCH DECEPTIONS IN APPEARANCES, HOWEVER, ARE MEASURING, COUNTING, AND WEIGHING, WHICH ARE FUNCTIONS OF THE REASONING PART OF THE SOUL, AS CAN BE SEEN FROM THE FACT THAT MEASUREMENT WILL SOMETIMES SHOW ONE THING TO BE BIGGER THAN ANOTHER, FOR EXAMPLE, WHEN THE APPEARANCE SUGGESTS THE CONTRARY. SO THE RESULTS OF IMITATION MUST BE INFERIOR TO THOSE OF REASON, BEING THE PRODUCTS OF AN INFERIOR PART OF THE SOUL.

A.   The aim of this section is to show that not only does imitation not produce the truth about things, but it produces results that are in conflict with the deliverances of reason (603a–b), and so is not a function of reason but in some sense inferior to it. This claim will be applied to imitative poetry in the following section.

B.   The passage shows us something further about what Plato believes is left out when we are presented only with the appearances of things, as when we see just one aspect of a thing from a single standpoint (598a–b), or see a thing as having one size from one distance and another from another distance (602c). For he maintains that measuring, counting, and weighing can come to our aid, so that appearances will not "rule" in us (602d). It is clear that in his view the results of reason are to be judged superior to those of appearance. He has in mind, for example, a case in which we have two sticks of equal length, but which are at unequal distances from us so that one appears longer than the other. His point is that the superior judgment will be that they are not of equal length, and that this judgment is not arrived at simply on the basis of the sensory appearance of the sticks, but on the basis of something else, which he calls reason. (It is helpful to remember yet again that one of his standard words for the "reasoning" part of the soul is *logistikon*, derived from the verb *logizesthai*, which means "to calculate"; cf. 590c–591a, n. D, with 522c, e, 525a–c.) It is important to Plato's point that, at least in many cases, the rational realization that one is being confronted by a deceptive appearance does not change the appearance. In the present example, the awareness that two unequally distant sticks actually are of equal length does not make them start to *look* equally long.

It is not clear whether Plato's view is compatible with the idea that there are, as they are sometimes called, "veridical appearances," or appearances that do represent a thing as it is, or as at least much closer to the way it is than other, "deceptive" appearances do. Such an idea is certainly suggested, even if Plato does not express the matter in this way, by the case of the stick that "really is" straight (as indeed it looks when not partially submerged in water) but does not look straight when it is submerged. If Plato did accept this idea, then his point about sensory appearances here would be, not that every one of them is somehow defective by contrast to the facts gleaned by rational reflection on them, but simply that they are *sometimes* deceptive by contrast to those facts. However, the foregoing section indicates what seems a reason for deeming *all* appearances unsatisfactory, in that none of them presents all of the features of a thing relevant to its use. Plato's point, I think we should conclude, is as follows: although some appearances are (more or less) accurate indicators of *some* features, nevertheless, no appearance is an accurate indicator of *all* of them; so (he infers) to understand the use of a thing, we have to add to the appearances of it some sort of reasoning process which gives us the true facts, so far as they can be gleaned. Thus, a look at the stick when it is out of water will not be deceptive with regard to the fact that it is straight, but neither that look nor any other will tell us all there is to know about the stick (and its use, whatever it might be).

C.   It should not be thought that in drawing this contrast between appearances and certain kinds of reasoning about facts in the sensible world, Plato is going back on his earlier assertion that there is knowledge only of Forms and that only Forms have "being" in the strict sense (see 476d–480a, nn. B–C); nor should one conclude that he is allowing that certain attributes, namely, the attributes detected by such things as measurement, are attached to sensible objects without qualification. As we have seen, he does believe that certain sensible objects are more correctly labeled by certain terms than are others (*ibid.*, n. C, fifth point), in the sense that the former are better or closer approximations of the Form of *F* than others. Moreover, when this is so, we can tell that it is so in part by our knowledge of the Forms, to which we compare sensible objects, this knowledge being a possession of the reason. But this does not mean that sensible objects have attributes that attach to them unqualifiedly in the way that attributes attach to Forms. Thus, even a stick that has been determined by measurement to be large compared to another stick, and is accordingly closer to being unqualifiedly large than the second stick and perhaps many other things, is nevertheless not unqualifiedly large. For, in the first place, it is small compared to still other things, and, in the second place, it will quite certainly not be permanently large and has not been so for all past time; so there are clear qualifications attached to its largeness (see *ibid.*, and Introd., sec. 3).

D. In 602e–603a, Plato's argument for the non-identity of reason with the part of us that can be deceived by imitation rests on the principle enunciated at 436d and thereafter used to distinguish the parts of the soul, the principle that the same object cannot do or suffer contrary things at the same time in the same part of itself in relation to the same object.

E. Plato does not directly confront the most notable problem in his contrast between appearance and measurement, which is that measurement (weighing, etc.) quite clearly involves appearances. For example, one measures by *looking* at measuring rods or the like. (This is not to say that Plato's view, as explained in n. B, cannot be made to accommodate this fact, but only that he does not here deal with it explicitly.)

F. Sight, Plato thinks, presents to us only single views of objects without the full range of information that gives an understanding of their use (cf. 597e–598d, n. B). It is accordingly obvious but important that the understanding that reason can have of an object, when it has information about its use, is not to be thought of as a "mental picture" of the object. For although Plato sometimes speaks of knowledge as analogous in a certain way to sight, he nevertheless regards it as far more complex than the replication in the mind or imagination of visual impressions. [See, e.g., White, pp. 91–2.]

G. As I have interpreted the Simile of the Cave at the beginning of Book VII, Plato is saying there that most people are unable to understand clearly the idea of objects in the world, above and beyond the kinds of appearances that sight is said in the present passage to deliver to us. These appearances are the things that we apprehend if we rely on our sight alone (Plato presumably thinks that the analogy holds for the other senses too), without any accompanying calculation of the objects from which they arise, and the things that painters represent in their paintings. See 514a–517d, n. B.

603b–605c: WE MUST NOT RELY ON THE ANALOGY WITH PAINTING, BUT MUST SEE DIRECTLY WHETHER THE FOREGOING POINT, ABOUT THE INFERIORITY OF IMITATION, APPLIES DIRECTLY TO IMITATIVE POETRY. IMITATIVE POETRY IMITATES MEN WHO THINK THAT THEY HAVE FARED WELL OR ILL AS THE RESULT OF THEIR ACTIONS, AND THEREFORE EITHER GRIEVE OR REJOICE. A MAN IN SUCH A SITUATION IS OFTEN AT ODDS WITH HIMSELF, AS WE HAVE SEEN (esp. 439ff.). FOR EXAMPLE, IF A GOOD MAN HAS LOST SOMETHING DEAR TO HIM, HIS SUFFERING TENDS TO MAKE HIM GIVE WAY TO GRIEF, WHEREAS HIS REASON URGES HIM TO REMAIN QUIET AND CALMLY PLAN HOW HE MAY MAKE THINGS BETTER IN THE FUTURE—CALMLY, BECAUSE GRIEVING DOES NO GOOD AND IS AN IMPEDIMENT TO EFFECTIVE THOUGHT AND ACTION. BUT THE PART OF A PERSON THAT LENDS ITSELF TO EASY AND UNDERSTANDABLE IMITATION IS JUST THE PART THAT LEADS ONE TO DWELL ON AND EXPRESS ONE'S GRIEF; WHEREAS THE INTELLIGENT AND QUIET PART IS STABLE AND IS NEITHER EASY TO IMITATE NOR READILY UNDERSTOOD, ESPECIALLY BY THOSE GATHERED AT FESTIVALS. THE IMITATIVE POET THEREFORE DOES NOT ATTEND MUCH TO THE REASONING ELEMENT, BUT INSTEAD TO THE OTHER PART, AND SO IT IS THAT PART THAT HE STRENGTHENS. IT IS, ACCORDINGLY, JUSTIFIABLE TO COMPARE HIM TO THE PAINTER, BECAUSE HE ESTABLISHES POOR GOVERNANCE WITHIN EACH SOUL, BY PLEASING THE UNINTELLIGENT PART RATHER THAN THE PART THAT DISCERNS WHAT IS LARGE AND IMPORTANT AND WHAT IS SMALL AND UNIMPORTANT, AND BY MAKING IMAGES THAT ARE VERY FAR FROM THE TRUTH.

A. The purpose of this very complex section is to cement the comparison between painting and imitative poetry and so to show the way in which the latter is indeed a misleading kind of imitation (cf. 595c–597e, n. A).

B. The basic point of comparison between the two is as follows. Our visual perspective, which painting renders, shows things as they appear from a particular standpoint, not as they are, so to speak, as wholes. Similarly, Plato thinks, tragedy shows us situations in that manner in which they produce an immediate emotional reaction, not as they would be looked on by reason, that is, as requiring a calculated and rational response designed to make the best of them and to plan for the future as well as can be done under the circumstances. A situation requiring human action and presented to a person's capacity for planning is thus analogous to a view presented to one's vision. Just as the latter will present objects that appear to be larger than others simply because they are closer, so the former will present events in a manner that distorts our estimation of their value and the value of the actions that might be performed. Thus, for example, a harmful event in the immediate future might seem more harmful, and seem to be worthy of more effort to avoid it, than a truly much more harmful event in the distant future; or, as Plato has explained in 583b–585a, our idea of the degree of pleasantness of a thing can be distorted by the circumstances in which we observe it. So, then, just as in the case of sight we can use measurement and the like to determine what the true relative sizes of things are (602c–603b), in cases requiring action we can make a rational calculation of advantages and disadvantages to see what course is the best one. Moreover, just as a preoccupation with appearances may prevent us from calculating the facts, so by succumbing to emotions we may be prevented from the calculation that is needed to improve the situation (604b–d). For example, Plato sometimes cites death as an example of something to which one's emotions react differently from reason and wrongly, so that one greatly fears it even though rational calculation shows that one should not (386a–387d, 485d–487a; cf. 514a–517d, n. C). Emotions arise only on the basis of a superficial view of some of the features of the situation; only rational calculation can take account of all of the pertinent facts. [Nettleship, p. 350.]

C. Portrayal of situations seen emotionally, so to speak, strikes Plato as being the stock in trade of imitative poetry, typified by tragedy. He thinks that this is so because the portrayal of such varied and capricious reactions is more superficially interesting to most people than the

representation of a man who, in the face of misfortune, simply calcu-
lates how he may make the best of it and proceeds to act accordingly.
(The parallel fact in the case of visual art might be that a picture
rendering a given aspect of an object is more interesting to most people
than, say, a calculated specification of all of its true measurements;
cf. 528e–531d.) Accordingly, imitative poetry tends to be about people
whose behavior is governed by their passions, arising from the lowest
part of the soul, rather than by reason.

We can see now just why Plato thinks of tragedy as the paradigm case
of the usual imitative poetry (though comedy is dealt with briefly at
606c). For grief and allied emotions, and their precipitate consequences,
do play a considerable role in tragedy.

D.   We can also see why, although he recognizes the possibility of a
kind of poetry that represents good men (397d, 607a), he does not
include that sort of poetry in the indictment of imitative poetry presented here (cf. 595c–597e, n. B). For the representation of good men
acting well would not portray situations in an irrationally emotional
light, and so would not resemble painting in the way in which, he
thinks, tragic poetry does. Rather, representation of this salutary kind
would be representation of the genuine advantages and disadvantages of
a situation and of the courses of action that might be taken in it, perhaps including a conclusion about what the best course would be. As
such, it would not be imitation at all, in the pejorative sense, because it
would not simply be the rendering of the appearance of something
(597e–598d), but rather a true account of how certain facts actually
stand (cf. 473a). [Grube, *PT*, p. 190.]

E.   In addition, we have the answer to the question how Plato can
regard his own works, which are after all a sort of literary portrayal, as
immune to the charge of being imitations in a pejorative sense. He can
respond that an imitation in that sense is something that only presents
the appearances of things, as represented by emotional reactions, but
that his own works are accurate representations of the facts, enabling us
to make correct assessments about how we should act. This response is
not affected by the fact that Plato's works sometimes contain characters,
such as Thrasymachus, who are rather far from being good men. For
even though such men would not be suitable characters for prospective
guardians to mimic in their education (see 595c–597e, n. B), the whole
works of which they are parts nevertheless have the salutary features
that exclude them from the class of imitations which Plato is con-

demning. (Nor is the response affected by the presence in Plato's works of myths, such as the Myth of Er in 614a–621b, because although he often treats them as conjectural, there is nothing preventing them from having the same salutary features: notice esp. 621b–d.) [E.g., Grube, *PT*, p. 206.]

F.   The present passage shows more clearly than others in the *Republic* how Plato can believe that, although in his technical sense there can be no *knowledge* of the sensible world (476d–480a, esp. nn. B–C), there is nevertheless a clear-cut form of expertise having to do with it, something that we, adopting standards different from Plato's, might well be content to call knowledge. Cf. 475e–476d, n. B.

G.   The adoption by Plato of his view of imitative poetry explains why he speaks so disapprovingly of the use of rhythm and the like, which he thinks of as poetic ornamentation (see 598d–601b, n. B). For these devices, he thinks, simply heighten the misleading effects of imitation.

605c–608b: THE MOST SERIOUS CHARGE AGAINST IMITATIVE POETRY, HOWEVER, IS THAT IT CORRUPTS EVEN GOOD MEN. FOR ONCE THEY ENJOY THE SPECTACLE OF GRIEF AND LAMENTATION IN THE THEATER, THEY SOON COME TO TAKE THE SAME ATTITUDE TOWARD IT IN THEMSELVES. MOREOVER, POETIC IMITATION ENCOURAGES OTHER EXCESSIVE EMOTIONAL REACTIONS IN US, TOO. SO WE MUST KEEP TO OUR RESOLVE TO EXCLUDE SUCH POETRY FROM OUR CITY AND ALLOW ONLY HYMNS TO THE GODS AND EULOGIES OF GOOD MEN—UNLESS, OF COURSE, THE IMITATIVE POETS CAN, EITHER IN POETRY OR IN PROSE, DEFEND THEIR WORK AND SHOW THAT IT NOT ONLY BRINGS PLEASURE BUT IS BENEFICIAL TO CITIES AND TO HUMAN LIFE. OTHERWISE, WE MUST EXCLUDE SUCH POETRY, BECAUSE IT IS IMPORTANT FOR A PERSON TO BE GOOD, AND NOT TO BE LED ASTRAY EITHER BY HONORS, OR BY WEALTH, OR BY POETRY.

A.   The final part of Plato's attack on imitative poetry rests on the contention that, in addition to appealing to the ignorant multitude and being misleading in the manner described, it can also corrupt good men, by habituating them to manifestations of emotion, which they will then be willing to tolerate in themselves at the expense of the rule of reason, so that they will come to view situations emotionally, so to speak, rather than by rational calculation. [Bosanquet, p. 401.]

B.   In 607a it is reiterated (from 397d) that certain kinds of poetry will
be allowed in Plato's city, namely, hymns to the gods and praises of good
men. But although such poems would in a broad sense plainly represent
gods and good men, they would not be imitative in the sense that Plato
has in mind (cf. previous n. D).

C.   The offer to the poets of a chance to vindicate their work is doubt-
less ironic, in the sense that Plato hardly expects them to produce a
reply that will convince him. It is dictated, no doubt, partly by the
desire for a certain politeness toward those with whom he is debating.
But it is also a reminder of the grounds on which he thinks that they
must rest their argument: they must try to show that imitative poetry is,
contrary to his contention, a *salutary* thing.

608c–611a: BUT GREATER PRIZES THAN THESE ARE AVAILABLE
TO EXCELLENCE OR VIRTUE, AS WE CAN SEE WHEN WE REAL-
IZE THAT THE SOUL IS IMMORTAL, AND THAT WHAT IS IM-
MORTAL SHOULD BE CONCERNED WITH ETERNITY RATHER
THAN WITH THIS SHORT TIME DURING WHICH WE ARE ALIVE.
THAT THE SOUL IS IMMORTAL CAN BE SEEN FROM THE FACT
THAT, WHEREAS EVERYTHING THAT PERISHES IS MADE TO
DO SO BY ITS OWN PECULIAR EVIL, THE SOUL IS NOT MADE
TO PERISH BY ITS OWN PECULIAR EVIL, WHICH IS INJUSTICE,
AND SO COULD NOT BE MADE TO PERISH BY ANYTHING ELSE.
(SO THERE IS NEVER ANY DIMINUTION IN THE NUMBER OF
SOULS; NOR CAN THEIR NUMBER INCREASE, BECAUSE IT
WOULD HAVE TO INCREASE BY THE ADDITION OF WHAT WAS
PREVIOUSLY MORTAL, IN WHICH CASE EVERYTHING WOULD
BECOME IMMORTAL EVENTUALLY.)

A.   The beginning of this section marks the major break in Book X
(see 595a–c, n. A). Plato now turns to discuss the immortality of the
soul and its consequences for one's efforts to calculate how one may
gain the greatest possible welfare.

B.   Plato's far-from-cogent argument for the immortality of the soul
rests on, among other things, the claim that injustice is the peculiar evil
of the soul, in being that which, when it attaches itself to the soul, makes
it bad (*ponēros*, 609a). The identification of injustice as the peculiar

evil of the soul has not been argued for quite explicitly. It is probably intended to rest, however, on Plato's earlier argument about the importance of justice to the goodness of the soul (433b–e). A chief weakness of the present argument, however, is its dependence on the unargued claim that for each thing there is precisely one "peculiar evil," and that for the soul it is injustice.

C.   In 611a, Plato claims, though arguing only cursorily, that there is a fixed number of souls, which is never diminished or augmented. That it is never diminished follows from the claim that each soul is immortal. That it is never augmented is argued for in one sentence, at 611a6–8. The latter point is not of much importance to him here, but it is presupposed in the Myth of Er in 614a–621b.

611a–612a: WE HAVE ARGUED THAT THE SOUL IS IMMORTAL. IT IS, HOWEVER, DIFFICULT TO MAINTAIN THAT ANYTHING COMPOSED OF MANY PARTS COULD BE IMMORTAL IF IT IS NOT PUT TOGETHER IN THE BEST WAY. IT IS DIFFICULT TO DISCERN THE TRUE NATURE OF THE SOUL WHEN IT IS ASSOCIATED WITH THE BODY. IF ONE CONSIDERS ITS LOVE OF WISDOM, AND HOW IT IS AKIN TO WHAT IS DIVINE AND IMMORTAL, ONE REALIZES THAT IF IT COULD BECOME FREE OF BODILY INFLUENCE, THEN ONE COULD TELL CLEARLY WHETHER IT IS REALLY COMPOSITE OR SIMPLE. AS IT IS, HOWEVER, WE HAVE SATISFACTORILY DISCUSSED IT AS IT EXISTS IN HUMAN LIFE.

A.   Plato here briefly describes a difficulty with which he is faced, arising out of a possible incompatibility between his contention that the soul is immortal and other things that he wishes to say about it. He tends to believe (see e.g., *Phaedo* 78c, with *Rep.* 382e) that a thing can be destroyed only by being somehow broken apart, and that anything indestructible must be so by virtue of lacking parts that are separable from each other. If the soul is immortal, he sees difficulty in any belief about it that might represent it as composite. The first problem would arise from his claim that it has three parts (434d–442d). But Plato lays this problem to rest by suggesting that if the soul can be said to be immortal, it is really only the rational part of it that is immortal (611e–612a). But can the rational part of the soul really be said to be incomposite? From Plato's description of it, it is not at all clear that it can be. For that description depicts it as having a plurality of tendencies and functions, and even a conflict of sorts concerning its activities of ruling and philosophizing (519d–521b), which would, in conjunction with the assumption enunciated in 436b–437a, show that it is actually composite. (That assumption was that the same object cannot do or suffer contrary things at the same time in the same part of itself in relation to the same object.) Plato does not resolve this problem here, but he has left two ways open to his solution. One is to say that unless we have a clearer notion of what the soul is like when detached from bodily influences, we cannot tell whether it is composite or not. The suggestion is that the apparent conflicts within reason may be the result of its association with the body, so that it somehow takes on certain concerns that it would not have by itself. The other possibility is that the assumption made in 436b-437a is wrong, and that a thing could tend in contrary directions without thereby being composite. That Plato wishes to leave this way open is evident from the fact that, as noted (*ibid.*, n. A), he called the contents of 436b–437a merely an assumption and emphasized that it can be questioned. No doubt one of the reasons why he did that, and probably the chief reason, is that he had in mind the problem arising here.

The Myth of Er, to follow in 614a–621b, raises this problem insistently, for it ascribes to souls after death all sorts of motivations, even conflicting ones (e.g., at 619b–c). So it is suitable that before presenting the myth, in which he is to express some of his beliefs about the rewards of justice after death, he should here indicate his awareness of the major difficulty affecting the picture of the soul to be exhibited there. [Dodds, *PI*; Dodds, *PIS*, pp. 213ff.; Guthrie, *PNS*; Guthrie, *HGP*, pp. 554–7; Szlezák.]

B.   At several points in earlier parts of the *Republic*, notably at 543c–544d (see n. B), Plato has hinted that the ideal state for a human soul might be to be disembodied. But although certain points in the following discussion may be intended to suggest the same idea, Plato does not explore the matter extensively in this work.

612a–e: WE HAVE SEEN THAT JUSTICE ITSELF IS BEST, AND THAT ONE MUST DO WHAT IS JUST EVEN IF ONE COULD ESCAPE DETECTION WITH A RING OF GYGES. LET US NOW LOOK AT THE REWARDS OF JUSTICE BOTH FROM GODS AND FROM MEN, AND IN PARTICULAR AT THE CONSEQUENCES OF THE REPUTATION THAT IT IN FACT HAS AMONG BOTH.

A.   Plato returns to the classification of goods expounded at the beginning of Book II, in 357a–358a. He maintained there that justice was to be welcomed both for its own sake and for its consequences. His argument that it was to be welcomed for its own sake took him all of the way to the end of Book IX. He now begins a discussion of its consequences.

B. The relative brevity of this discussion of consequences probably shows that it is of less interest to Plato than the treatment of the goodness of justice for its own sake. Moreover, what he has to say about consequences is far less convincing and carefully argued than what has gone before. The arguments in 612e–613b and 613b–614a are hardly arguments at all, but mere assertions, with little support, of what Plato wishes to maintain. One of the reasons may be that the considerations offered in Book X as praise of justice are perhaps intended for a less philosophically accomplished audience than the complex demonstration in Books II–IX. (As is suggested in sec. 4 of the Introduction, this may be because the earlier treatment *presupposes* in its audience some exceptional ability to come to grasp Plato's conception of the Good, or—what for Plato comes to much the same thing—a temperament basically suited to philosophy.)

C. The kind of consequence of justice with which Plato is especially concerned in Book X has to do with the reputation that one gains for being just (612c–d). That this is so fits with what we saw earlier of his major motivation in setting up his classification of goods (see 362d–368c, n. A, and 358a–362c, n. C), which was largely to distinguish between what one gained from justice because of reputation and what one gained apart from reputation.

612e–613b: AS FAR AS THE GODS ARE CONCERNED, THEY NOTICE WHO IS JUST AND WHO IS UNJUST AND SEE TO IT THAT THE FORMER, EVEN IF THEY SOMETIMES MEET MISFORTUNE, ARE REWARDED EVENTUALLY, EITHER DURING THEIR LIFETIMES OR AFTERWARD, FOR THE GODS WOULD NOT NEGLECT ONE WHO ATTEMPTS TO BECOME LIKE THEM.

A. This brief passage cannot be thought of as a genuine argument and would not convince anyone who was at all inclined to believe otherwise. What, then, is its purpose?

We must remember that Plato has not generally pictured the Thrasymachean view, that people usually lose by being just, as the view that is generally held. The general view, as Plato sees it, is represented by the prudently pious Cephalus in Book I (328c–331d), and also by Glaucon at the start of Book I, where he represents most people as holding that justice is in the class of goods welcomed not for themselves but for their consequences (358a). Moreover, even Thrasymachus readily admitted that the man committing petty injustices is usually made worse off because he is punished, and that it takes large-scale injustice to produce real advantages (343a–344c with 358a–362c, n. B, which shows Socrates accepting this claim for the sake of his argument).

The conclusion to draw is plainly that those whom Plato is addressing are supposed to be in basic agreement with what he is saying here. They needed to be convinced that justice is good for its own sake and apart from reputation, and so Plato wrote Books II–IX for them. But they do not need to be convinced that in conjunction with circumstances justice *generally* has good consequences, and so Plato's discussion of that point is brief and, especially in the Myth of Er, mainly exhortatory rather than argumentative. [Grote, pp. 121–126.]

613b–614a: AS FOR REWARDS FROM MEN, ALTHOUGH UNJUST MEN MAY GAIN MANY BENEFITS AT THE START AND WHEN THEY ARE YOUNG, NEVERTHELESS, THEY ARE LATER CAUGHT IN MISFORTUNES AND FAILURES, WHEREAS JUST MEN HOLD OFFICES AND HAVE OTHER SUCH ADVANTAGES.

A.   Like the previous section, this section has little force as an argument. Also like the previous section, however, it is directed at people who are inclined to accept its conclusion (see previous note).

Plato believes, however, that there are notable exceptions to his contention that just men are usually rewarded, and unjust men usually punished, by their fellows. One notable exception, in his view, must have been Socrates. No doubt this is the reason why he carefully qualifies his contention and says that such rewards and punishments *generally* occur (*to polu*, 613c), in the majority of cases (613d). (Presumably, his belief in the goodness of the gods—cf. 379b–380c—leads him to think that they are more reliably correct dispensers of rewards and punishments than men are.)

614a–617d: THE MYTH OF ER: BEGINNING

A.   As always in Platonic myths (such as we find in, e.g., the *Gorgias* and the *Phaedrus*), it is difficult to tell which features convey essential points and which do not. In a very rough way, the message of this myth is clear enough: there is punishment of a sort after death for injustice and reward for justice. The nature of the punishments and rewards, however, is not entirely plain. One sort of punishment and reward is expounded in the present section; in the following section, a different one appears.

B.   The present section describes (in a manner leaving many details unclear) punishments and rewards that are meted out to souls by agents other than themselves, in some kind of proportion to their bad and good deeds in their previous lives (615a–c). The chief difference between these punishments and rewards and those described in the following section, as we shall see, is that these are not, or at least not directly, chosen by the souls themselves, whereas the later ones in some degree are.

C.   In the present section, Plato leaves it quite unclear whether the effects of the punishments and rewards are important to him, and whether, e.g., the punishments are valuable in having a deterrent effect.

D.   The description of the structure of the universe as seen by the traveling souls (616b–617d) has been the subject of much scholarly debate and puzzlement. It contains much that is unclear. Plato, however, obviously did not consider it his main need here to expound his cosmology, though the problems involved in explaining the motions of the heavenly bodies were obviously regarded seriously by him.

617d–621b: THE MYTH OF ER: CONCLUSION

A.   This section deals with the second sort of consequences of justice and injustice after death (see previous nn. A–B). It presents the procedure whereby reincarnation is planned, to decide what sort of life each soul will subsequently have. This aspect of the matter appears to have a much more important place than the previous one, because Plato describes it much more elaborately with much more explanation of its rationale. Not only that, but also the punishments described in the previous section appear to have no impact on the decisions that souls are said here to make about what sorts of lives to live.

B.   The main burden of the passage, voiced by Lachesis in her message to the souls, is that their choice is their own responsibility (though chance does have some part to play in it, in 617e and 619b). Indeed, Plato issues a rebuke to those who try to place the responsibility elsewhere (619c). In this respect, the consequences of the souls' justice or injustice appear to be quite different from those described in 614a–617d, where the punishments and rewards were apparently imposed from outside.

C. The consequence of this message is that the rewards and punishments in this part of the myth are simply the results of the souls' continuing to follow the various desires that are part of their characters (620a). Plato does allow for the possibility that some souls will improve and learn from experience, as Odysseus does at 620c–d (though as noted, nothing is said to suggest that the rewards and punishments of the first part of the myth have any important effect). But the main point seems to be that, at least in many cases, the reward or punishment of having a certain character is to continue to live in accordance with that character.

What, then, would be the advantage of having a good (and just) character, and the disadvantage of having a bad (and unjust) character? Wherein, that is, would living in accordance with a good character be a *reward*, and living in accordance with a bad character be a *punishment?* What Plato seems to be saying, or close to saying, is that a life in accordance with virtue is its own reward, in the sense that by acting in accordance with virtue one gets the chance to do more of the same, and that in a precisely analogous way a life in accordance with vice is its own punishment. And this is close to saying what he has been maintaining in Books II–IX, that justice and, in general, virtue are to be welcomed for their own sakes. If this is something like what he has in mind, then this part of the myth's argument, that justice is good for its consequences, is arguing something not so different from his claim that justice is good for its own sake.

D. This section of the myth makes clear the main connection between the two main parts of Book X (see 595a–c, n. A). By contrasting the rational with the imitative view of the way in which human beings should regard situations in which they must act (603b–605c, n. B), the first part of the book has constituted a lesson on human prudence and foresight. The second part of the book, culminating in the myth of Er, is an application of this lesson, showing the way in which prudence and calculation must be applied to the problem of how to live one's whole life. Through the eyes of Er, who is made to understand the picture of the afterlife which is being presented to him, Plato is showing how a rational, non-tragic understanding of death (which he would clearly wish to contrast with poetic descriptions of death and the afterlife, such as the one in Book XI of the *Odyssey*) will deal with what he conceives to be the problem that it raises. For he thinks that death should not call forth an emotional response of grief or fear but should be treated as something forcing one to render an account of one's life and to choose how best one may live.

621b–d: CONCLUSION

In a brief and eloquent summation, Plato insists on the importance of keeping these things in mind in one's deliberations.

Bibliography

The following is a list of works referred to elsewhere in this book. As noted in the Preface, it is but a small and sometimes arbitrary selection of the works on or relevant to the *Republic*.

Summaries of the *Republic* abound. I have written the present book because I do not think that any of them follows the main line of Plato's argument adequately, nor that any of the more specialized studies in existence allows us to piece it together correctly. Still, the reader should consult other summaries beside this one in order to see other versions of Plato's most important themes, which not infrequently invite a variety of interpretations. I particularly recommend Grote's treatment, which for all its faults and harshness seems to me by far the best and most intelligent account of the ideas of the *Republic* which I have encountered, and particularly of those aspects of it which concern me here. After Grote, the next best work to consult is Shorey's Loeb translation (reprinted in the Hamilton and Cairns collection of translations), with its introductions and copious notes, which, although they often seem to me quite mistaken, are nevertheless unfailingly stimulating. Also interesting and especially worthwhile are Bosanquet's book, after which the present work is partially named, Nettleship's, and the relevant parts of Crombie, *EPD*, and of Guthrie, *HGP*. Among the summaries that I have not had occasion to refer to here, the reader should take note of some of those mentioned by Shorey, *Rep.*, I, p. vii, n. *a*, of those accompanying Jowett's and Cornford's translations, and of the as yet incomplete one by Gigon (*Gegenwärtigkeit und Utopie*, Bd. I (Zurich and Munich, 1976), covering the first half of the *Republic*. For many other works to which I have not referred, the reader should see especially the bibliography by Cherniss in *Lustrum*, 1959–60. I should also mention here two works that are insufficiently attended to by historians of Greek philosophy, namely, the two works by the great Sidgwick listed below. (Those who need an introduction to the historical background of Plato's work might best begin with Antony Andrewes, *The Greeks* (London, 1967), or with C. M. Bowra, *The Greek Experience* (London, 1957), or with M. I. Finley, *The Ancient Greeks* (N. Y., 1963). For a full-scale history, they might try J. B. Bury and Russell Meiggs, A *History of Greece*, ed. 4 (London, 1975).)

James Adam, ed., *The Republic of Plato*, ed. 2 (Cambridge, Eng., 1963), vols. I and II.

Arthur W. H. Adkins, *Merit and Responsibility* (Oxford, 1960).

R. E. Allen, ed., *Studies in Plato's Metaphysics* (N. Y., 1965).

R. Bambrough, *New Essays on Plato and Aristotle* (N. Y., 1965).

Bernard Bosanquet, *A Companion to Plato's Republic for English Readers* (N. Y., 1895).

Harold Cherniss, *ACPA, Aristotle's Criticism of Plato and the Academy* (Baltimore, 1944).

Harold Cherniss, *SEAP*, "The Sources of Evil According to Plato," *Proceedings of the American Philosophical Society*, 98 (1954), 23–30, reprinted in Vlastos, *Plato II*, pp. 244–57, and cited in the latter pagination.

John M. Cooper, "The Psychology of Justice in Plato," *American Philosophical Quarterly*, 14 (1977), 151–7.

I. M. Crombie, *EPD, An Examination of Plato's Doctrines*, vol. I (London, 1962).

I. M. Crombie, *PMA, Plato: The Midwife's Apprentice* (London, 1964).

R. C. Cross and A. D. Woozley, *Plato's Republic: A Philosophical Commentary* (London, 1964).

Raphael Demos, "A Fallacy in Plato's *Republic?*" *Philosophical Review*, 73 (1964), 395–8, reprinted in Vlastos, *Plato II*, pp. 52–6, and cited in the latter pagination.

Auguste Dies, introd. to Emile Chambry, ed., *Platon, La République*, vol. I (Paris, 1959).

E. R. Dodds, *PI*, "Plato and the Irrational," *Journal of Hellenic Studies*, 65 (1945), 16–25.

E. R. Dodds, *PIS*, "Plato and the Irrational Soul," Ch. VIII of *The Greeks and the Irrational* (Berkeley, 1951), reprinted in Vlastos, ed., *Plato II*, pp. 206–229, and cited in the latter pagination.

K. J. Dover, *Greek Popular Morality in the Time of Plato and Aristotle* (Berkeley and Los Angeles, 1974).

Gerald F. Else, "The Structure and Date of Book 10 of Plato's *Republic*," *Abhandlungen der heidelberger Akademie der Wissenschaften*, Phil.-hist. Kl., 1972, 3. Abh.

William K. Frankena, *E, Ethics*, 2nd ed. (Englewood Cliffs, 1973).

William K. Frankena, *PEV*, "Prichard and the Ethics of Virtue," *Monist*, 54 (1970), 1–17, reprinted in K. E. Goodpaster, ed., *Perspectives on Morality: Essays of William K. Frankena* (Notre Dame, 1976).

Paul Friedländer, *Plato*, trans. H. Meyerhoff, vol. III (Princeton, 1969).

J. C. B. Gosling, *Plato* (London, 1973).

George Grote, *Plato, and the Other Companions of Socrates*, new ed. (London, 1888), vol. IV.

G. M. A. Grube, *PT, Plato's Thought* (London, 1935).

G. M. A. Grube, *Rep.*, trans., *Plato's Republic* (Indianapolis, 1974).

Norman Gulley, *Plato's Theory of Knowledge* (London, 1962).

W. K. C. Guthrie, *PNS*, "Plato's Views on the Nature of the Soul," *Fondation Hardt, Entretiens sur l'antiquité classique*, vol. III (Vandoeuvres-Genève, 1955), 3–19, reprinted in Vlastos, *Plato II*, pp. 230–243, and cited in the latter pagination.

W. K. C. Guthrie, *HGP, A History of Greek Philosophy*, vol. IV (Cambridge, Eng., 1975).

R. M. Hackforth, *Plato's Examination of Pleasure* (Cambridge, Eng., 1945).

R. M. Hare, "Plato and the Mathematicians," Bambrough, pp. 21–38.

Terence Irwin, *RPT*, "Recollection and Plato's Moral Theory," *Review of Metaphysics*, 27 (1974), 752–772.

Terence Irwin, *PMT, Plato's Moral Theory: The Early and Middle Dialogues* (Oxford, 1977).

Charles H. Kahn, "The Meaning of 'Justice' and the Theory of Forms," *Journal of Philosophy*, 69 (1972), 567–579.

H.-J. Krämer, *Arete bei Platon und Aristoteles* (Heidelberg, 1959).

Richard Kraut, *ELP*, "Egoism, Love, and Political Office in Plato," *Philosophical Review*, 82 (1973), 330–44.

Richard Kraut, *RJR*, "Reason and Justice in Plato's *Republic*," E. N. Lee, A. P. D. Mourelatos, R. M. Rorty, eds., *Exegesis and Argument* (Assen, 1973).

David Lyons, "Mill's Theory of Morality," *Nous*, X (1976), 101–120.

G. E. Moore, *Principia Ethica* (Cambridge, Eng., 1903).

Alexander Nehamas, "Plato on the Imperfection of the Sensible World," *American Philosophical Quarterly*, 12 (1975) 105–117.

Richard Lewis Nettleship, *Lectures on the Republic of Plato*, 2nd ed. (London, 1901).

G. E. L. Owen, *PPI*, "A Proof in the *Peri Ideōn*," *Journal of Hellenic Studies*, 1957, pt. 1, 103–111, reprinted in Allen, pp. 293–312.

G. E. L. Owen, *PTP*, "Plato and Parmenides on the Timeless Present," *Monist*, 50 (1966), 317–340.

G. E. L. Owen, *PNB*, "Plato on Not-Being," Vlastos, *Plato I*, pp. 223–267.

Terry Penner, "Thought and Desire in Plato," Vlastos, *Plato II*, pp. 96–118.

H. A. Prichard, "Moral Obligation" and "Duty and Interest," pp. 87–163 and 203–238 of *Moral Obligation, and Duty and Interest* (Oxford, 1968).

Hans Reiner, *Die Grundlagen der Sittlichkeit, Monographien zur Philosophischen Forschung*, Bd. 5 (Meisenheim, 1974).

Constantin Ritter, *The Essence of Plato's Philosophy*, trans. A. Alles (London, 1933) from *Kerngedanken der platonischen Philosophie* (Munich, 1931).

Léon Robin, *Platon* (Paris, 1935).

Richard Robinson, *PED*, *Plato's Earlier Dialectic*, 2nd ed. (Oxford, 1953).

Richard Robinson, *SRD*, "Plato's Separation of Reason from Desire," *Phronesis*, XVI, 2 (1971), 38–48.

W. D. Ross, *Plato's Theory of Ideas* (Oxford, 1953).

Bertrand Russell, *EE*, "The Elements of Ethics," *Philosophical Essays* (London, 1910).

Bertrand Russell, *PP*, *The Problems of Philosophy* (New York, 1912).

David Sachs, "A Fallacy in Plato's *Republic*," *Philosophical Review*, 72 (1963), 141–158, reprinted in Vlastos, *Plato II*, pp. 35–51, and cited in the latter pagination.

P. A. Schilpp, ed., *The Philosophy of George Santayana* (Evanston and Chicago, 1940).

Friedrich Schleiermacher, *Schleiermacher's Introductions to the Dialogues of Plato*, trans. W. Dobson (Cambridge, Eng., and London, 1836, reprinted N. Y., 1973).

Paul Shorey, *IG*, "The Idea of the Good in Plato's *Republic*," *University of Chicago Publications in Classical Philology*, 1 (1895), 188–239.

Paul Shorey, *UPT*, *The Unity of Plato's Thought* (Chicago, 1903).

Paul Shorey, *WPS*, *What Plato Said* (Chicago, 1933).

Paul Shorey, *Rep.*, trans. and comm., *Plato, Republic*, vol. I, rev. ed. (London, 1937), vol. II (London, 1935).

Henry Sidgwick, *ME*, *The Methods of Ethics*, 7th ed. (London, 1907).

Henry Sidgwick, *OHE*, *Outlines of the History of Ethics*, 6th ed. (London, 1931).

Thomas Szlezák, "Unsterblichkeit und Trichotomie der Seele im zehnten Buch der Politeia," *Phronesis*, 21 (1976), 31–58.

A. E. Taylor, *Plato: The Man and his Work*, 4th ed. (N. Y., 1936).

H. S. Thayer, "Plato: The Theory and Language of Function," *Philosophical Quarterly*, 14 (1964), 3–18.

Gregory Vlastos, *DRP*, "Degrees of Reality in Plato," Bambrough, pp. 1–19, reprinted in Vlastos, *Platonic Studies* (Princeton, 1973), pp. 58–75.

Gregory Vlastos, *JHR*, "Justice and Happiness in the *Republic*," Vlastos, *Plato II*, pp. 66–95.

Gregory Vlastos, ed., *Plato I: A Collection of Critical Essays* (N. Y. 1971).

Gregory Vlastos, ed., *Plato II: A Collection of Critical Essays* (Garden City, 1971).

A. Wedberg, *Plato's Philosophy of Mathematics* (Stockholm, 1955).

Nicholas P. White, *Plato on Knowledge and Reality* (Indianapolis, 1976).

Eduard Zeller, *Die Philosophie der Griechen in ihrer geschichtlichen Entwicklung*, II, 1, ed. 5 (Leipzig, 1922).

Index